DAMES IN THE DRIVER'S SEAT

REREADING FILM NOIR

Dames in the Driver's Seat

Jans B. Wager

University of Texas Press ◆ Austin

Requests for permission to reproduce material
from this work should be sent to:
    Permissions
    University of Texas Press
    P.O. Box 7819
    Austin, TX 78713-7819
    www.utexas.edu/utpress/about/bpermission.html

⊗ The paper used in this book meets the minimum requirements
of ANSI/NISO Z39.48-1992 (R1997) (Permanence of Paper).

Library of Congress Cataloging-in-Publication Data
Wager, Jans B., 1958–
Dames in the driver's seat : rereading film noir / Jans B. Wager.— 1st ed.
      p.   cm.
Includes bibliographical references and index.
ISBN 0-292-70694-4 (cloth : alk. paper) —
ISBN 0-292-70966-8 (pbk. : alk. paper)
1. Film noir—History and criticism.   2. Sex role in motion pictures.
3.Race in motion pictures.   4. Social classes in motion pictures.   I. Title.
PN1995.9.F54W34   2005
791.43'6552—dc22
                                                            2005010564

For Jane Wager, my mother;
Tracy Wager, my sister;
and Bill Nicholson, my partner.

Their love, support, and insight provide me with security and freedom.

CONTENTS

ACKNOWLEDGMENTS

Many people assisted me in completing this project. Two anonymous readers for the University of Texas Press provided cogent critique. Wendy Moore and Jim Burr at UTP remained encouraging throughout the process. Thanks also to Lynne Chapman and Kip Keller from UTP. J. D. Davidson at Utah Valley State College consistently supported my scholarship. His sustained advocacy has been instrumental. I thank Dr. William Cobb for his encouragement and his integrity. Dr. Elaine Englehardt facilitated my work. Dr. Lucille Stoddard provided generous and supportive mentorship. Additionally, thanks to the Faculty Center for Teaching Excellence, the Office of Scholarship and Outreach, the dean of the School of Humanities, the Presidential Scholarship Fund, and the Board of Trustees of Utah Valley State College.

I thank my many colleagues and friends, including Channing Lowe, Lee Mortenson, Laurie Wood, Drs. Rob Carney, Laura Hamblin, Christa Albrecht-Crane, William Cobb, Tamara Fritze, Ryan Simmons, Shannon Mussett, Maria Pramaggiore, and Lisa Flores for their help and support. Dr. Rick McDonald deserves special thanks, as does Dr. Anne Scott. Thanks also to my students at UVSC, including Nanette Pawelek, Amie Davies, Rich Roberts, and Pat Jacobson.

Thanks to my family, and especially my sisters Deidra and Tracy Wager. My mother, Jane Wager, remains my ideal reader. My partner, Bill Nicholson, made me tea, and made me laugh.

DAMES IN THE DRIVER'S SEAT

DAMES AND DRIVING

By arguing episodically for the presence of a noir sensibility—a pulp politics—throughout twentieth-century America, I improvise a method for theorizing its peculiar modernism, not as a seamless grand narrative, nor as a tightly focused case study, but as the chaotic repetition of the familiar.

PAULA RABINOWITZ, *Black and White and Noir: America's Pulp Modernism*

But if we think, as we sometimes do, that we are uncovering "subversion" in the midst of [Hollywood production], that subversion will usually have much more to do with the contradictory conditions of cultural production than with any genuine attempt at counterideological statement. In the first instance Hollywood is a force for social stability and must be understood as such.

PHILIP GREEN, *Cracks in the Pedestal: Ideology and Gender in Hollywood*

The 1946 film noir *The Big Sleep* has a brief sequence featuring a professional dame in the driver's seat, a taxi driver played by Joy Barlow (Figure I.1). Barlow's name does not appear in *Femme Noir: Bad Girls of Film*, nor in *The Film Encyclopedia*. Hers is a bit part. She is a secure and far from demure version of femininity. Like all the female characters in *The Big Sleep*, she displays an overt attraction to detective Philip Marlowe (Humphrey Bogart). She helps Marlowe tail a suspect and then suggests that if he can use her again, he call her. He asks, "Day or night?" and she responds, "Night's better; I work days." There is much to like about this sequence. The character—white, dark-haired, and beautiful—

1

Figure I.1. A professional dame in the driver's seat (*The Big Sleep*, 1946)

follows the suspect expertly and without chatter, with Marlowe looking over her shoulder from the back seat. When she does take her turn to talk, she wields her language with wit, innuendo, and competence — much like Marlowe himself.[1] Although Marlowe never gets back together with this woman at the wheel, she epitomizes one of the most potent pleasures that classic film noir, and later post-classic noir, has to offer: a smart, capable, verbally astute, often beautiful female character who goes after, and sometimes gets, what she wants.[2]

The femme fatale who often drives the narrative in classic film noir remains a feature of my fascination with noir. But Barlow's brief appearance in this 1946 film noir also represents a dramatic change in work-related gender roles brought about by World War II. These changes affected all women, although white women benefited most, as women flooded into previously male-dominated professions. As William Chafe notes in *The Paradox of Change: American Women in the 20th Century*, "the Japanese attack on Pearl Harbor swiftly erased opposition to hiring women workers."[3] According to Chafe, "women hackies took to the wheel" in New York City and the *New York Times* detailed "the 'Adventures of a [female] Hackie.'"[4] Barlow's character reflects changing women's roles, and underscores film noir's enduring focus on class. While she seems content with her job, noir narratives often tell the story of working-class people seeking to escape their economic situation, a story that resonates deeply with movie audiences, both in the classic noir years and today.

Film noir continues to fascinate, and to serve as a durable feature of many Hollywood narratives, as a bankable advertising mode, and as an ongoing inspiration for consumers, students, and scholars of popular culture. Film noir provides spectators with the "chaotic repetition of the familiar" governed, in general, by what cultural critic bell hooks calls the white supremacist capitalist patriarchy.[5] One might add heterocentric to this already daunting phrase, to really take into account the dominant ideological discourses of twenty-first-century U.S. culture. Although "Hollywood is a force for social stability," a crucial element in noir's abiding appeal remains the hint of ideological subversion exhibited by classic noir, and the aura of subversion that persists in postclassic texts.[6] This project builds on the work begun in *Dangerous Dames: Women and Representation in the Weimar Street Film and Film Noir* and considers how femininity, masculinity, class, and race articulate in classic films noirs, and late-1990s postclassic films that reflect a noir sensibility.[7] I separate postclassic noir into two categories: retro-noirs (made in the present but set in the classic noir period, the 1940s or '50s) and neo-noirs (made and set in the present but referring to classic noir narratively or stylistically). My exploration of these categories suggests that, in their treatment of gender, retro-noirs fulfill a reactionary function while neo-noirs often seem to reflect revisionary views. For class and especially race, the issue is less black-and-white.

Classic films noirs are Hollywood crime movies made in the 1940s and '50s. The films often feature a femme fatale and hard-boiled male protagonist. Low-key lighting, with minimal fill light, and night-for-night photography provide atmospheric shadows and stark pools of light.[8] Extreme and unsettling camera angles, voice-over narration, and episodic narrative structure may also appear in classic film noir.[9] The crime films of postclassic noir usually include some of these visual and narrative elements. Postclassic noir includes both reactionary retro-noir and somewhat revisionary neo-noir films.

I analyze these films as a way of charting the resistance to and strength of the white supremacist capitalist patriarchy in the early twenty-first century. My heterosexual, middle-class, academic, white, feminist, visual, and narrative predilections no doubt inform my scholarship. Nevertheless, through thinking, theorizing, writing, and teaching about movies, I imagine a future where Hollywood gratifies my visual and narrative pleasures instead of thwarting them with conservative sex, gender, race, or class politics.

Dangerous Dames explored the connection between the femmes fatales in German street films of the early twentieth century and American films noirs of the mid-twentieth century, concluding with a brief analysis of some postclassic

German and Hollywood noirs of the 1990s. That project also discusses another female character often featured in these films: the passive, domestic antithesis to the femme fatale, which I name *femme attrapée* to foreground her imprisonment in the patriarchal system. In *Dangerous Dames*, I follow other feminist film scholars and suggest that although female characters in the Weimar street film and film noir may well have reflected unstable postwar male subjectivity, these characters also implied other possible readings, readings that related to women's lived experiences. The visual and narrative pleasures of these movies, especially for female spectators, derives from their representations of cultural changes in gender roles, changes that often provided women with more agency. In Weimar street films and classic films noirs, the femme attrapée does not resist the patriarchy and therefore survives the narrative. The femme fatale, meanwhile, fights against male economic and social domination, usually at the cost of her life or her freedom. She is murdered, tortured, jailed, or at the very least contained by marriage in the final reel of the film. The femme fatale's resistance is fatal, sometimes to the men who fall for her, almost always to herself.

These antithetical female characters continue to appear in noir narratives today, reflecting the contradictions inherent in a supposed postmodern, post-feminist existence, in the same way the classic dames once reflected the contradictions of U.S. culture in the forties and fifties. But masculinity figures powerfully in noir narratives as well. Once I recast the femme attrapée as trapped by the patriarchy and the femme fatale as doomed by her resistance to it, I saw an analogous reading of the male protagonists. Almost every film noir features men who function much as the typical female archetypes do. Like the femme fatale, the *homme fatal* wants more than he should, more money and often a dangerous dame as well. Like the femme attrapée, the *homme attrapé* does not resist society's demands, and usually he survives the noir narrative. These male characters are also endemic to today's noirs.

Both femmes and hommes fatals pay for their visibly antisocial desires in classic film noir. The ideologically conservative Production Code, in effect from the 1930s through the 1960s, ensured their punishment.[10] A joint effort between Hollywood executives and religious leaders designed to mitigate the possibility of external censorship, the code required that "no picture shall be produced that will lower the standards of those who see it. Hence, the sympathy of the audience should never be thrown to the side of crime, wrongdoing, evil or sin."[11] Femmes and hommes fatals pay for their power, money, or sexual lust in *The Killers* (1946) and *Out of the Past* (1947), discussed here, as well as *The Postman Always Rings Twice* (1946), *Gun Crazy* (1950), *The Killing* (1956), and countless other classic films noirs. Despite the constraints of the code, films noirs still managed to portray the ambiguities and difficulties involved in both acquiescence in and resistance to societal demands, in part by portraying those choices affecting both male and female protagonists.

While the cabby in *The Big Sleep* is not a protagonist, she does reveal cultural changes in what constitutes women's work; she represents the working class, and she signifies Hollywood's dominant interest in whiteness. Classic noirs virtually always tell stories about whiteness, stories that both rely on and elide nonwhiteness. As Eric Lott notes in defining film noir, "Leave it to white folk to turn chiaroscuro into a racially coded metaphor for the 'dark' places of the white self."[12] In "The Whiteness of Film Noir," Lott sees film noir as concerned, above all, with race. He suggests that "film noir is . . . a sort of whiteface dream work of social anxieties with explicitly racial sources, condensed on film into the criminal undertakings of abject whites."[13] Lott analyses the blacks and other nonwhites at the periphery of various classic noir narratives, seeing these "characters of color [as those] who populate and signify the shadows of white American life in the 1940s."[14]

Paula Rabinowitz makes a similar assertion in *Black and White and Noir: America's Pulp Modernism;* she views "film noir *as* the context; its plot structure and visual iconography make sense of America's landscape and history."[15] Rabinowitz provides an evocative discussion of the pulpy nature of popular, political, and personal culture in the United States, using film noir as inspiration rather than primary text. Yet her central point also proves Lott's complaint. According to Rabinowitz, "modernity in America is structured around two poles, each working to suppress a hidden history of state violence: racial codings (hence the black-and-white motif) and class melodrama (hence the recourse to noir sentimentality and nostalgia)" (18). Instead of interrogating how race, class, and gender materially appear in specific films noirs, Rabinowitz suggests that race and class conflate and "are revealed in the femme fatale—that dark lady who glows in the bright key lighting of B-movies" (18). Various cultural fears might be reflected in the generic figure of the femme fatale; however, this project reads specific films to articulate the representations of gender, class, and race, and charts some of the changes in how noir represents race, including whiteness.

Looking forward to 1990s noir, Barlow's taxi driver serves as a precursor to the sexy, barefooted taxi driver Esmarelda Villalobos (Angela Jones) in *Pulp Fiction* (1994) but also to more interesting female protagonists in late-1990s neonoir: Catherine (Susan Sarandon) in *Twilight* (1998), Jackie Brown (Pam Grier) in *Jackie Brown* (1997), and even Marge Gunderson (Frances McDormand) in *Fargo* (1996). These films exhibit a change in the representation of the femme fatale. In the early 1990s, the sexualized performances of characters such as those played by Sharon Stone in *Basic Instinct* (1992) and Linda Fiorentino in *The Last Seduction* (1994) dominate noir narratives. According to Kate Stables in "The Postmodern Always Rings Twice: Constructing the *Femme Fatale* in '90s Cinema," the early 1990s femme fatale is a woman motivated by "her enormous appetite for power, money, sex."[16] Stables suggests that the classic film noir femme fatale existed as "sexual *presence*," while the early 1990s femme fatale "is redefined as sexual *performer*."[17] Slavoj Zizek, in "The Art of the Ridiculous Sublime," agrees with Stables, asserting that "the neo-noir *femme fatale* is to be located in the context of the dissolution of the . . . Production Code: what was merely hinted at in the late '40s is now explicitly rendered thematic."[18]

In the late 1990s, a different sort of femme fatale appears, one such as Jackie Brown who relies less on sexual performance (although her sexuality remains appealing) and more on other abilities. She suggests a shift in direction for at least some of the noir narratives in the twenty-first century. This new femme fatale appears in neo-noirs, those films made and set roughly in the late 1990s. Neo-noirs can undermine the institutions of the white supremacist capitalist patriarchy, at least with regard to gender.

Yet in addition to the attractions of the late-1990s neo-noir, the last half of the decade also produced a series of reactionary films noirs that feature a pastiche, or imitation, femme fatale. These more reactionary films, made in the late 1990s but set in the classic noir years, I call retro-noirs. The pastiche femmes fatales of the retro-noir have little or no ability to drive the narrative. They include Lynn (Kim Basinger) in *L.A. Confidential* (1997), Allison (Jennifer Connelly) in *Mulholland Falls* (1996), and Marla (Helena Bonham Carter) in *Fight Club* (1999). These characters seem designed to prove Laura Mulvey's thesis in "Visual Pleasure and Narrative Cinema": women function solely as objects of the male gaze and signifiers of castration and, as such, must be punished or controlled.[19]

Under the influence of a rating system more concerned with policing sexuality than morals, postclassic noirs continue to represent cultural shifts in gender roles and in women's and men's lived experiences, expressing both the fears and benefits of these shifts. The noir of the late 1990s becomes a paradigm for understanding the conflicting nature of lived experience. These films provide spectators with "a pulp politics" of gender, class, and race.[20] The focus here is not just the oppression and resistance of women under the patriarchy, but also the ways that the capitalist patriarchy — even the white supremacist capitalist patriarchy — determines all film form. In this project, femininity, masculinity, race, and class enter the discussion. As Teresa Amott and Julie Matthaei assert in *Race, Gender, and Work: A Multicultural Economic History of Women in the United States,* "race-ethnicity, gender, and class are interconnected, interdetermining historical processes, rather than separate systems."[21]

The first of four sections, "Contents and Contexts," explores some of the theoretical and ideological currents informing contemporary film noir and feminist scholarship. Chapter One, "Manning the Posts," provides a discussion of classic film noir and postclassic noir's mutable generic status and explains some of the terminology. The chapter concludes with an inquiry into how the discourses of postmodernism inform current cinema, and late-1990s noir in particular, perhaps accounting for both the reactionary and revisionary aspects of these films. Chapter Two, "Sexing the Paradigm: Women and Men in Noir," and Chapter Three, "Racing the Paradigm: The Whiteness of Film Noir," provide a brief historical examination of how masculinity and race articulate with the representations of women in movies. Chapter Two reconsiders gender representations in classic and postclassic noir and discusses the influences of third-wave feminism, sometimes referred to as postfeminism, on current media practices. Then, beginning with Patrice Petro's study of Weimar cinema and working forward to late-1990s noir, I suggest a series of oppositions that seek to organize and understand the discourses of gender in retro- and neo-noir. Chapter Three concentrates on the representation of race in film noir and adds race to the gendered paradigms. Although drawn primarily from film noir and postclassic noir, the binary oppositions of revisionary and reactionary trends suggested here also provide a possible model for thinking about Hollywood film beyond the confines of noir.

After this academic orientation, we go off to the movies. The next three sections explore first classic film noir, then retro-noir, and finally neo-noir. Most of the people I talk with about film are not cinema scholars: they are medievalists, creative writers, my mother and family, ski patrollers, office managers, and undergraduate students. These moviegoers make up an important part of my intended audience. For many of these film lovers, A. O. Scott, Janet Maslin, Ebert and Roeper, and even Joe Bob Briggs provide useful criticism. My academic colleagues who regularly utilize film in the classroom have not read Laura Mulvey, Kaja Silverman, or even Béla Balázs. A lot of filmgoers, although not film scholars, are experts at watching and thinking about movies. They enjoy engaging in critical and complex analysis, enjoy working to understand their responses and to build their own interpretations. Film scholars share a canon of theoretical texts and a specialized language that often exclude the expert nonscholar. I invite both film aficionados and film scholars into this discussion by moving obliquely away from scholarly discourse and toward more personal and popular responses, especially in the later chapters that focus on recent Hollywood movies.

For the classic films, in addition to scholarly writings and reviews from the classic period, I also include commentary from one of the first works of noir criticism, *A Panorama of American Film Noir: 1941–1953* by Raymond Borde and Etienne Chaumeton. In this wonderfully exuberant discussion, published in 1955 and finally translated into English in 2002, two French intellectuals make noir exemplary of their own surrealist ideology.[22] The language they use to talk about the movies remains as vibrant and evocative as the films themselves. For Borde and Chaumeton, classic film noir begins with *The Maltese Falcon* (1941) and ends with *Kiss Me Deadly* (1955). I follow other noir theorists who see *Citizen Kane* (also 1941) as an additional inaugural film, since *Citizen Kane* has the complex narrative structure, unsettling camera work, and dramatic lighting often identified with film noir. From this perspective, another film directed by Orson Welles, *Touch of Evil* (1958), brings classic film noir to a close. Instead of a hard-boiled detective and femme fatale, this film features a grotesque and corrupted detective, a host of other perversions, and takes the noir camera work and lighting to extremes.

The second section examines "Prototypes in Classic Noir" and provides close readings of three classic film noir texts: *The Killers* (1946), *Out of the Past* (1947), and *Kiss Me Deadly* (1955), each in some way quintessential. These films, well known and often cited in scholarly and popular texts on film noir, provide a basis for understanding classic noir. Chapter Four examines *The Killers,* starring Ava Gardner and Burt Lancaster. Gardner functions as both femme fatale and femme attrapée, although the dominant reading of her character dooms her to jail at the end. Lancaster portrays the passive yet powerful masculinity of an homme fatal, doomed by his desire for both economic wealth and the femme fatale. Chapter Five discusses *Out of the Past,* starring another passive and powerful homme fatal played by Robert Mitchum, as well as an exemplary femme fatale played by Jane Greer. Kirk Douglas—father of Michael Douglas, the exemplary American man in numerous postclassic noirs—also stars. Finally, Chapter Six looks at the famous late-classic noir *Kiss Me Deadly.* Much has been and continues to be written about this film, which ends with the femme fatale opening a box that unleashes a nuclear explosion. My analysis, inspired by feminist theorist Laura Mulvey, reads the investigative competence and unstylized appearance of the female characters as a revision of cinematic conventions. This revision makes it possible to interpret the film as a postmodern feminist text despite its generalized misogyny and misanthropy. Both *Out of the Past* and *Kiss Me Deadly* feature a black jazz club sequence, but the latter invests the sequence with more meaning than most classic noirs do. These quintessential texts set up a discussion of postclassic noir.

For postclassic films noirs, I use current voices—newspaper reviews, popular film journals, directors' and actors' commentaries, scholarly responses, and others—to calibrate reaction to these films relative to issues of gender and race. I ask what the films and the responses to them circulating in popular texts suggest about cultural relationships, and thereby explore how spectators might understand, internalize, or resist these suggestions. As the opening epigraph from Philip Green implies, these films and the responses to them reflect, above all, "the contradictory conditions of cultural production."[23] Yet the effectiveness of these films as reactionary or revisionary texts is reflected in the cultural responses discussed here; these responses have some potential to determine the future of film form.

Every decade since the close of the classic noir period (1958) has had its share of noir-inspired films, including, to name only a few, *Harper* (1966), *Klute* (1971), *The Big Sleep* (1978), *Body Heat* (1981), *Fatal Attraction* (1987), *Point Break* (1991), *Fargo* (1996), *Mulholland Drive* (2001), and *Femme Fatale* (2002). Postclassic noirs proliferated in the 1980s and '90s, and that proliferation continues today. Late-1990s noir provides the primary texts for this discussion, since these often successful films starring well-known actors reflect both a change from the early 1990s and serve to usher in a noir sensibility for the twenty-first century. The films analyzed in Sections Three and Four do not seek to provide an exhaustive selection of retro- and neo-noir. Instead, a sampling of late-1990s films allows the noir aficionada to fill in the taxonomy with other texts and contexts.

Section Three, "Return of the Repressed in Retro-Noir," focuses on retro-noirs, those ideologically reactionary films noirs made in the present but set in the past. Chapter Seven, "Does Anything Change as Time Goes By?" begins by comparing one celebrated non-noir text of the classic period, *Casablanca* (1942), to a retro-noir, *L.A. Confidential* (1997), and highlights the nostalgic and conservative impulses of retro-noir. Despite the intervening years and the social gains made by women and people of color, the 1942 non-noir and 1997 retro-noir tell remarkably similar stories about homosocial and heterosexual relationships and about whiteness, masculinity, and nonwhite marginalization. Chapter Eight, "Nuclear Noir as Numbskull Noir," analyzes the retro-noir *Mulholland Falls* (1996). This film, which promotes muscular and violent white masculinity and passive and doomed white femininity, serves as the antithesis to classic noir's active women and passive but powerful men. Nonwhite characters disappear almost completely from the narrative. Finally, in Chapter Nine, retro-noir masquerades as neo-noir. Binary oppositions are never absolute; according to my own taxonomy of retro- and neo-noir, *Fight Club* (1999), set in a vague and not too distant future, should be neo-noir. Instead, the film achieves retro-noir status because of its reactionary treatment of gender, class, and race. *Fight Club* promotes a white supremacist patriarchy.

Section Four, "Revision of the Repressed in Neo-Noir," discusses the visual and narrative pleasures of three neo-noirs, films made and set in the mid- to late 1990s, including *Twilight* (1998), *Fargo* (1996), and *Jackie Brown* (1997). Neonoirs often revise, at least somewhat, gender representations. As noted earlier, the sexual performance aspect of early-1990s femmes fatales gives way to more interesting and complex characterizations in the late 1990s.[24] Although I enjoyed watching Linda Fiorentino, as femme fatale Bridget in *The Last Seduction,* use and discard men and then drive off with a fortune, Pam Grier's Jackie Brown and Susan Sarandon's character Catherine in *Twilight* offer spectators a more nuanced and socially relevant femininity.[25] Neo-noir generally revises sex or gender representations and, like classic noir, focuses on class, yet often seems ambivalent or reactionary with regard to race. In *Twilight* a nonwhite character serves as a racist stereotype. In *Fargo,* the representation of nonwhites seems somewhat ambiguous, although racist elements appear. Of the three neo-noir films discussed, only *Jackie Brown* provides nonwhite characters with larger and more complex roles.

All the films discussed here represent mainstream Hollywood filmmaking, written, produced, directed, and marketed primarily by white men. As Green notes, any subversion here "will usually have much more to do with the contradictory conditions of cultural production that with any genuine attempt at counterideological statement."[26] Although these texts do not threaten social stability, neo-noirs occasionally subvert ideologies that bolster the white supremacist capitalist patriarchy, whereas retro-noirs more insidiously support those ideologies. Film noir, with its focus on the mythologies of class, sex-gender, and race, continues to reflect the ambiguity and extremes of postmodern experience. These texts provide a unique site for exploring the comforts and threats implicit in Hollywood production. In the conclusion, "Doing It for bell," I discuss bell hooks's potential influence on film and filmmakers and promote the importance of culturally engaged and aware scholarship and teaching as a vehicle for social change. Late-1990s noir seems the perfect vehicle to initiate a discussion of gender, race, and class in the new millennium. Where do the paths in late-1990s noir lead? And how will we — as film spectators, theorists, and filmmakers — modify those directions in the twenty-first century?

PART 1

CONTENTS AND CONTEXTS

CHAPTER 1

MANNING THE POSTS: CLASSIC NOIR, POSTCLASSIC NOIR, AND POSTMODERNISM

Film noir belongs to the history of ideas as much as to the history of cinema. . . . film noir is both an important cinematic legacy and an idea we have projected on the past.

JAMES NAREMORE, *More than Night: Film Noir in Its Contexts*

And about the *post* of *modernism:* It was conservative politics, it was subversive politics, it was the return of tradition, it was the final revolt of tradition, it was the unmooring of patriarchy, it was the reassertion of patriarchy . . . and so on.

ANNE FRIEDBERG, *Window Shopping: Cinema and the Postmodern*

One of the characteristics that distinguishes the film noir scholar from the film noir devotee, in addition to the language each uses to talk about the movies, might be the scholar's ambivalence and the devotee's confidence about the definition of film noir. The scholar struggles under the weight of over forty years of accumulated academic discourse on the nature of noir as genre, cycle, style, series, or system.[1] Meanwhile, the devotee can often reel off a definition, and film reviewers in the popular press regularly use *film noir* as a defining term in identifying the style and content of new movies. For the movie buff, films noirs are crime films, mostly black-and-white, made in Hollywood in the 1940s and 1950s, often featuring a hard-boiled male and a beautiful, duplicitous female protagonist, usually set in urban surroundings. The occasional use of complex narrative structures and dramatic visual effects, including night-for-night photography, low-key lighting, and bizarre camera angles, also appear in this standard definition, along with a mention of subversion.[2] As Richard Martin notes in *Mean Streets and Raging Bulls: The Legacy of Film Noir in Contemporary American Cinema,* for many, whether scholars or devotees, film noir has always represented "a body of work which offered a bleak and, to a certain degree, subversive worldview that contrasted starkly with the self-promoting American myths that characterized many . . . Hollywood films."[3]

Martin points to the widespread popularity of the idea of noir, suggesting that "the term *noir,* having gained currency outside the domains of film criticism and academia, holds some significance for twentieth-century popular culture in general."[4] He sees the prolific academic and critical investigations of film noir as fueled by its ability to become "many things for many people."[5] In addition to these investigations, Martin asserts that it is the

> parallel cinematic investigation and revival of film noir in the Hollywood cinema of the late sixties and its subsequent transformation through the cinema of the seventies, eighties, and 1990s that has most significantly contributed to an evolving concept of what film noir actually is. The industrial assimilation of the term film noir, moreover, has contributed to its establishment as a contemporary Hollywood genre irrespective of how one is inclined to define the generic status of the classic films of the forties and fifties.[6]

For Martin, postclassic noir cinema has itself contributed to popular culture's understanding of film noir. Although he admits that classic noir's status remains a subject of debate, he nevertheless identifies both classic film noir and neo-noir as genres.

In *Genre and Hollywood,* Steven Neale devotes a chapter to film noir. He outlines the scholarly approaches to classic noir's status since the 1970s, and then discounts each approach by asserting that whether concerned with issues of gender, literary antecedents, narrative style, or expressionism, each attempt to delineate film noir fails. Neale sees those failures primarily in the difficulty of locating the distinctive element (whatever it might be) in all films identified as classic noirs and in "the extent to which [the elements] are exclusive" to noir.[7] Neale concludes his discussion by asserting that as "a single phenomenon, *noir* . . . never existed" but that "the phenomenon of neo-*noir* . . . is much more real, not only as a phenomenon but also as a genre."[8] For Neale, classic film noir avoids generic status, while neo-noir achieves it. According to Neale, neo-noir "is now the most widely accepted term for those films which, from the late 1960s on, relate to or draw upon the notion, the image and the punitive conventions of film noir and, directly or indirectly, on some of the films featuring centrally within most versions of the basic noir canon."[9]

Both Neale and Martin see neo-noir as a genre that draws upon film noir, although the status of the source, classic film noir, remains indeterminate. In *More than Night: Film Noir in Its Contexts,* James Naremore astutely notes that film noir "has less to do with a group of artifacts than with a discourse — a loose, evolving system of arguments and readings that help to shape commercial strategies and aesthetic ideologies."[10] He goes on to insist that "film noir is both an important cinematic legacy and an idea we have projected onto the past."[11] As I noted in the introduction, for Paula Rabinowitz, film noir provides *the* context. According to Rabinowitz, "cultural sensations coalesce around the spectacles of crime in part due to the conventions film noir provides; it's the template."[12] She goes on to suggest that, "film noir, rather than reflecting these [cultural sensations and] changes . . . prefigures them, encodes them, and makes them intelligible."[13] I see film noir and postclassic noir fulfilling both functions — both reflecting the cultural sensations circulating around gender, race, and class, as well as making them intelligible.

All these attempts to interpret film noir simultaneously recognize noir's power to move and the inability to concretely define it. Nevertheless, film noir has firmly established itself in the discourse of popular culture, film buffs, film critics, scholars, and the advertising and film industries. Perhaps film noir achieves genre status by default, just as grammar changes are imposed over time, through popular usage. Indeed, in his "Definitions of Genre" section, Neale quotes Andrew Tudor's suggestion that genre "notions . . . are not critics' classifications made for special purposes; they are sets of cultural conventions. . . . Genre is what we collectively believe it to be."[14]

Film noir gained currency thanks to cultural critics and scholars who named and defined it sometimes years or decades after production and initial audience consumption. The discourses surrounding film noir, and especially classic noir, reveal two tendencies Ihab Hassan identifies as central to postmodernism: indeterminacy and immanence. In *The Postmodern Turn: Essays in Postmodern Theory and Culture,* Hassan defines "indeterminacy, or better still, indeterminancies, [as] . . . a complex referent that these diverse concepts help to delineate: ambiguity, discontinuity, heterodoxy, pluralism, randomness, revolt, perversion, deformation."[15] Certainly, film noir functions as an indeterminate referent, rife with ambiguity, discontinuity, and deformation. At the same time, the desire to understand film noir, to name it and then categorize it, has more to do with immanence, with the "capacity of the mind to generalize itself in symbols, intervene more and more into nature, act upon itself through its own abstractions and so become, increasingly, immediately, its own environment."[16] The cultural discourses surrounding film noir reveal more about our ideas of ourselves, the critics' and scholars visions' of themselves, and my understanding of myself, than anything to do with the actual group of films produced roughly between 1941 and 1958. Film noir marks a postmodern turn: it marks our inability to definitively define ourselves and serves as a symbol of what we imagine ourselves to be. The discourses surrounding classic film noir reveal incipient postmodern uncertainty, just as the films themselves reflect, predict, and make clear cultural concerns while simultaneously defying a unified reading.

In this study, I use the term *film noir,* but instead of narrowing the definition down to some generic set of characters or features, *classic film noir* means any black-and-white Hollywood crime film made in the 1940s and 1950s — any crime film made roughly postgangster and precolor. As noted briefly in the introduction, for the sake of this study I separate *postclassic noir* into *neo-noir* and *retro-noir. Neo-noir* describes crime films made after the classic period, but primarily those films made and set in the same general time frame, such as the 1970s postclassic noir *The Long Goodbye* (1974) and 1990s films such as *Jackie Brown* (1997) and *Twilight* (1998).[17] The term *retro-noir* indicates a crime film made after the classic period but using that time frame, the 1940s and 1950s, as a setting — films such as *Chinatown* (1974), *Mulholland Falls* (1996), *L.A. Confidential* (1997), and *The Man Who Wasn't There* (2001).[18]

Postclassic Hollywood noir capitalizes on the enduring fascination of film noir, selling both reactionary and revisionary narratives of gender. The late-1990s noir films discussed here reflect the contradictory impulses of postmodernism: retro-noir reverberates with reactionary gender images, while neo-noir portrays some revisionary possibilities. Using Anne Friedberg's assessment of postmodernism in *Window Shopping: Cinema and the Postmodern* to discuss gender relationships in postclassic noir, I take retro-noir to present the return of the repressed and to serve as the locus of conservative politics, the return of tradition, and the reassertion (with a vengeance) of patriarchy, while neo-noir, to a certain extent, features subversive politics, an attempted revolt against tradition, and a least a partial unmooring of patriarchy.[19] For example, in the retro-noir *Mulholland Falls,* the thoroughly objectified white female protagonist is thrown from a plane for daring to investigate a nuclear secret, while the thoroughly muscular and well-dressed white male protagonist ignores the same important secret and survives the narrative. In the neo-noir *Jackie Brown,* the black female protagonist manages to get the best of a number of dangerous and capable male antagonists, yet she survives the narrative and drives off with half a million dollars.

Both retro- and neo-noirs are made by an industry interested in making an effective appeal to consumers. As Shugart, Waggoner, and Holstein note in "Mediating Third-Wave Feminism: Appropriation as Postmodern Media Practice," for the most part, postmodern media practices support capitalism and seek to deflect and defuse resistance.[20] The success of postclassic noir today points to nostalgia, another concept connected to postmodern media practice. Both retro- and neo-noirs can be identified as nostalgic. As Fredric Jameson suggests in "Postmodernism and Consumer Society," a nostalgia film seeks to reinvent "the feel and shape of characteristic art objects of an older period . . . it seeks to re-awaken a sense of the past associated with those objects."[21] This type of film "does not reinvent a picture of the past in its lived totality."[22] In the case of postclassic noir, and especially retro-noir, the past represented is itself a cinematic past: the nostalgia is not for a lived past but for a representation of a past, a time when men were men, women were dames, and whiteness reigned supreme.

Jameson sees nostalgia films "invading and colonizing even those movies today which have contemporary settings, as though, for some reason, we were unable today to focus on our own present . . . [to achieve] aesthetic representations of our own current experience."[23] The inability to deal with "time and history" marks postmodernism for Jameson, who sees *Body Heat* (1981), discussed in Chapter Two here, as exemplary of this trend.[24] Retro-noirs do exhibit an inability to deal with time and history, featuring instead a past that never existed. Neo-noirs, however, reflect both past and present, and the present represented has to do with current cultural conditions. In her discussion of neo-noir, focused primarily on the films of the early 1990s, Yvonne Tasker comes to a similar conclusion. According to Tasker, "in its articulation of the vulnerable, persecuted hero of *film noir* and the sexually aggressive and independent figure of the *femme fatale* . . . new *film noir* addresses contemporary culture in its own appropriate paranoid fashion . . . both ahistorical and very precisely of its time."[25] The neo-noirs of the late 1990s revise the sexual and cultural politics of the films of the early 1990s, but are also precisely of their time.

Friedberg, like Jameson, focuses on history and representation, or rather the perception of representation in discussing the postmodern. She describes an "epistemological tear along the fabric of modernity" that ushered in postmodernity.[26] For Friedberg, this tear was the "*mobilized 'virtual' gaze*" created by "cinematic and televisional apparatuses."[27] She notes that the virtual gaze is "not a direct perception but a *received* perception mediated through representation."[28] Similarly, then, the past evoked or represented in postclassic noir is a *virtual* past. Postclassic noir trades, to a certain degree, on nostalgia, but as Friedberg suggests in this chapter's opening epigraph, postmodern texts can reveal both revisionary and reactionary tendencies. In the more reactionary retro-noirs, the spectator sees a recreation of a style of movie making popular in the 1940s and '50s and a physical recreation of that past. In retro-noirs, however, the classic noir femme fatale is often replaced by a pastiche femme fatale, an empty and powerless imitation of the female character who once drove noir narratives. The homme fatal disappears as well, replaced by a confident supporter of the white supremacist capitalist patriarchy. In the more revisionary neo-noir, the spectator enjoys the narrative or stylistic flourishes of classic noir but in a contemporary setting, and the gendered relationships portrayed often reflect satisfying revisions to classic noir's obligatory containment of the femme fatale.

It seems self-evident to suggest that all these texts "represent stereotypes about the past" more than they accurately document the past, which remains "forever out of reach."[29] Friedberg skillfully makes a connection between cinema spectatorship and the postmodern condition, noting that "postmodernity is marked by the increasing centralization of the feature implicit (from the start) in cinema spectatorship: the production of a virtual elsewhere and elsewhen, and the commodification of the gaze that is mobilized in both time and space."[30] Postclassic noir then becomes the epitome of the postmodern cinema experience, an experience that does not seek to represent a past as much as it seeks to reproduce a representation of a cinematic past. Yet postclassic noir films, relying on a virtual represented past, speak to us about our present. The present these films address ripples with gender, racial, and class tensions, tensions repressed, worked through, and expressed on the screen. The next chapters take a closer look at gender and race in noir.

CHAPTER 2

SEXING THE PARADIGM:
WOMEN AND MEN IN NOIR

As shifts in regulation made it at least *possible* for the *femme fatale* to profit by
her crimes, the *noir* hero . . . emerges as inept in, if possible, a more thorough-
going way than their 1940s' predecessors.

YVONNE TASKER, *Working Girls: Gender and Sexuality in Popular Cinema*

A historical moment called "postmodernism" contributes to the third wave . . .
[feminism's] distinction from the first and second waves in that "the simultaneous
confidence and uncertainly about what constitutes feminism doesn't have to be
conceptualized as a problem." Instead, the condition of ambiguity is understood as a natural consequence of the proliferation of feminisms.

EDNIE KAEH GARRISON, REFERENCED BY DEBORAH L. SIEGEL,
"The Legacy of the Personal: Generating Theory in Feminism's Third Wave"

In the introduction, I discuss the two antithetical female characters common to
film noir and suggest that parallel male characters exist as well. Historically, in
scholarly and popular texts, the term *femme fatale* implicates the female character in the downfall of the male protagonist; for me, it implies her own inevitable
demise. The femme fatale almost always causes her own destruction or, at the
very least, containment within prison walls or marriage. I also rename her passive, nurturing opposite, identified by Janey Place in "Women in Film Noir," as
the "woman as redeemer."[1] This female character becomes a femme attrapée, de-

noting her situation in the gendered economy of the film instead of implying her role as a potential savior for the male character.

With both terms, *femme attrapée* and *femme fatale,* the goal is to focus attention on the female character, on her survival through acquiescence in the requirements of the patriarchy, or on her destruction through resistance. This removes the male subject from his central position in the descriptive nomenclature for the female characters predominant in film noir. A large part of the appeal of classic film noir comes from its portrayal of the choices available to these mostly working-class female characters. These women are either trapped in the realm of domestic labor, economic hardship, and drab dullness, or they are criminal, sexy, exciting, and doomed. Both characters remain bound by patriarchal culture, and classic film noir clearly delineates the ambivalent nature of the choices available to them.

This project also recognizes and discusses male characters analogous to the femme fatale and femme attrapée in classic films noirs: the homme fatal and homme attrapé. Noir theorists do occasionally discuss the homme fatal as fatal to the women whom he seduces. *Film Noir: An Encyclopedic Reference to the American Style* identifies Joe Sullivan in *Raw Deal* (1948) as an homme fatal, a man who seduces a woman "into a world filled with violent action and murder, enticing her with a promise of sexual fulfillment that goes beyond the realm of normal relationships."[2] I retain the terminology but, as with the femme fatale, redefine the homme fatal to suggest that he is, above all, fatal to himself. Whereas the femme fatale resists a society that requires her containment in marriage and domesticity, the homme fatal resists a culture that insists on his participation in capitalism through a job and a modest paycheck. Like the femme attrapée, the homme attrapé accepts that participation. In exchange, society offers him the fiefdom of the domestic realm, one place he can reign supreme. The homme fatal wants either a more lucrative lifestyle than participation in legal forms of capitalism enables, or a sexually dominant and worldly woman rather than a submissive wife. He guarantees his demise in classic noir by wanting both big money and a dangerous dame.

Other views of masculinity in film noir also circulate. Chris Straayer, in "*Femme Fatale* or Lesbian Femme: *Bound* in Sexual *Différance*," identifies the classic film noir couple as the "phallic *femme fatale* and emasculated protagonist."[3] This terminology serves to reinscribe rather than disrupt gender binaries, but the woman often dominates in film noir and the male protagonist often wants to be dominated. Not everyone sees male protagonists as emasculated, although many of them, such as Bart Tare in *Gun Crazy* and Christopher Cross in *Scarlet Street* (1945), might easily earn that descriptor. In " 'New Hollywood,' New *Film Noir* and the *Femme Fatale*," Yvonne Tasker comments on more recent versions of movie masculinity, but also notes that "while the 1940s' *noir* hero was perpetually losing consciousness/control, contemporary scenarios exaggerate this sense of vulnerability."[4] In contrast, Philip Green asserts that "films noirs were usually movies about strong men brought to their knees by a malignant fate, most often coded as 'woman.' "[5]

Whether emasculated, vulnerable, or strong, the male protagonist in film noir, the homme fatal, defies the capitalist patriarchy, and both hommes and femmes fatals pay for their excessive desires with their lives or freedom. They are, above all, fatal to themselves. Straayer notes the diversity of gender representations noir provides and speculates on the liberatory potential of those images, exploring the way classic film noir, although coded heterosexually, "maintain[s] difference-based coupling while deconstructing gender-sex alignment and allowing for gender inversion, gender trading, and same-gender couplings."[6] For Straayer, this "gender fluidity now facilitates queer readings of and representations in neo-noir."[7] Straayer also provides an illuminating discussion of the anomalous neo-noir *Bound* (1996), a film which features a lesbian in the role of the homme fatal. The femme fatale in *Bound* proves fatal to the men who fall for her, but she and her lover, a woman who "offers a masculinity much more attractive to a femme," drive off in a red pickup with two million dollars at the end of the film.[8] Females fair better in neo-noir than men. Queer readings also surface in the more typical, heterocentric noirs discussed here.

Critical readings of noir focus almost exclusively on white heterosexual male subjectivity. Most scholars ignore female subjectivity, or treat it only in relation to the more central issue of male subjectivity. Martin, for example, in *Mean Streets and Raging Bulls,* presents a fine discussion of the legacy of film noir in contemporary cinema. Martin omits a discussion of race, and like many scholars he also overlooks female subjectivity in favor of male subjectivity.

Whereas I identify postclassic noir as either neo- or retro-noir, Martin sees two strands of neo-noir cinema existent in the early 1970s and persisting to the present. He calls these strands "revisionist" and "formulaic" and ties them into his penetrating discussion of industrial influences. Martin sees revisionist noir as "inspired by the nouvelle vague's experimental/investigative approach to film" and "a staple of low-budget independent feature film production."[9] He views formulaic noir as "a manifestation of renewed cinematic interest in a popular narrative pattern" and "a staple of both mainstream major studio production and low-budget straight-to-video and made-for-television production."[10] Martin's terminology proves useful, although, as we shall see, his oppositions revive a problematic binary.

Many films I identify as neo-noirs, those crime films made after the classic period and set in approximately the same time in which they were produced, function as revisionist noir, especially with regard to gender—even those, such as *Body Heat* (1981), that contain elements Martin identifies as formulaic. In contrast, retro-noirs are almost solely formulaic and reactionary with regard to gender. Retro-noirs promote a fantasy that never existed to the same degree in the fantasy of classic noir—a fantasy of violent and repressive white male power and female passivity.

Martin provides an illuminating discussion of 1970s, '80s, and '90s noir, in which whiteness is implicit. He sees 1940s noir as "founded on male-female relationships, with *the woman serving as the locus of male psychological dislocation and sexual dysfunction*" (emphasis added), and ties 1970s noir into 1950s noir, suggesting that both decades concentrated "*more overtly on masculinity* and the corruption of patriarchy" while marginalizing the femme fatale (emphasis added).[11] For Martin, a film such as *Taxi Driver* (1976) exemplifies the revisionism of the 1970s, whereas *Sea of Love* (1989) represents the pastiche of the 1980s, and both films represent "the danger of *masculinity's entropic trajectory* toward alienation and psychosis" (emphasis added).[12] *Romeo Is Bleeding* (1994) embodies the irony of the 1990s and is "*thematically concerned with the notion of masculinity in crisis* and the broader social implication of patriarchal corruption" (emphasis added).[13] Martin's taxonomy of noir is both effective and useful, placing an emphasis on masculinity and patriarchal corruption. But in addition to race, Martin overlooks another important focus: female subjectivity. The omission of race as a determinant will be taken up in greater detail in the following chapter. Martin's discussion of *Body Heat* exemplifies his focus on masculinity.

The popular 1980s neo-noir *Body Heat,* a film cultural critic Fredric Jameson sees as exemplary of postmodern nostalgia, nevertheless revises classic noir's insistence that the femme fatale be punished for her agency. Instead, she survives, an important change for spectators interested in female subjectivity. Martin suggests that in the 1980s and '90s a cultural shift took place "from the neomodern to the postmodern with an attendant focus on style, surface, and playfulness; a commodification . . . of the stylistic experimentation, formal revisionism and self-referentiality of Scorsese and his fellow Hollywood renaissance filmmakers."[14] For Martin, *Body Heat* "marks the beginnings of the postmodern era," positing a "return to genre and the reaffirmation of the myth of the film noir crime melodrama."[15] For him, this film and other 1980s noirs' "evocation of the iconography, narrative patterns, and character types of the classic film noir constitutes little more than a superficial, primarily visual re-creation of film noir rather than the dynamic thematic reinvention of the genre represented by the no less allusive texts of the sixties and seventies."[16]

Martin cites noir scholar Leighton Grist's rather damning assessment of the film: according to Grist, in "place of the reflexive interrogation and reinflection of the New Hollywood period, the generic self-consciousness of *Body Heat* is superficial, and not at all analytical."[17] Likewise, in *Genre and Hollywood,* Neale appears to share Grist's and Martin's assessment of eighties and nineties noir, suggesting "most of the 1980s and 1990s films use [the idea and image of noir] as a basis for uncritical pastiche."[18] Naremore, in *More than Night,* does not spend much time on *Body Heat,* although he does note in discussing the film that "most examples of neo-noir are less artistically sophisticated and politically interesting than the films they emulate."[19] Here, then, under the guise of neomodern noir and postmodern noir, an essential debate resurfaces and swirls around *Body Heat.*

Perhaps *Body Heat* does, as Martin suggests, "reaffirm the myth of the film noir crime melodrama," but instead of understanding that as a reproach, Martin's use of the term *melodrama* is auspicious.[20] In *Dangerous Dames,* I explored the connection between the Weimar street film and film noir—both are postwar cinematic phenomena overtly concerned with unstable masculinity, while simultaneously featuring a new type of powerful female subjectivity. Both film noir and the Weimar street film serve as forms of melodramatic representation concerned just as much with issues of white femininity as with white masculinity, although with differing ways of addressing those issues.

The neo-noir *Body Heat* addresses these concerns by ending with the homme fatal Ned (William Hurt) in jail and with the femme fatale Matty (Kathleen Turner) on an exotic beach, with money and handsome, apparently Latin American, male company (Figure 2.1). Unlike the classic film noir femme fatale, Matty survives and thrives, an outcome often shared by other femmes fatales in neo-noir. Ned, however, suffers the same fate as the classic homme fatal; his desire for a dangerous woman and financial wealth dooms him to jail. As Tasker notes, "Ned doesn't have the authority of a voice-over, but we know he is doomed in any case."[21] Obviously, the dangers and pleasures involved in a filmic narrative such as *Body Heat* vary substantially. Although some viewers see the same old film noir crime melodrama, others see an important and agreeable difference from classic film noir, which insisted on the containment or elimination of both the homme and femme fatals; here, only the homme fatal takes the fall. Martin's focus on the superficial, formulaic aspects of *Body Heat* devalues the films he labels as postmodern in favor of neo-modern, and masculine, films such as *Taxi Driver.*

Let me be perfectly clear here. I am not suggesting that *Body Heat* is a better-made, higher-quality film than *Taxi Driver.* However, the criticisms of Martin et al. imply a value system that sanctions subjectivity easily identified as male. The same essentialist debate surfaced around whether Germany's Weimar cinema was modernist or mass cultural. In the same way that many formidable critics, in-

Figure 2.1. The unexpected narrative pleasure of the neo-noir (*Body Heat*, 1981)

cluding Martin Heidegger and Anton Kaes, discounted the value of mass cultural production, and even stressed the potential for this type of production to do harm, so too Martin discounts films he labels postmodern and formulaic. And although the subject of both Weimar modern and what Martin terms neo-modern production is only implied, as Patrice Petro shows in *Joyless Streets: Women and Melodramatic Representation in the Weimar Street Film* and as I show in Martin's taxonomy of postclassic noir, it is both implicitly white, and more central to this discussion of gender, implicitly male.[22] Petro's delineation of the discourses circulating around Weimar cinema and Martin's delineation of the discourses of postclassic noir suggest a series of oppositions.

Weimar Cinema (Petro)

Popular	*Avant-garde*
Realist	Experimental
Mass cultural	Modernist
Passivity	Activity
(white) Male subject (confirmed)	(white) Male subject (destabilized)
(white) Female subject implied	(white) Female subject ignored

Petro devotes the first two chapters of *Joyless Streets* to outlining the history and critical reception of Weimar cinema. The debates surrounding Weimar cinema focused on whether or not it was mass cultural or modernist. According to Petro, after "defining radically different objects of analysis," critics and cultural theorists then "insist on a remarkably similar subject—the male subject whose identity is seen either as confirmed by mass culture or as destabilized by modernist practices."[23] The final pair of oppositions delineating Petro's view of Weimar history suggests that the female subject is at least implied by the mass cultural view of Germany's early cinema. As Petro notes, "mass culture itself was commonly personified as 'feminine,' as having the capacity to induce passivity, vulnerability, even corruption," whereas "modernism was often construed as 'masculine,' as providing an active and productive alternative to the pleasures of mass cultural entertainment."[24] Martin makes a similar move.

Postclassic Noir (Martin et al.)*

Postmodern	*Neomodern*
Formulaic	Revisionist
1980s and 1990s neo-noir	1970s neo-noir
(*Body Heat*)	(Scorsese)
(white) Male subject	(white) Male subject
(confirmed or destabilized)	(destabilized)
(white) Female subject	(white) Female subject
(confirmed)	(ignored)

*Martin identifies what I call postclassic noir as neo-noir.

As the oppositions delineating Martin's view of postclassic noir indicate, the focus on male subjectivity and the marginalization of female subjectivity continues. Although the early critics might have associated the female spectator with the passive and potentially dangerous pleasures of the mass-cultural product, Martin leaves that overt sexism out. The neomodern product is simply better than the postmodern one, more intelligent, more complex, and more masculine. The pleasures of the less demanding postmodern text, by implication only, evoke femininity.

Martin sees the shift from neomodern to postmodern noir coming in the 1980s; others see the postmodern turn coming with the cinema itself. In a sense, the appearance of women in the cinema audience does correspond with the disruption of the stable, modern, and masculine subject. In *Window Shopping*, Friedberg discusses "history and memory" as "endangered forms" and "cinematic and televisual apparatuses . . . not just as symptoms of a 'post-modern condition,' but as contributing causes."[25] She suggests that if "feminisms have had as one of their prime agendas the reordering of the relations of power and difference, then appropriation and its aesthetic underbelly, nostalgia, must be interrogated for the ways in which these strategies in representation DO reorder relations of power and difference."[26] Friedberg goes on to assert that "postmodern aesthetic practice does not always undermine that authority, it can reassert it."[27]

By examining the postmodern phenomena of postclassic noir—looking at what is appropriated and why, at how nostalgia works, and at where and how relations of power and difference are reordered or reasserted—I hope to disrupt the reinscription of the model that Martin implies. His model does not consider race, and continues to marginalize the feminine subject while rearticulating the values of self-conscious intellectualism, experimentation, and revisionism, associating those qualities with a subject that Martin identifies as neomodern and that is implicitly masculine. Below is a possible sexed paradigm for postclassic film noir, one that allows male and female subjectivity a place; race comes next.

Postclassic Noir

Retro-noir	*Neo-noir*
(*L.A. Confidential,*	(*Body Heat, Jackie Brown,*
Mulholland Falls)	*Twilight*)
Reactionary (gender)	Revisionist (gender)
Male subject confirmed	Female subject confirmed
Female subject marginalized	Male subject destabilized
Nostalgia (Friedberg)	Appropriation (Friedberg)

In this provisionary sexed paradigm, retro-noirs feature a reactionary vision of gender: male characters become more violent and female characters more powerless than they usually were in classic film noir. Both retro- and neo-noir films reflect postmodern nostalgia, drawing on a cinematic past that has more to do with current conditions than the historical moment of classic noir. Friedberg builds on this notion, suggesting that the reactionary impulse of nostalgia has a revisionary opposite, appropriation.

In retro-noir, then, nostalgia implies a reactionary call for the return, with a vengeance, of masculinity and the repression of femininity, whereas neo-noir appropriation implies revisions that allow for new conceptions of masculinity and femininity within the mythologies of gender in postclassic noir. Neo-noir appeals to certain spectators by appropriating the concept of the powerful female character embodied by the femme fatale in classic noir and revising that character in ways that provide visual and narrative pleasures for those who enjoy seeing a female character triumph. In these revisions, the female protagonist often survives and thrives instead of winding up dead, in jail, or married, containments of female agency insisted upon by classic film noir. In contrast to the neo-noir femme fatale, the homme fatal suffers the same fate he once did in classic noir: he is jailed or killed. Marriage does not appear as a viable survival strategy for the neo-noir homme fatal.

Just as these representations reflect the ambiguities and indeterminancies of postmodernism, they also reflect and prefigure current cultural discourses in what is often called third-wave feminism. Third-wave feminism, far from a monolithic movement, follows previous feminisms. According to Brenda O'Neill in "What Do Women Think?" the "first wave of the feminist movement in the early twentieth century won basic legal rights such as the right to own property, to vote and sit in the Senate [and] the second wave in the 1960s and 1970s fought for substantive equality."[28]

Like first- and second-wave feminism, third-wave feminism has numerous disparate camps, as Amanda Lotz delineates in "Communicating Third-Wave Feminism and New Social Movements: Challenges for the Next Century of Feminist Endeavor."[29] According to Lotz, reactionary third-wave feminism, popular in the media, primarily attacks the second wave "on such grounds as constructing women as victims rather than empowering them, and overemphasizing the epidemic of acquaintance rape," and for the most part ignores the cultural advances for women won during middle phase of feminist activism.[30] What Lotz and others call reactionary third-wave feminism is often called postfeminism.[31] Leslie Heywood and Jennifer Drake, in *Third Wave Agenda: Being Feminist, Doing Feminism,* suggest that " 'postfeminist' characterizes a group of young, conservative feminists who explicitly define themselves against and criticize feminists of the second wave."[32] Shugart also sees the media as promoting another version of reactionary postfeminism, in the mass-market personas of Alanis Morissette, Kate Moss, and television character Ally McBeal. According to Shugart, while representing some of the characteristics of third-wave feminism such as an awareness of and confrontation with the exploitation of women, androgyny, and confident sexuality, these media images also defuse third-wave feminism in favor of a patriarchal femininity.[33]

Retro-noir representations of gender support the same sort of patriarchal femininity. By setting these narratives in the past, these films avoid direct confrontation with feminism, and can instead present a past in which no one questions reactionary versions of gender. If film noir once suggested a discourse of gender that implied resistance to patriarchal norms, retro-noir instead provides what Shugart calls a " 'genuine imitation' — something whose code appears strikingly similar to the resistant discourse but, by virtue of strategic repositioning, is rendered devoid of challenge."[34] The pastiche femme fatale is also a genuine imitation. She looks like, but does not act like, a classic noir femme fatale. The retro-noir imitation supports instead of challenges the patriarchy.

Third-wave feminism also includes other approaches that do challenge dominant discourse, approaches more in tune with the ongoing need for feminist activism and conscious of the identity politics that alienated many from second-wave feminism. According to Lotz, these feminisms critique "the race and ethnicity-based exclusion" of second-wave feminism, while also focusing "on theorizing variant access to privilege among women, expanding the theoretical framework to include other factors defining identity, such as sexual orientation and class."[35] Third-wave feminism includes both reactionary postfemininist and progressive camps. The progressive branches embrace a diversity of racial, sexual, and class identities and seek to work both inside and beyond the academy promoting the ongoing value of feminist practice.

Third-wave feminism, like postmodernism, reflects inherent cultural contradictions, appearing discursively in the culture as both reactionary and revisionary. Reactionary postfeminism also implies, like postmodernism, that feminism (like modernism) is a phenomenon of the past. The discourses of third-wave feminism and postfeminism circulated in the late 1990s and continue to do so today. While retro-noir exhibits the reactionary and conservative elements, neo-noir reflects, at least in the representation of gender, the more positive impulses of third wave feminism, and the more revisionary aspects of postmodernism.

The sudden appearance — although he was always there — of the homme fatal and the homme attrapé in film noir also provides a significant benefit for re-reading gender in film noir. The presence of these hommes, and their analogous relationship to the femmes of film noir, makes explicit how the capitalist patriarchy affects both male and female characters. Neither classic nor postclassic film noir, nor the criticism surrounding noir, seems concerned with race. Implicit in most of the discussion above has been white heterosexual subjectivity, whether male or female. The next chapter adds race to the paradigm and enhances the complexity and significance of these explorations.

CHAPTER 3

RACING THE PARADIGM: THE WHITENESS OF FILM NOIR

Racial Others . . . keep coming back into white lives in film noir. Untoward behavior and its seeming inevitable racial echoes indelibly mark the white homes—and films—for which race typically exists somewhere else.

ERIC LOTT, "The Whiteness of Film Noir"

Issues of race do not seem to dominate film noir narratives; issues of gender and class do. As noted in the introduction, these films usually narrate the efforts of working-class women and men who struggle to escape their economic situation not through legal and less profitable means but through scams, heists, and seductions that promise (but in classic film noir never yield) financial nirvana. The male noir protagonist, the homme fatal, often has nothing but disdain for the working man willing to punch a clock and bring home a small paycheck, and the femme fatales are equally unwilling to raise a brood of children and work in the domestic realm. As Straayer notes, "the American dream of home, family, and 'security' is precisely the feminine fulfillment which the femme fatale intended to elude."[1] These characters resist a society that seeks to contain their desires for a better life, although the final reel of the classic films noirs makes sure that resistance is futile.

Class and race are, of course, articulated intimately in U.S. culture. As David Roediger notes in *The Wages of Whiteness: Race and the Making of the American Working Class,* "working class formation and the systematic development of a sense of whiteness went hand in hand for the U.S. white working class."[2] He

29

goes on to discuss how this sense of whiteness prevents large-scale class wars in which whites and other races unite. Roediger paraphrases W. E. B. DuBois, who suggests that "white labor does not just resist and receive racist ideas but embraces, adopts, and, at times, murderously acts upon those ideas," adding that the "problem is not just that the white working class is at critical junctures manipulated into racism, but that it comes to think of itself and its interests as white."[3] Working-class whites, the dominant characters in classic films noirs, must be read and understood relative to how other races and classes appear in the films. This project attempts to read these images carefully, in both classic and postclassic noir, and includes an examination of race that does not elide whiteness.

The birth of classic film noir in 1941 also heralded the demise of an industry that produced race films in the United States. Although World War II opened economic doors for women and people of color by allowing them into employment areas previously dominated by white men, as these economic pathways opened up, others closed. As Thomas Cripps notes in "Hollywood's High Noon: Moviemaking and Society before Television," prior to World War II, in the 1920s and '30s, "race movies challenged Hollywood movies in that they took black aspiration seriously and formulated it into generic melodramas of scaling a black ladder of success, struggling against demons of cupidity with the race (never any off-screen white demons), and reworkings of white genres such as musicals, westerns, and film noir."[4]

Cripps adds, these race movies would face "the same fate the Negro National Baseball League faced after Jackie Robinson signed on with the white Brooklyn Dodgers: both Hollywood and major league baseball, by holding out a promise of black integration into a classier product than blacks could provide for themselves, ensured that the black audience would desert in favor of an integrated future."[5] In 1919, black filmmaker Oscar Micheaux expressed the desire to film "plays that deal in some way with Negro life as lived by Negroes in that age or period, or day."[6] Instead, with social integration, black audiences settled for Hollywood cinema that represented them less negatively but only obliquely or as a small part of white narratives. As Anna Everett makes clear in *Returning the Gaze: A Genealogy of Black Film Criticism, 1909–1949,* "Hollywood's short-lived and limited reformulation of cinematic blackness was the result of a necessary capitulation to the demands of generating pro-war sentiments in the hearts of all Americans, including blacks."[7] This partial glimpse of black culture is exactly what most classic films noirs offer.

But a further marginalization takes place, as Judith Mayne suggests in her chapter on white spectatorship in *Cinema and Spectatorship.* In movies, "one of the most efficient ways to evoke and deny race simultaneously is to make a black character a projection of white anxieties about race."[8] Much film noir criticism engages in an additional projection. In "Noir by Noirs: Towards a New Realism in Black Cinema," Manthia Diawara notes that in classic film noir "women, bad guys, and detectives are . . . considered 'black' by virtue of the fact that they occupy indeterminate and monstrous spaces such as whiteness traditionally reserves for blackness in our culture."[9] Diawara sees feminist criticism as exposing "film noir's attempt to paint white women 'black' in order to limit or control their independent agency, their self-fashioning."[10] Diawara makes an interesting point, one echoed by Lott and Rabinowitz. Not only are black characters a representation of white anxieties about race, but even white characters acquire blackness through their association with darkness, the underworld, and evil. In postclassic noir, white anxieties about race, about class, about power, and about gender are again projected onto nonwhites.

Yet those familiar with classic film noir know that the black culture represented there often connotes something other than darkness, evilness, and a criminal underworld. The white male protagonist's familiarity with and acceptance into black culture often indicates his hipness. Black culture seems, in some classic film noir sequences, to represent not a source of evil but an ideal if stereotypical world of sophistication, of feelings reflected in music, and of community that, at least liminally, includes the white protagonist. Naremore suggests these hints about black culture "give the protagonist an aura of 'cool.' "[11]

In "Racial Cross-Dressing and the Construction of American Whiteness," Eric Lott goes further, suggesting that "white American manhood" could "not exist without a racial other against which it defines itself and which . . . it takes up into itself as one of its own constituent elements."[12] The white male noir protagonist, unlike lesser male characters, is apparently secure enough in his masculinity to enter into a realm where he could be measured against the "potent fantasies of the black male body."[13] His familiarity with black culture enhances his hipness and his white masculinity. The two ways that classic film noir represents blackness, as extreme and threatening otherness internalized by whites and as desirable difference externally, illustrate Lott's thesis about the "combined vigilance and absorptive cross-racial fascination of North American whiteness."[14]

Lott also discusses the historical and cultural context of classic film noir in "The Whiteness of Film Noir." He details the racial tensions of the 1940s, noting the "massive March on Washington Movement against discrimination in the wartime defense plants," as well as that "the ranks of the NAACP began to grow in tandem with rising black political and economic desires" and that "Hollywood itself . . . agreed to reshape black movie roles in accord with the new times."[15] Lott mentions the "zoot suit" riots of 1943, in which "black and Mexican youths . . . were convenient targets of attack for white service men and police whose violence often sparked such street combat."[16] Although these tensions rarely appear explicitly in classic film noir, they inform the vision of whiteness and nonwhite culture represented in these films.

The classic noir white male protagonist's access to and acceptance by nonwhite culture represent a social liberalism that was not culturally widespread. In postclassic noir, things appear to change. Just as retro-noir contains the threat represented by the white femme fatale, so too the white male protagonist's access to black culture, and associated social liberalism, is also contained. Retro-noirs, for the most part, forgo the inclusion of the generic noir sequence that suggested the hipness and stable white masculinity of a male protagonist through his contact with black culture. Instead, even the suggestion of such a measure being taken is absent from most retro-noir, perhaps because the retro-noir male's portrayal of hypermasculinity cannot withstand the suggestion of tolerance and empathy that such contact implies. White masculinity in retro-noir can no longer risk social contact with black culture. Although neo-noir displays appropriation and revision with regard to gender, many neo-noir texts remain reactionary with regard to race, perhaps because attention to gender enables a lack of attention to race in some narratives.

Naremore, in *More than Night,* devotes a chapter to "The Other Side of the Street," where white male "characters on the margin of the middle class encounter a variety of 'others': not savages, but criminals, sexually independent women, homosexuals, Asians, Latins, and black people."[17] Naremore then charts the history of each racial category, beginning with Asians. According to Naremore, "the Far East was repeatedly associated in film noir with enigmatic and criminal behavior" and was treated "as a kind of aestheticized bordello, where one could experience all sorts of forbidden pleasures."[18] In the cold war era, "propaganda images of sadistic Asians persisted," and by the end of the 1980s, "as Tokyo became an economic rival of the United States, old stereotypes [of mystery and Eastern decadence] began to reappear in thrillers."[19] Naremore concludes with a brief discussion of Japanese cinema, Chinese-American director Wayne Wang, and Hong Kong-influenced John Woo. Naremore does not mention two recent and ubiquitous Asian stereotypes—the hardworking convenience store owner in urban areas, and the Asian overachiever in the academic realm—although hints of both stereotypes appear in the late-1990s postclassic noirs *Fight Club* and *Fargo.*

Like Asian environs, Latin America exerts a similar exoticism in film noir, but with a stress, according to Naremore, on "relief from repression" and "a mélange of sentimental pastoralism and chic primitivism."[20] He notes that little has changed in the characterization of Latin America in postclassic noir, although the setting now extends to Miami. He concludes with a brief discussion of Latin America's own film noir tradition and Robert Rodriguez's *El Mariachi*

Figure 3.1. Diegetic hints of black culture in classic film noir (*The Maltese Falcon,* 1941)

(1997). Naremore laments that "few pictures in this [Miami noir] vein have made significant use of Latin characters."[21] Postclassic noirs such as *L.A. Confidential* and *Twilight* do include minor Latin characters, characters who both represent and contain a potential threat to white male dominance. African American characters play a similar role in postclassic noir.

Naremore does not really discuss Africa, although his heading and previous discussions of Asia and South America lead the reader to expect it. Instead, he begins with a discussion of the relative liberality of the hard-boiled writers, who often implied the "blacks and whites might be brothers under the skin."[22] He goes on to assert that "most films noirs of the 1940s are staged in artificially white settings, with occasional black figures as extras in the background."[23] One such sequence occurs in *The Maltese Falcon* (1941) when Sam Spade (Humphrey Bogart) takes the newspaper-wrapped falcon to the bus station to check it. In the background, a sophisticated, well-dressed black couple engages in an animated conversation (Figure 3.1). The man gesticulates and speaks while the woman smiles and listens—the passive woman and active man stereotype firmly in place. Nevertheless, these black citizens of San Francisco seem somewhat different from the "black Pullman porters, musicians, shoeshine boys, janitors, maids, and nightclub singers" who, Naremore suggests, usually appear in classic film noir.[24] Of course, as Everett and other scholars point out, these sequences also perpetuate the false image of a racially integrated U.S. society, one that served Hollywood during "this time of national crisis."[25] Film noir's forays into nightclubs do serve to suggest, as does the couple in the bus station in *The Maltese Falcon,* that a vibrant black culture exists just offscreen.

Other scholars have documented the history of black actors in Hollywood productions throughout the twentieth century.[26] As Donald Bogle notes in *Toms, Coons, Mulattoes, Mammies, and Bucks: An Interpretive History of Blacks in American Films,* nightclub scenes emerged in the 1930s and '40s as a "special platform for displaying the [black] entertainer to his best advantage."[27] Nat "King" Cole, Louis Armstrong, Duke Ellington, or Hazel Scott could perform in these locales without directly affecting the narrative. The sequences reflect Hollywood's attempt to integrate blacks and black entertainers into films in less obviously stereotypical ways. Black women become singers and chic nightclubbers instead of cooks and mammies, although many still portrayed maids. Black men become musicians and sophisticated, well-dressed patrons instead of porters or servants, although many still work as waiters or bartenders on screen. At the same time, many of these musical scenes "were not integrated into the script," and therefore "blacks could be cut from the films without spoiling them should local (or Southern) theater owners feel their audiences would object to seeing a Negro."[28] In films noirs the jazz club scenes, although brief, are usually integral to the plot and therefore not expendable. These scenes may provide entertainment for the film spectator and often yield information for the hard-boiled white male protagonist. They may serve to prefigure some impending threat to him or to bolster his liberal white masculinity.

Naremore moves from the films of the 1940s to discuss the black culture featured in the films of Melvin Van Peebles and Gordon Parks (*Shaft*), briefly mentions white directors Martin Scorsese and Quentin Tarantino, and then the "noirs by noirs," including directors Charles Burnett and Carl Franklin.[29] Diawara explores these films as well. He sees *Rage in Harlem* (1991) as paradigmatic of black film noir, which includes films like *Boyz N the Hood* (1991), *Malcolm X* (1992), *Juice* (1992), and *Deep Cover* (1992). For Diawara, "black *film noir* is a light (as in day*light*) cast on black people."[30] He reads these noirs as socially conscious, often ending with the transformation of the protagonist into a person cognizant of the "need for blacks to care for blacks, for resistance to colonizing structures, and for a movement towards a good life society founded on an amelioration of existing material conditions."[31]

These films may mark a return to the thriving black film industry of the early twentieth century, but the films I discuss here align more closely with classic noir, and like those earlier films, are mostly white written, produced, directed, and marketed. Although some reviewers and critics regret the lack, almost no one sees social consciousness in the films of Tarantino. Instead, as Susan Fraiman argues in *Cool Men and the Second Sex,* Tarantino's films promote a distinctly antifeminist violence, even as the director capitalizes on the coolness associated with black culture.[32] As Naremore observes, *Pulp Fiction,* directed by Tarantino, does arouse various responses from spectators with regard to racism. The neo-noir *Jackie Brown,* also directed by Tarantino, with its black female protagonist and black male antagonist, also provides ample room for a variety of reactions. If the representation of blacks and whites in *Jackie Brown* seems somewhat more nuanced and revisionary than that of *Pulp Fiction,* in retro-noir *L.A. Confidential,* Hispanic and black culture serves only as a marginalized criminal backdrop for white, homosocial, masculine, and much more profitable criminality.

To start to understand race in these late-1990s noirs, it can be added in a rudimentary way to the paradigm suggested in the previous chapter.

Postclassic 1990s Noir

Retro-noir	*Neo-noir*
(*L.A. Confidential*)	(*Jackie Brown*)
Reactionary (gender, nostalgia)	Revisionist (gender, appropriation)
Reactionary (race, nostalgia)	Reactionary or revisionist (race, nostalgia, or appropriation)
White male subject confirmed	Black and white female subjects confirmed
White and nonwhite female subjects marginalized	Black and white male subjects destabilized

As this provisionary raced and sexed paradigm shows, although certain postclassic noirs appear as revisionist or reactionary, even within a single text, contradictions surface that prevent facile characterizations. Appropriation remains associated with revisionism, and nostalgia with the reactionary impulse, and some postclassic films noirs may well contain both elements. Indeed, by its nature as a derivative of a series of conflicting ideas, postclassic noir embodies these types of contradictions, making it a complex but fascinating object of study. One reason postclassic noir remains such a vibrant source of visual and narrative pleasure no doubt has to do with the complexity noir continues to offer scholars, moviegoers, and moviemakers. The discourses of race, gender, and class in retro- and neo-noir are investigated later in the book; the next three chapters explore these elements in three classic film noir texts.

PART 2

PROTOTYPES IN CLASSIC NOIR

CHAPTER 4

THE KILLERS (1946): QUINTESSENTIAL NOIR?

The second evening we wanted to see *The Killers*, the film based on the new Hemingway novel, which was playing in an outlying district [of San Francisco]. We set out on foot in the evening. . . . Suddenly, we were on a dark road lined with tracks, unmoving trains, and hangars, crossed now and then by other deserted streets. . . . It began to rain violently, and in the wind and rain, we felt as forlorn as on a treeless plain—no shelter, no cars in sight. At last we saw a light and rang the bell at the gate of some kind of depot. . . . Men busy with boxes and bales of merchandise led us to a telephone so we could call a taxi, and we waited a good quarter of an hour under their roof. After two miles we were again in a district full of lights and drugstores. We even arrived in time to see *The Killers*.

SIMONE DE BEAUVOIR, *America Day by Day*

At nightfall, in a peaceful American small town, two men with cruel and scornful expressions have just arrived by the main highway. After a brief scene of clipped violence in one of those diners that in the United States spring up alongside the road, they make off for the house of their victim.

The man they are going to kill listens, panting, to footsteps resounding on the stairs. The door is suddenly opened, a blast of air obliterates the darkness and the silence, then the shadows are restored.

RAYMOND BORDE AND ETIENNE CHAUMETON,
A Panorama of American Film Noir, 1941–1953

The Killers (1946) features nearly all the elements constitutive of noir—a white cast of mostly working-class characters that includes the doomed homme fatal alluded to in the second of the opening epigraphs; a femme fatale who, true to type, destroys both the male protagonist and herself with her duplicity; a femme and an homme attrapé functioning within the patriarchal system, both of whom offer the protagonist a redemption he cannot accept; and a depiction of domestic life that does not glorify that realm. The film has an investigator seeking to discover the mystery of the femme fatale and a cadre of low-life thieves and hoodlums working for a suave criminal mastermind. Half of what makes *The Killers* classic film noir includes this typical cast of characters. Indeed, *Film Noir: An Encyclopedic Reference to the American Style* identifies *The Killers* as "a quintessential noir," citing the "disjointed and at times overlapping" narrative threads that contribute to the "alienating disjunction felt by Swede [the protagonist] and his subsequent surrender to the nightmarish trap of a classic *femme fatale,* Kitty Collins."[1]

But the other half of the film's appeal lies in the ambiguity with which it treats many of the tropes of noir. The femme fatale, although narratively locked in position as a duplicitous, sexy woman by her initial appearance on the screen, takes on more and more of the trappings of a femme attrapé as the film proceeds. The femme attrapé herself becomes more domesticated, but her allure early in the film belies her label, which generically insists she be visually dull and unappealing. This film noir also includes the male characters common to classic noir: an homme fatal and an homme attrapé. The homme fatal pays with his life for his desire to escape working-class existence; the homme attrapé acquiesces in the demands of society and survives. The investigator, unlike the private detective characters played by Bogart in *The Maltese Falcon* and *The Big Sleep,* arouses almost no interest. Spectators can scarcely remember what the investigator in *The Killers* looks like, nor do we care that much about him. *The Killers* is classic noir, and what makes it quintessential is how interestingly and ambiguously its supposedly classic characters develop.

Based on a short story of the same name by Ernest Hemingway, directed by German émigré Robert Siodmak, and starring Burt Lancaster and Ava Gardner, *The Killers* reconstructs the past of Swede (Lancaster), a man who, in the opening sequence of the film, passively allows himself to be shot to death by two killers, one a burly Hemingway look-alike, the other a menacing tall man (Figure 4.1). In their formative *A Panorama of American Film Noir, 1941–1953,* French cultural critics Borde and Chaumeton describe the "dark absurdism" of the opening scene: "a couple of hired gunmen walk into a small-town diner on the road to nowhere and complain about the menu" and "terrify the clients with contemptible self-confidence."[2] The Hemingway short story ends with the gun-

Figure 4.1. The killers in the diner, with superb noir lighting (*The Killers,* 1946)

men killing their victim, but the film narrative goes on to fill in the questions left by the murder.

This opening sequence is also the only place in the film where a nonwhite character appears, a black cook named Sam (Bill Walker). Sam works in the diner where the killers first seek Swede and consummately plays the frightened bystander; he threatens no one's masculinity (Figure 4.2).[3] After this brief sequence, the world of *The Killers* becomes almost exclusively white, although in "Film Noir: Outside History, but Historically So," Oliver Harris discusses the ethnic aspects of that whiteness.[4] Whereas other films noirs often use black culture to suggest something about the white male investigator, this does not occur in *The Killers,* and the investigator is not the male protagonist. Swede is the object of our interest, and Kitty appears to lead to his doom.

Kitty (Gardner) seems to function as a classic femme fatale. The convoluted story of Swede's involvement with Kitty, her urbane criminal boyfriend "Big Jim" Colfax (Albert Decker), and a gang of thieves develops through a series of character-linked, homodiegetic flashbacks.[5] Much of the information provided by the narrative encourages both the movie spectator and, apparently, the insurance investigator, Riordan (Edmond O'Brien), to pin growing suspicion on Kitty as the author and perpetrator of a profitable double-cross that leaves Swede broke

Figure 4.2. Hollywood stereotype of the black cook (*The Killers*, 1946)

and a shell (albeit a handsome shell in a torso-revealing undershirt) of a man. In the penultimate sequence of the film, Riordan solves the mystery surrounding Kitty. Her boyfriend, Colfax, who in the course of the film has become her husband, is the mastermind behind the double-cross and even the subsequent murder of Swede. Colfax uses Kitty, planning on her seduction and abandonment of Swede as the endgame in a robbery scam that leaves Kitty and Colfax with the take and the rest of the gang, including Swede, empty-handed. Nevertheless, Riordan saves most of his derision at the end of the film for Kitty, taunting her as her husband dies, saying, "Your would-be fall guy is dead."

Typical of a film noir femme fatale, Kitty is beautiful, duplicitous, and willing to use her erotic appeal to manipulate and destroy men in order to get what she wants (or, in Kitty's case, what Colfax wants). In classic film noir, the femme fatale's actions almost always prove fatal to her as well as her male victims. But in *The Killers,* Kitty only appears invested with power—Colfax actually engineers her duplicity, just as he uses Swede in the initial robbery. Kitty, in this supposedly quintessential film noir, does not have the power many classic noir femmes fatales wield, although she still pays the price for appearing to drive the narrative. Kitty at first looks like the femme fatale within the narrative space of *The Killers,* but the visual information provided by the film alerts spectators to another aspect of her character, to the awareness that Kitty increasingly becomes a femme attrapé as well. In his discussion of the fascination of film noir, Harris provides insightful psychoanalytic readings of the male characters and their actions, yet completely ignores the ambiguous characterization of Kitty. Harris continues the tradition, delineated in Chapter Two, of omitting female subjectivity from his analysis by focusing on male characters and, by implication, male spectators. Harris misses a crucial aspect of *The Killers,* one central to reading gender in the film. Although Kitty certainly functions as a femme fatale, importantly, she does less than that as well. She does not drive the narrative; Colfax does.

Kitty's first appearance on the screen contains all the familiar iconography of a film noir femme fatale—indeed, the visual force of that initial sequence, despite its brevity, serves to carry the spectator toward the conclusion of the film fully convinced of Kitty's essential greed and duplicity. Kitty is first seen about forty minutes into the film in a flashback narrated by Lilly (Virginia Christine), Swede's childhood girlfriend, explaining to Riordan why she and Swede stopped seeing each other.[6] In a sequence lasting approximately four minutes, Lilly and Swede enter a party in a luxurious apartment, peopled with women in evening dresses and shady men with "mean eyes" and names like Jake and Blinky, and featuring Kitty, sitting at the piano in a striking black gown that accentuates her dark hair and voluptuous figure. Swede is instantly and totally smitten, and Lilly admits it, saying that she left the party and he "never even missed me; he'd never been in love before."[7] The sequence concludes with a shot of Kitty in the sexy evening gown, leaning on the piano, drink and cigarette in hand as she sings a love song, obviously aware of Swede's mesmerized gaze behind her (Figure 4.3).

In Kitty's second appearance, she sits laughing and chatting vivaciously in a restaurant, wearing a light-colored sophisticated dress and an exotic hat. In both of these sequences, early in the chronology of the film, Kitty is a femme fatale. Kitty's boyfriend, Colfax, languishes in jail as she first seduces Swede and then, in the restaurant scene, convinces Swede to "take the fall" for a jewelry theft that she apparently committed.[8] But Colfax gets out of jail, and in each of her subsequent appearances in the film, Kitty is increasingly deglamorized—she appears in various seedy motel rooms, first in a fitted sweater and skirt; then visibly tired, without makeup, in a checked shirt (Figure 4.4); and, finally, as a character in her own flashback of her eventual betrayal of Swede, in a wrinkled shirt and skirt. By the end of the film—supposedly nine years after Lilly's introductory flashback—Kitty looks like an attractive, well-dressed, middle-class housewife (Figure 4.5).

In her essay "Lounge Time: Postwar Crises and the Chronotype of Film Noir," Vivian Sobchack comments on the fact that "not a single scene in [*The Killers*] occurs in what could be considered normal (that is, culturally normative) domestic space."[9] For Sobchack, classic film noir represents, in a material way, the

Figure 4.3. Swede mesmerized by Kitty, an apparent femme fatale (*The Killers*, 1946)

postwar American loss of "the intimacy and security of home and the integrity and solidity of the home front."[10] She sees the spaces of film noir as places where "women . . . are rarely mothers . . . nor are men fathers" and where "no weddings, no births, no natural deaths (although plenty of unnatural ones), no familial intimacy" can occur.[11]

Sobchack does not focus on the fact that the fantasy of domestic space works primarily as a male fantasy of successful patriarchy—the stakes involved in such a fantasy (or the loss of it) were certainly different for a woman.[12] The visual domestication of the femme fatale in *The Killers* takes place completely outside the domestic realm, except possibly for the penultimate scene of Colfax's death, which occurs on a grand staircase in "the huge empty vestibule marked by a cold and geometrically tiled floor" of the Colfax mansion.[13] I agree with Sobchack's assessment of the types of spaces in which film noir plays itself out, yet *The Killers* represents both the allure of the femme fatale and her containment and confinement by men even in the nondomestic spaces of film noir. Kitty enjoys a modicum of freedom during the prison term of her boyfriend, Colfax. Once he gets out of jail, she seems to do his bidding, and the film records her domestication visually. Her ability to actively function as a femme fatale becomes increasingly restricted even by the offscreen presence of Colfax, and this is reflected in her attire and

Figure 4.4. Kitty's deglamorization in the course of the film (*The Killers,* 1946)

Figure 4.5. Kitty's total transformation into a femme attrapée (*The Killers,* 1946)

her surroundings. Kitty is, nevertheless, a femme fatale; she seduces Swede into doing what she wants over and over again, and even attempts to seduce Riordan at the end of the film.

In a late sequence in *The Killers,* Kitty meets Riordan outside a theater, and they take a taxi together to a nightclub called The Green Cat. In many classic noirs, this lounge milieu might include black musicians. No musicians make it into the mise-en-scène here, although the dissonance of the background music increases as the tension in the scene crescendos. Kitty's efforts to portray herself as a married woman who will do anything to protect her new life fail, and she abruptly asks Riordan to take her to his hotel room. He practically leaps from his seat. Robert Porfirio, in "*The Killers:* Expressiveness of Sound and Image in *Film Noir,*" provides a shot-by-shot analysis of this scene and suggests the sequence sustains "her identification as the *femme fatale* by the viewer."[14] Kitty tells Riordan to wait for her, goes to the restroom, and the insurance investigator barely escapes a violent shoot-out with the gunmen who shot Swede. Kitty does portray a classic femme fatale; she wants the threat Riordan represents removed and will go to any length to do that. But the end of the film, when Kitty begs her husband to clear her name before he dies, proves she is also a femme attrapée. Kitty is trapped in a domestic economy that, although outside the usual space of the home, nevertheless insists a woman obey her husband.

Lilly, Swede's childhood sweetheart and the character whose flashback introduces Kitty, serves as the more typical femme attrapée of a noir narrative. Often called the "woman as redeemer," as I noted previously, the femme attrapée stands opposed to the femme fatale, offering acceptance and redemption instead of seduction and destruction.[15] Lilly does not put a great deal of pressure on Swede; she offers complete acceptance, and the way of life she represents probably does

Figure 4.6. Lilly, vibrant and elegant (*The Killers*, 1946)

lead to redemption if one reads male redemption as a low-paying job and domestic life. In her essay, "How Hollywood Deals with the Deviant Male," Deborah
Thomas suggests that both types of women in film noir present the male with
divisive threats, the femme attrapée with the oppression of "prescriptive normality," and the femme fatale with dangerous transgression.[16] Yet the normality
that Lilly offers seems less than oppressive, and she never really pressures Swede.
If he does not want to go out to dinner with her after a boxing match, she says she
understands. If he dumps her mid-date for an obvious femme fatale, she quietly
and independently goes home. Lilly is not portrayed as dull and passive, the way
femmes attrapées in classic films noirs often appear.[17] She seems vivacious, attractive, smartly dressed, and intelligent (Figure 4.6).

Later in the story line of the film, she has married a childhood friend of
Swede's, cop Sam Lubinsky, the homme attrapé. Now she does look the part of
the femme attrapée—she wears a checked housedress and apron as she offers
her husband and the investigator, Riordan, a pitcher of lemonade. But even here
the domestic economy that seems to drain the life out of many femmes attrapées has not enervated Lilly. For example, in *Gun Crazy*, femme attrapée Ruby
(Anabel Shaw) is always exhausted. Once she marries, she is surrounded by an
ever-increasing brood of kids and never seen with her husband.[18] Lilly's nine-

Figure 4.7. Lilly and Sam, the epitome of middle-class normalcy (*The Killers,* 1946)

year marriage to Sam does not seem to have produced children, and she confirms her relative satisfaction with her domestic life both visually, sitting comfortably in his lap, and verbally (Figure 4.7). Sam tells Riordan that Lilly was always in love with Swede; Sam was always in love with Lilly, and it worked out pretty well for him, since Sam is now married to Lilly. But Lilly asserts fondly, "I haven't been too unhappy myself." Although the statement cannot be read as a wholehearted endorsement of married life, Lilly seems adjusted to her situation.

The Killers never implies that Lilly or Kitty work at jobs in the public realm, but many women, both white and nonwhite, were recruited to work in the war industries and then pressured just as strenuously to return to the domestic sphere after the war. Julie Wosk, in *Women and the Machine: Representation from the Spinning Wheel to the Electronic Age,* reports that the propaganda used to encourage women to enter the previously male-dominated labor force revealed the "complex social agendas women were being asked to fill."[19] According to Wosk, women had to be convinced that they could work as "riveters, welders, mechanics, and pilots" and that "they could still retain an aura of glamour and femininity."[20] They were also expected to "keep in mind . . . that they were expected to return to their domestic duties as housewives and mothers after the war."[21] Classic film noir often reveals the difficulties inherent in fulfilling society's postwar demands. Some texts, such as *The Blue Dahlia* (1946) and *Dead Reckoning* (1947), deal explicitly with the difficulties faced by returning veterans. Others show, less obviously, the stresses on women. *Life* magazine in 1943 promoted "Postwar Living" that included "a visionary image of a well-dressed woman in the 'ultra-modern kitchen' of the future, a sparkling clean kitchen of gleaming smooth surfaces," but *The Killers* in 1946 provides Lilly with the most mundane of living arrangements.[22]

Nothing even vaguely glamorous taints the domestic realm that attrapés Sam and Lilly inhabit. Indeed, included as background on the rooftop patio where this scene takes place is a caged bird, symbolic of both the safety and the confinement of domestic life. Sobchack makes much of the fact that Lilly, whom she calls only Lubinsky's wife, "steps out of a door holding a pitcher of lemonade that seems to have come from another dimension," a dimension that must remain "forever off screen" in the film noir universe.[23] True, domestic spaces in film noir rarely appear, and when they do, threats to domestic security often surface as well. In *The Killers,* the oppression implicit in domesticity gains screen time on the patio — in the characters' unglamorous appearances, in the everyday nature of the tasks in which they are engaged (Sam paints furniture, Lilly serves lemonade), and in the caged bird in the background. The spectator does not need to see more of the realm from which Lilly emerges with the lemonade: the mise-en-scène explains the context completely — the realm exists just as powerfully as it would if it had been painstakingly delineated on screen. Both Sam and Lilly made choices. Both of them saw the other life — Sam through his career as a cop and Lilly through her relationship with Swede — yet both chose the security of middle-class life. The film does not gloss over the mundane nature of that life, nor does it particularly glorify it. Domesticity seems only slightly more oppressive for femme attrapée Lilly than for homme attrapé Sam, since Sam, not Lilly, does get to venture out into the spaces of film noir to track down Kitty with the insurance investigator.

Sam and the insurance investigator, Riordan, who decides to investigate why Swede allowed himself to be killed, serve as two more versions of masculinity. Riordan, remarkable for an investigator-hero in a film noir, barely registers as a character. Unlike Humphrey Bogart in *The Big Sleep* (1946) and *The Maltese Falcon* (1941), Robert Mitchum in *Out of the Past* (1947), or Glenn Ford in *The Big Heat* (1953), Edmond O'Brien, the actor who plays Riordan, arouses interest only because his character serves as the vehicle through which the spectator finds out about Kitty and Swede. Riordan's obsession with finding out why Swede allows himself to be gunned down speaks to Riordan's need to escape the ordinary. Neither his boss at the insurance agency nor the cops in the small town where the killing occurs seem very interested in the case. Various brief scenes make lukewarm attempts to establish him as a dashing Sam Spade figure. The secretary in the insurance office calls him "Dream Boy" and competently tracks down his leads, and Kitty, as I note above, in a final attempt to escape the trap he has set for her, does tell him to "Take me back to your hotel." Even in these scenes, however, Riordan seems more ordinary than dreamy and in no way an object of desire. In keeping with his focus on masculinity, Harris discusses Riordan as Swede's "dream double" and suggests that by the end of the film Riordan has "made sense out of the sensual [the femme fatale] and liquidated the experience."[24]

His incompetence almost liquidates him. One sequence shows him as inept with a gun; he loses it to the small-time crook Dumb Dumb, who beats him up and manages to escape Riordan's trap (losing one's gun to Dumb Dumb speaks for itself). In "Eastwood Bound," Paul Smith delineates three stages through which the male action hero must progress, "from eroticization, through destruction, to reemergence and regeneration."[25] Smith sees these stages as an "orthodox structuring code" for action movies.[26] He discusses primarily Clint Eastwood movies, but this structuring code also functions in films noirs, both classic and postclassic, when the hero survives. It exists, in muted form, in *The Killers*. Riordan first appears as competent and whole, if not actually eroticized. He then loses his primacy, his gun, and is beat up—not quite destroyed but certainly damaged. Finally he emerges again, triumphant. Yet we never really care about Riordan at all, and his cute salute to the boss in the final sequence of the film practically occurs after we have stopped watching; after all, Kitty is in jail and Swede's murder has been solved (Figure 4.8). Just as the investigation Riordan engages in was not about the money, the movie is not about the investigator. Even though Riordan's character has to go through the same stages as a genuine film noir action hero, the narrative avoids conferring hero status upon him except in a peripheral way.

The homme attrapé provides another peripheral, but more interesting, version of masculinity. Sam, Lilly's husband, a childhood friend of Swede's and a cop, competently assists Riordan in the investigation of Swede's murder. Sam, although a relatively minor character, invites more consideration than Riordan. Sam seems to understand Swede, both Swede's desire for big money and his fascination with "dynamite" of the feminine sort, Kitty. Kitty and Lilly function as femme fatale and femme attrapée, respectively. Swede and Sam represent the male versions of those archetypes, an homme fatal who, like the femme fatale, will pay with his life or freedom for his desires, and an homme attrapé who resists the lure of the wild life and survives the narrative. Of course, male domination is part of what the femme attrapée and the femme fatale either submit to or resist. In the case of the hommes, their resistance or submission is more closely

Figure 4.8. The uninteresting investigator (*The Killers*, 1946)

related to economic status and class. Nevertheless, Swede, as the homme fatal, submits both to his desire for more than a working-class income can offer and to the sexual allure and domination of Kitty.

Sam, the homme attrapé, accepts his role in the gendered and classed economy; he functions as head of the household and is willing to work for an insubstantial but honest dollar. A police detective, Sam backs up Riordan, saves him in a shootout in a restaurant, and helps revenge the murder of his friend, Swede. Sam leads the life, with the femme attrapée Lilly, that both he and Lilly seek to convince Swede to live early in the story of the film. At one point, Sam attempts to convince Swede to take a job as a cop. Swede cannot stand the thought of such a modest income and rejects the idea. Lilly and Sam do not suffer from any illusions about the dull but safe nature of their lives and seem content with the choices they have made. Swede was unable to make those choices, and the film charts the price he pays for refusing both Sam's offer of a $2,200-a-year job as a cop and Lilly's offer of herself.

Homme fatal Swede offers a particularly Lancastrian version of masculinity, one that embodies passivity, physical strength, and beauty. As Justine Elias comments in the *Village Voice*, Lancaster first appears in *The Killers* as "a defeated figure reclining on a bed in a seedy motel room . . . [with] his Adonis-like

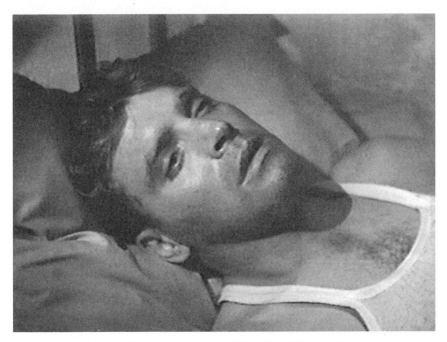

Figure 4.9. Swede's muscular but passive masculinity (*The Killers*, 1946)

physique, half-dressed . . . visible, but his face remains hidden by shadows."[27] Elias sees Lancaster as "an ethereal presence despite his imposing physique" and notes that, with the actor, "half was enough."[28] Lancaster, the actor, and Swede, the character, do seem half-asleep throughout the film (Figure 4.9). Swede never really rises from his bed as the killers approach to do their work, and in various flashbacks the film shows him passively stretched out on his jail bed, in bed in various cheap hotel rooms gazing at the ceiling, and even just waking up from sleeping in the course of planning the robbery caper. Swede's still, sleepy passivity renders him attractive and safely desirable, despite his muscularity and his expertise as a fighter.

Swede does not seem particularly smart but does operate according to a code of conduct that would prevent him from harming a woman. Swede defends Kitty when Colfax threatens her, and in a charming final gesture to a certain kind of womanhood, he leaves his $2,000 insurance benefit to an elderly hotel maid. She had grabbed him by his belt to prevent him from jumping out a window as he tried to commit suicide after Kitty betrayed him for the final time. Like his femme fatale counterpart in film noir, Swede is offered to the cinema spectator as a sexually attractive person willing to engage in criminal activities to achieve a better lifestyle, and like many femmes fatales, Swede pays, first with his freedom and then with his life, for his desires. Unlike the femme fatale, Swede does not actively seduce within the narrative of the film; but his passive appeal nevertheless works on Lilly, Sam, perhaps even Kitty, and certainly me.

In most films noirs, the white characters act out their narrative in front of a backdrop that includes at least some racial diversity. In *The Killers* that sort of background information seems remarkably absent. Harris makes a powerful case for the ethnicity of the whiteness portrayed here. As he notes, "ethnic or national origins are everywhere in this film, but they pass unnoticed—we never think of 'Swede' as Swedish, or his friend [Sam] Lubinsky as Semitic or Polish," and the green "handkerchief represents Kitty [Collins] via its traditional Irish motifs."[29] For Harris, the handkerchief "signifies a forgotten homeland," and the loss of that homeland structures Riordan's obsessive investigation and the film's meaning.[30] Harris links this loss to director Siodmak's own background as "a German Jew (whose family came from Poland) . . . [who] erased his origins and claimed American birth specifically to secure his Hollywood career."[31] Though this astute analysis does point to white ethnicity as part of the story *The Killers* has to tell, perhaps the German director's sense of American culture did not include nonwhites once the inspiration of the Hemingway narrative had been used up. After the cook, in the opening sequence, leaves the screen, we never see any person of color; there are no nonwhite waiters, street sweepers, musicians, or urban dwellers, although those bit parts exist in most other films noirs, including *The Maltese Falcon* as well as those discussed here. *The Killers* removes any hint of nonwhite experience by removing all references to it from the screen. The dominant ethnic subtext teased out by Harris remains exclusively white.[32]

The standard cast of exclusively white characters appears on the screen. Kitty and Lilly can easily be read as femme fatale and femme attrapée, respectively, but cracks in those readings appear. Swede falls for Kitty just as the male protagonist in a film noir should; yet as an homme fatal, he has already voiced his desires for a life beyond the one that Sam and Lilly represent. Sam represents the homme attrapé mate for Lilly's femme attrapée, yet Sam seems to understand and respect Swede's choices. This depth of characterization and visual and narrative awareness of the risks involved for the female and male characters in both the world of working-class domesticity and the world of film noir all appear on-screen in *The Killers.*

In classic film noir, the characters are what they appear to be, and, as I have shown, often much more than that as well. In the classic noir *Out of the Past,* the femme fatale dominates, working only for her own gain; the femme attrapée has desires that mirror those of more dangerous women. Another homme fatal and homme attrapé gain screen time, and nonwhite characters serve peripheral narrative functions—more quintessential noir.

CHAPTER 5

OUT OF THE PAST (1947): PASSIVE MASCULINITY AND ACTIVE FEMININITIES

Out of the Past raises the extravagance of film noir to its highest pitch. This absurd restlessness, these useless murders, this odd nocturnal atmosphere, and these episodes of a fulgurating brutality could only end in the death of the three protagonists.

RAYMOND BORDE AND ETIENNE CHAUMETON,
A Panorama of American Film Noir, 1941–1953

O ut of the Past (1947) has always been one of my favorite films noirs. It is quint-essential noir because, in addition to the ambiguity of the characterizations of the standard cast of noir characters, it also features a true femme fatale rather than a femme attrapée masquerading as a femme fatale. Set primarily in California (Bridgeport, San Francisco), Nevada (Lake Tahoe), and Mexico, *Out of the Past* features the wonderful, passive, powerful masculinity of Robert Mitchum, who plays the doomed homme fatal; Kirk Douglas as a wealthy, unscrupulous gambler; and Jane Greer as the femme fatale. Directed by Jacques Tourneur and adapted by Daniel Mainwaring from his novel *Build My Gallows High*, the film features a notoriously complex plot, one that actually caused a reviewer in the 1947 *New York Times* to close with the comment, "If only we had some way of knowing what's going on in the last half of this film, we might get pleasure from it. As it is, the challenge is worth a try."[1] The plot resonates with many noir themes, and the white male protagonist's investigation takes him to various exotic locales, including Acapulco, Mexico, and a New York jazz club. Jeff Bailey (Robert

Mitchum), like Swede in *The Killers,* has escaped a past that includes a dangerous dame. He now runs a gas station (Swede only works at one) in the small California mountain town of Bridgeport. He fishes, and romances a local girl.

In the first sequence of the film, a man from the past shows up and insists Jeff make the past his present. Although homme fatal Jeff does not motionlessly wait for his demise, he seems just about as sure as Swede was in the earlier film that he cannot escape it. Spectators learn of Jeff's past in a long flashback sequence (introduced and occasionally narrated with his voice-over) during which Jeff tells his Bridgeport girlfriend, femme attrapée Ann (Virginia Huston) just how bad he has been. In his earlier life as a private detective, Jeff agreed to help a smooth gambler, Whit Sterling (Douglas) find a woman who had shot him and run off with forty thousand dollars. Jeff does find the woman, Kathie Moffett (Greer), in Acapulco. She is beautiful; he falls for her, and they seek to hide out from Whit together. While they are hiding in plain sight in San Francisco, Jeff's former partner sees them and winds up dead, shot by Kathie. Kathie drives off.

Jeff ends up in Bridgeport, and now, as the film opens, Whit wants to talk. Jeff discovers that Kathie has returned to Whit and that Whit wants Jeff's assistance in beating a tax rap. The caper involves stealing some tax documents from a San Francisco accountant. But the plan really involves murdering the accountant and pinning the blame on Jeff. Jeff realizes this too late, and the accountant winds up dead. Jeff hides out, meets with Whit again, and asserts that Kathie should take the fall (she has been instrumental in all of the criminal activities). Whit agrees, but Kathie shoots him and insists that Jeff go off with her, leaving Bridgeport and the woman he supposedly truly loves behind. Jeff acts as though he is going along with Kathie's plan, but arranges for the police to stop them in their escape attempt. Kathie shoots him in anger and is killed by a barrage of gunfire. No wonder noir critics Borde and Chaumeton claim that the film "raises the extravagance of film noir to its highest pitch."[2]

None of the eventually well-known actors who played the leads were huge stars at the time *Out of the Past* was filmed. Some critics suggest that Greer was a neophyte, a claim that her filmography, as delineated by Karen Burroughs Hannsberry in *Femme Noir: Bad Girls of Film,* disputes.[3] Just prior to the release of *Out of the Past,* in which she plays femme fatale Kathie Moffett, Greer had appeared in *They Won't Believe Me* (1947), receiving rave reviews from a number of Hollywood trade journals. Douglas had acted in only one movie before 1947, the melodramatic noir *The Strange Love of Martha Ivers* (1946), and according to Tom Flinn, his "mannerisms had not yet become affectations."[4] Douglas plays gambler Whit with well-dressed urbanity and only once reveals the character's sadistic side, toward the end of the film, when he slaps and threatens Kathie. Despite the underplaying of this aspect of Whit's personality, spectators understand and take seriously his malevolence. Whit might have someone else carry out his unspeakable acts, but he is certainly capable of doing them himself.

Like Douglas, Mitchum had one major success before he played former private eye Jeff Bailey in *Out of the Past;* according to *The Film Encyclopedia,* he was nominated for an Academy Award as best supporting actor for his role in the 1945 film *The Story of G.I. Joe.*[5] *Out of the Past* was filmed a year prior to Mitchum's arrest and fifty-day imprisonment for possession of marijuana, although Daniel Mainwaring claimed, "He smoked marijuana all the time on the set."[6] The mention of marijuana in 1947 surprises me, but it shocked me to read a reviewer's comment on the amount of cigarette smoking in the film; I thought everyone in the 1940s and '50s smoked a lot. According to the 1947 review in the *New York Times,* Mitchum consumes "an astronomical number of cigarettes in displaying his nonchalance."[7] Despite his habits, Mitchum had not yet firmly established his "persistent reputation as Hollywood's Bad Boy."[8]

The erotic-triangle plot of *The Killers* also appears in *Out of the Past.* Here, the disruptive force is Kathie. Still trapped by her apparent need for men (or for their physical or financial prowess), Kathie nevertheless operates according to her own needs and desires rather than those of her husband or lover. Kitty, in *The Killers,* only appears to direct the action; her husband actually drives the narrative forward. No hint of eroticism between Kitty and her husband ever gains screen time. Instead, the focus is on the sexually charged relationship between Kitty and Swede, whom she betrays. Similarly, in *Out of the Past,* Whit never displays erotic desire for Kathie; she seems more like a prized possession to him. Jeff Bailey (Mitchum) freely admits his overwhelming attraction to Kathie, and she appears to reciprocate, especially when it suits her plans. One crucial difference in the similar erotic triangles of *The Killers* and *Out of the Past* remains, perhaps the one that accounts for Kathie's independence from Whit. Whit may feel as if he owns Kathie, but they are not married. Kathie's entanglements have much to do with her need to maximize her financial potential and relative independence and nothing to do with middle-class values, such as marriage. In this, she distinguishes herself from a character such as Kitty Collins. Kathie's activity, wholly selfish, seeks to secure her own future.

The hommes fatals, the male leads in the two films, display similar characteristics. Jeff exerts slightly more effort to secure his future than Swede does, but like Lancaster in *The Killers,* Mitchum plays Jeff with a solid, powerful, and attractive passivity. Not all critics agree with my taste in male actors. Film critic James Agee suggests that "Mitchum is so very sleepily self-confident with the women that when he slopes into clinches you expect him to snore in their faces."[9] Agee goes on to assert that although Mitchum plays well opposite other men, he should not play romantic leads: "In love scenes his curious languor, which sug-

Figure 5.1. Contrasting masculinities: alert Whit and languorous Jeff (*Out of the Past,* 1947)

gests Bing Crosby supersaturated with barbiturates, becomes a brand of sexual complacency that is not endearing."[10] For many spectators, Mitchum's almost sleepy persona proved extremely appealing (Figure 5.1). According to Ephraim Katz, Mitchum attributed "his most pronounced physical feature, sleepy eyes that a generation of female audiences found so sexy, to a combination of chronic insomnia and a boxing injury that caused astigmatism in both eyes."[11]

Jeff Bailey looks carefully out at the world from hooded eyes, not always understanding what he sees. He seems smarter than Swede, but never as smart as he needs to be to escape the traps set for him by the femme fatale. As he laconically remarks to his cab driver buddy, "I think I'm in a frame," but "all I can see is the frame." Unlike many hommes fatals in classic film noir including Swede, Jeff does not seem all that interested in money. More than anything, he wants, or at one time wanted, femme fatale Kathie, and he pays for his willingness to step outside the requirements of the patriarchy and be dominated by a woman.

In the final sequence of the film, Jeff makes himself into part of the frame in order to stop Kathie from kidnapping him. She makes it clear that running away from the past with him constitutes her plan; she has shot Whit, rendered Whit and Jeff's plan to make her the "fall guy" moot, and packed some clothes for Jeff from Whit's wardrobe. Although she definitely expects to drive their narra-

Figure 5.2. A glimpse of vibrant black culture separate from the white film noir narrative (*Out of the Past,* 1947)

tive from now on, even telling Jeff, "I'm running the show, don't forget," she also wants him to love her again. As with the motivation of many femmes fatales, her reason for wanting his love remains difficult to ascertain. For Nicholas Christopher, in *Somewhere in the Night: Film Noir and the American City, Out of the Past* functions as a model film noir, and the ambiguous nature of the femme fatale's feelings about the male protagonist constitutes part of the formula for film noir.[12]

Likewise, the film's ambiguous treatment of race serves as a model. As suggested above, the male protagonists in classic film noir often exhibit a familiarity with black culture that lends them an additional air of hipness. In *Out of the Past,* this occurs as Jeff, investigating Kathie for Whit, seeks out her maid in a jazz club. In this sequence, the black patrons of the club remain oblivious to the white interloper until Jeff gains an introduction to the maid, Eunice (Theresa Harris), and her male companion (Caleb Peterson), via a black man who introduces Jeff as a friend of his (Figure 5.2). As Naremore notes, Eunice "responds to Jeff's questions without a trace of subservience, all the while conveying a wry intelligence."[13] For Naremore, the whole scene "is played without condescension, and whether it intends to or not, it makes a comment on racial segregation."[14] Jeff, the only white person in the club, is virtually ignored by the dancing and chatting patrons, and he "lies to the maid about working for [Whit] and she lies to him about Kathi's [sic] destination."[15] This sequence not only suggests the liberal white masculinity of the male protagonist; it also suggests that a vigorous black culture exists just offscreen and focuses briefly on black femininity as well.

In *Black and White and Noir,* Rabinowitz reads the black maid Eunice relative to the white femme fatale. She suggests that Eunice's "visual position between two men — one white, the other black — is critical to understanding the different complexion of the femme fatale" (60–61). For Rabinowitz, "the black women is rarely the center of the action in film noir . . . but her presence appears necessary to the complex postwar sexual and racial dynamics that films noirs track by linking domestic melodrama to hard-boiled proletarian culture" (63). As in many films noirs, the domestic melodrama acted out in the *Out of the Past* features a rural household and small-town strictures as well as a hard-boiled, more sophisticated urban culture, and Eunice is part of the latter. Despite shifts in working-class urban culture for white women and for nonwhites, according to Amott and Matthaei, "the majority of Black women workers . . . [were] still employed as domestic and institutional servants."[16] Eunice, despite her elegance, probably continues to serve a white mistress.

Rabinowitz suggests an intriguing paradox — that the "white femme fatale has the potential to disturb the 'tradition' of racism" — but then admits that that potential "is limited because, as a 'mistress,' she still remains dependant on this tradition."[17] Similarly, during World War II, even as both white and minority women made significant gains in war-related industries, Wosk reports, "African American industrial workers . . . were often placed in segregated housing, and protest erupted when there were efforts at integration."[18] Racial, sexual, and class oppression fail to unite the oppressed.

In *Out of the Past,* after Eunice's brief appearance on the screen, black culture fulfills its narrative function and disappears completely from this classic noir. Despite Eunice's deception, Jeff discovers enough about Kathie's disappearance to trace her, via her excess baggage, to Mexico. Here, according to Naremore, his "pursuit of Kathie . . . takes him to a series of sun-baked Mexican towns that offer a temporary escape from the forbidding shadows of a northern metropolis."[19] The Mexican setting provides an exotic backdrop against which the white characters can anonymously act out their desires. None of the white characters interact with the Mexicans beyond the level of exchanges with waiters, bartenders, bellhops, or would-be guides.

Out of the Past does not use the white male protagonist's familiarity with black culture as powerfully as *Kiss Me Deadly* and other films noirs do.[20] Jeff does not gain a great deal of patina from his exchanges with black culture or from his lack of engagement with Mexican culture. He seems similarly laconic and detached, whether on a Mexican beach or in a New York jazz club. His character is enhanced, however, by his apparently strong relationship with a deaf-mute boy who works for him at the gas station in Bridgeport. Unlike the other people in *Out of the Past,* Jeff speaks, or at the very least understands, sign language. Jeff's relationship with the boy, played by Dickie Moore, works to assert his sympathetic masculinity. After all, by befriending a linguistic outsider, Jeff confirms his own status as outsider and suggests that another, more humane social order might prevail.

Jeff's connection with the deaf boy helps to humanize his masculinity in a sympathetic way and, at one point, even saves Jeff's life. In a murder sequence unlikely even for Hollywood, the boy, while fishing, sees one of Whit's henchmen taking aim with a handgun at the unsuspecting Jeff. The boy manages to cast, catch the man in the shoulder of his black overcoat with a lure, and then pull him off a cliff into the waters below![21] In his review of the newly released video version of *Out of the Past,* Chris Peachment calls the boy "the only honest male in the film," a notion that ignores the apparent honesty of Ann's local beau, the *homme attrapé.*[22] Like many of his female counterparts, the *femmes attrapées,* Ann's small-town boyfriend remains bland and dull; unlike Jeff, he is admired by the gossip who runs the lunch counter, but never really engages Ann's affections. At the end of the film, the deaf boy lies to Ann, indicating that Jeff did intend to stay with Kathie, apparently leaving Ann free to return the affections of her Bridgeport boyfriend, however reluctantly. For Peachment, the honest boy's lie is "the only lovely gesture in a doomed world."[23]

Kathie seems to understand instinctively that there is another woman in Jeff's life. She tells him, just before he betrays her, "If you're thinking of anyone else, don't. Wouldn't work. You're no good for anyone but me. You're no good, and neither am I." Her hard-boiled delivery of these lines resonates more truthfully than seductively, although she seeks to follow them up with a passionate kiss (Figure 5.3). For Blake Lucas, in *Film Noir: An Encyclopedic Reference to the American Style,* Jeff knows his relationship with Kathie dooms him, and the "film traces the course in which he gradually accepts this fate and even embraces it, spiritually if not physically."[24]

Naremore also asserts the "film is about fatal attraction or the fear of a woman's sexuality."[25] In his well-illustrated and perceptive discussion of the superb lighting effects in *Out of the Past,* Naremore reads a sequence in which Jeff roughly pushes Kathie into a chair. According to Naremore, the "reverse angle shows her landing roughly, her mink coat falling off and lamplight spilling across her bare shoulders; her black dress is outlined against the gray upholstery of the chair, and her seductive body functions almost like a return blow, countering Jeff's violence."[26] While astute, this reading of Kathie's body as a return blow ignores the fear in her eyes and the passivity of her pose: Kathie knows she is no match

Figure 5.3. Kathie insisting that Jeff stay with her (*Out of the Past,* 1947)

for Jeff in the realm of physical strength. But she does not know until the film's penultimate scene that she no longer has any sexual hold on him either.

In the present of the film, the femme attrapée Ann has a greater hold, one with closer ties to geography than sexuality. Janey Place sees Ann as an archetypal "woman as redeemer," "firmly rooted in the pastoral environment, static, undemanding and rather dull, while the other (Kathie) is exciting, criminal, very active and sexy."[27] On the surface, no one can deny this delineation of the female characters in *Out of the Past,* and the San Francisco double-cross sequence even includes another femme fatale, the secretary of the accountant who is murdered in an attempt to frame Jeff. But Ann's character deserves a closer reading. In his discussion of the complex narrative structure of *Out of the Past,* John Harvey makes much of the location shooting in the film, asserting that Bridgeport and Lake Tahoe (Nevada) reinforce a narrative about a "journey between two contrasting worlds."[28] For Harvey, Bridgeport aligns with the country, naturalness-normality (natural light), honesty-openness, family, and the present; Lake Tahoe aligns with artificiality-excess (artificial light), deviousness-deception, lack of family, and the past.[29] Implicitly then, Ann aligns with Bridgeport, her hometown, and Kathie with Lake Tahoe and Whit's realm.

These oppositions do not, however, present quite as unambiguous a picture as Harvey suggests, especially with regard to Ann. None of the scholarly discussions of the film note that Ann's home does not provide a safe haven for her. The spectator is invited into her home only once; otherwise we wait outside in the cold with Jeff, sensing the displeasure of her small-town parents (no Hollywood parents would approve of a man who pulls up in his car and honks the horn for his girlfriend). From inside the darkened Victorian-style house, Ann's mother castigates her father, saying, "John, are you letting her go out like this, with a man who won't even come to the door?" Ann insists Jeff not worry about it, but he knows "it's no good, is it?"

Later in the film, when Jeff has been framed for murder, the camera does venture into Ann's home, allowed in by her father, who retrieves a newspaper from the front porch, a newspaper that reports Jeff as a murderer and fugitive. The cozy, homey décor of hallway and kitchen unfortunately offer no comfort to Ann. While her mother complains ("he was no good; the police are hunting him for two murders"), and needles her daughter ("I told you, Ann"), her father attempts to offer comfort. But Ann rejects his offer and escapes the house to the outdoors with her mother's disdain for Jeff again ringing in her ears.

Despite scholars' and critics' consistent alignment of Ann with small-town values and a lack of desire, a careful reading of her character suggests another side to this femme attrapée. She chooses Jeff over her devoted Bridgeport boyfriend precisely because he represents something other than the small-town milieu she finds stupefying. Jeff has seen the world and does not want to have anything to do with it; Ann nevertheless sees Jeff as offering access to a world she will never see without him. Her devotion to him is complete, yet she does not exactly represent the supposedly standard femme attrapée's drive to reintegrate her man into a stable domestic environment. Because of her desire for Jeff, she has exiled herself from her home and family and alienated herself from domesticity. Ann cannot be at home anywhere; she takes refuge in nature, sitting bundled in a winter coat among leafless fall willows next to a small creek (Figure 5.4) or hiding in the bare woods at night waiting for Jeff. In neither of these sequences is nature warm, inviting, or comforting; instead it evokes coldness, discomfort, and alienation.

In a sense, both of the female leads in *Out of the Past* represent a flight from middle-class values. Kathie obviously has no desire for marriage; she wants money, power, and male companionship. Although what Ann wants is not really the concern of the narrative, the film hints that she too desires liberation from the values her hometown and family represent; her relationship with Jeff provides her with a possible means of escape. At the end of the film, both the femme attrapée and the femme fatale are foiled in their respective attempts to elude their destinies as women. Kathie dies in a barrage of gunfire for daring to suppose that she can control her life. And Ann's passions get reined in as well; she takes the

Figure 5.4. Ann, the femme attrapée, alienated and isolated in her family and in nature (*Out of the Past*, 1947)

arm of her small-town boyfriend in the final scene of the film. The femme attrapée and homme attrapé wind up together, just as they do in *The Killers*. Ann might be less satisfied with the arrangement than Lilly, but both films support the capitalist patriarchy by allowing the attrapé couple to survive. In *Out of the Past*, the concluding sequence was, as Flinn notes, "studio imposed."[30]

John Harvey sees the concluding coda as a condemnation of Kathie "in favour of the passive, patient and trusting figure of Ann — the apotheosis of 'the little woman'" and "the values she represents."[31] Perhaps Ann does represent those values generically, but Ann also stands for something other than honesty, openness, and family, perhaps even a sort of rebellion against those values. Harvey accurately notes that *Out of the Past* above all insists that "we admire Kathie's sexuality, her energy, the ways in which she dominates the frame," while it fails "to make any re-integration of woman's independence with the needs and desires for family."[32] The narrative of *Out of the Past* counters Kathie's moves for financial and sexual independence with violent death, just as it kills off the men with whom she associates, including the homme fatal, Jeff. The narrative also suggests that not even a woman as unthreatening as the supposedly quintessential femme attrapée Ann can successfully make a bid for more moderate independence. None of the women in *Kiss Me Deadly* (1955) succeed either.

CHAPTER 6

KISS ME DEADLY (1955): APOCALYPTIC FEMMES

This is the desperate flip side of the film that opened the noir series fourteen years earlier, *The Maltese Falcon*.

The theme is the same: the search for a treasure, a statue or an iron strongbox. The hero is the same: a private detective, both tough and vulnerable, who adores pounding a face, pummeling a belly, and who is the victim marked out by fate of she who will remain his objective counterpart: the grasping, desirable and frigid female.

But between 1941 and 1955 . . . the tone has changed. A savage lyricism hurls us into a world in manifest decomposition, governed by dissolute living and brutality; to these intrigues of wild men and weaklings, [the film] offers the most radical of solutions: nuclear apocalypse.

RAYMOND BORDE AND ETIENNE CHAUMETON
A Panorama of American Film Noir, 1941–1953

In choosing texts to include in the section dealing with classic film noir, I sought films that were both quintessentially noir and more than that as well. In *The Killers*, the femme fatale becomes a femme attrapée when her boyfriend returns to the narrative. In *Out of the Past*, the femme attrapée wants more than she should in her generic role as "woman as redeemer." In both *The Killers* and *Out of the Past*, the safety and security of domestic life includes an indisputable visual and emotional drabness, and in the case of *Out of the Past*, connotes a life devoid of love and comfort. The male characters in both texts, though typical of film noir, prove more than typical as well. The investigator in *The Killers* is neither particularly competent nor attractive. The investigator in *Out of the Past* is appealing, but unlike his precursors, Marlowe and Spade, he cannot reason or talk his way out of his troubles. The only way this homme fatal can make sure that the femme fatale gets what she deserves is by dying along with her. *Kiss Me Deadly* (1955), like these earlier films, stands as quintessential noir and as much more than that.

Directed by Robert Aldrich and based on a novel by hard-boiled writer Mickey Spillane, *Kiss Me Deadly* remains a perennial favorite of critics and scholars and may even be the most written-about classic film noir of all. It features a detective without a moral code. If Swede in *The Killers* and Jeff in *Out of the Past* needed to be smarter to survive their narratives, at least they seem like decent if doomed men. The less-than-brilliant male protagonist in *Kiss Me Deadly,* Mike Hammer (Ralph Meeker), abuses both his enemies and his friends. His predilection for violence explodes onto the screen throughout the film. Hammer is an homme fatal after money, and only money. He does not care about women, beyond needing to use them as his investigators; his own capabilities do not extend that far.

Kiss Me Deadly disrupts the usual pleasures of classic film noir by replacing the attractive male physicality and passivity of hommes fatals Burt Lancaster and Robert Mitchum with a violent, belligerent, but still doomed masculinity. It substitutes sweaty, whiny, desperate femmes fatales for the composed, sexy femininity of Ava Gardner and Jane Greer (Figure 6.1). Although I did not like *Kiss Me Deadly* at first viewing, perhaps the disruption of my visual and narrative pleasures enables a more complex and revisionary reading of gender. This reading culminates with the concluding sequence of the film, which features a Pandora's box of destruction opened by a femme fatale.

The film begins with a desperate woman, Christina (Cloris Leachman, in her Hollywood debut), flagging down the sleazy detective mentioned above. He gets beat up; she gets brutally tortured and murdered, and Hammer spends the rest of the complex and violence-infused narrative trying to figure out what she knew and the reason for its value.[1] For Stephen Prince, in *Classical Film Violence: Designing and Regulating Brutality in Hollywood Cinema, 1930–1968,* the stylized and "exceptional brutality and sadism" of *Kiss Me Deadly* effectively provide "pleasurable entertainment for the viewer that in practice renders almost all screen violence, of whatever apparent ideological inflection, into an easily consumed commodity."[2] The film ends with the ultimate form of violent destruction, a nuclear explosion; the box I refer to above contains a nuclear device.

Nuclear noir as a subcategory of noir has a venerable tradition, including titles such as *The House on 92nd Street* (1945), Alfred Hitchcock's *Notorious* (1946), *D.O.A.* (1949), and *The Atomic City* (1952). Nineties retro-noir *Mulholland Falls*

Figure 6.1. Disinterested masculinity and unstylized femininity (*Kiss Me Deadly*, 1955)

(1996) joins the list of nuclear noirs, and I analyze that text in Section Three. As Mark Osteen points out in "The *Big* Secret: Film Noir and Nuclear Fear," nuclear noirs illustrate "the results of the cultural obsession with secrecy, dramatizing our ambivalence about scientists and scientific knowledge, and depicting the psychic effects of nuclear fear."[3] He goes on to suggest that "the erosion of the ability to know, the ability to trust, and the fragmentation of the self are the real fallout of the nuclear age."[4] Certainly, Hammer trusts no one, and no one trusts him. Yet the secret Christina knew and dies for drives Hammer throughout the film. He figures anything important enough to kill for must be valuable, and he wants in on it.

Much has been written about *Kiss Me Deadly*, from Borde and Chaumeton's exultant praise through Silver and Ward's discussion in their *Encyclopedia of Film Noir* to a number of current essays, articles, and chapters in books. In *More than Night*, Naremore's discussion of *Kiss Me Deadly* focuses again on the male characters, although he notes that "the women characters [have] plenty of opportunity to criticize the phallic, self-absorbed private eye."[5] As the character's name suggests, Hammer relies on physical intimidation instead of intelligence to solve crimes and get what he wants. His only real friend seems to be a Greek car mechanic named Nick (Nick Dennis), which points both to his devotion to his playboy image and to the associated fast cars (Figure 6.2).

Figure 6.2. Hammer with Nick, the only person (other than himself) he truly cares about (*Kiss Me Deadly*, 1955)

Introducing a queer interpretation, Robin Wood suggests that Hammer's attachment to Nick indicates that "the American construction of 'masculinity' (together with its accompanying paranoia) is built upon not only the repression of the male's 'femininity' (which would account for Hammer's hatred of/ contempt for women . . .) but his innate homosexuality."[6] In *Masculine Interests: Homoerotics in Hollywood Film*, Robert Lang expands on Wood and provides a convincing reading of *Kiss Me Deadly* as an explicitly homoerotic text, a narrative motivated by the fear of women and, especially, "the fear of passive homosexuality."[7] Lang sees Hammer as "invested with an excess of phallic sexuality that converts to homoerotic obsession . . . [which] drives Mike Hammer to fascistic behavior."[8] Wood reads Hammer somewhat more sympathetically, suggesting Hammer's one moment of grace is his "grief over Nick's death, as he gets drunk in a bar: a moment that eloquently confirms one's sense that the emotional centre of the film is homoerotic."[9] The blame for Nick's death lies with Hammer, and this, as well as their homosocial attachment, may also account for his grief. But the bar scene hints at more than grace through grief.

As I have noted, access to and familiarity with black culture often serves to bolster the characterization of the male film noir protagonist, simultaneously enhancing his hipness, his status as outsider, and his masculinity. As Naremore

Figure 6.3. I'd rather have the blues than what I got (*Kiss Me Deadly*, 1955)

Figure 6.4. Hammer humanized by his association with black culture (*Kiss Me Deadly*, 1955)

comments in his discussion of race in *Kiss Me Deadly*, the bar sequence makes the otherwise despicable Hammer momentarily into "a relatively sympathetic embodiment of urban liberalism."[10] Naremore continues, "When we first meet Hammer he is listening to Nat Cole on the radio; later we discover that he is a regular customer at an all black jazz club, where his friendship with a black singer (Madi Comfort) and a black bartender (Art Loggins) helps to indicate his essential hipness."[11] In addition, his best friend is Greek — not black, but also not just white. Despite his grief over Nick's death, Hammer listens appreciatively, along with the sophisticated black customers at the club, as the beautiful entertainer sings, "I'd rather have the blues than what I got" (Figure 6.3). The bartender obviously knows Hammer well, asking him in stylized slang, "Hey, man, you sure look beat; you look real lean, real wasted. What's got you, man?" In *Kiss Me Deadly*, the bartender and the singer seem to know a different Hammer from the one otherwise portrayed on the screen. They appear to genuinely like him and to sympathize with his sorrow and fear (Figure 6.4).

The urban jazz club represents a dynamic aspect of U.S. postwar black culture. As Amott and Matthaei note, by the midfifties the dominant change in the economic status of African Americans "came about primarily as a result of movement out of agriculture and into cities."[12] This movement brought with it cultural trends and racial tensions. Rosa Parks, "a longtime activist in the National Association for the Advancement of Colored People," started the "Montgomery bus boycott" in 1955, the same year *Kiss Me Deadly* first appeared in theaters.[13] Racial tension does not emerge in the narrative of the film, but certainly circulated in the atmosphere at the time of its release. Hammer's almost tender relationship with these black characters seems remarkable, especially in the face of his overt misogyny and even misanthropy toward whites. Just as the earlier noirs I discuss both follow and disrupt generic standards, so too the narrative flow of this film, and the cohesive characterization of Hammer as a jerk, gets disrupted by this brief foray into black culture.

Kiss Me Deadly features a complex cast of male characters, but the few female characters are central to the big secret. Even those with only a reading knowledge of *Kiss Me Deadly* know that it ends with a nuclear explosion that may, or may not, destroy the male investigator and his girlfriend-secretary, along with a large part of California. But it certainly destroys the dominant femme fatale of the film. Gabrielle (Gaby Rodgers) bursts into flames as she opens the box containing the "great whatsit"—her uncontainable curiosity causing a nuclear holocaust (Figure 6.5). In *Feminisms in the Cinema*, Laura Mulvey takes up the myth of Pandora. She traces the size of the container Pandora carries from its original mythic and large proportions to a smaller box and suggests that "when the container shrinks from jar size, the approximate size of Pandora herself, to a small box, an extension of meaning takes place, a sexualization of the resonances associated with the box."[14] Mulvey goes on to note that "three 'cliché' motifs, elements of myth, are central to the Pandora's iconography":

1. Femininity as enigma.
2. Female curiosity as transgressive and dangerous.
3. The spatial or topographical figuration of the female body as an inside and an outside.[15]

Mulvey then moves to reformulate these "cliché" motifs, making Pandora a feminist icon by suggesting that:

1. Pandora's curiosity acts out a transgressive desire to see inside her own surface or exterior, into the inside of the female body metaphorically represented by the box and its attendant horrors.
2. Feminist curiosity has to pick up Pandora's look and transform the topography of the feminine through theoretical investigation, with the aim of understanding and decoding this duality that haunts the female body in patriarchal representation.[16]

Kiss Me Deadly almost prefigures Mulvey's theoretical seizing of the myth, especially in the representation of the female characters.

According to Mulvey, "the cinema has invested deeply in the concept of feminine seductiveness as a surface that conceals."[17] For Mulvey, in "its most perfect form . . . the figure of the woman on the screen is stylized to the point of artificiality, so that makeup and lighting combine to etch exquisite features onto a blank surface."[18] But in *Kiss Me Deadly*, very few of the female characters in the film function as blank surfaces etched with erotic features, like Kitty in *The Killers* and Kathie in *Out of the Past*. Christina — the possibly good woman who appears naked except for a trench coat in the opening scene (and who, less than eight minutes into the film, is naked while being tortured to death with pliers because of her knowledge) — and Gabrielle — the definitely bad woman who appears naked except for a terry cloth robe in her initial two scenes — seem strangely desexualized, especially when compared with the femmes fatales discussed previously.[19] David Thomson notes that Christina is "far from the pretty sexpot."[20] It sounds odd to say that these characters seem desexualized since their nakedness, and what is supposedly most fearsome about it, is actually pointed to by the opening of the trench coat or robe, respectively.

Their relative lack of erotic appeal contradicts the cinematic tradition of female "artifice par excellence, 'cosmetic' with all the word's resonance and connotation," and subverts this tradition more than maintains it.[21] Others also note the female characters' lack of visual appeal as well as their intellectual activity. In "Sound, Woman, and the Bomb: Dismembering the 'Great Whatsit' in *Kiss Me Deadly*," Caryl Flinn provides a perceptive discussion of sound in *Kiss Me Deadly* and suggests that "the film uses its female characters and elements associated with them in ways that sidestep film theory's routine claims to femininity's passivity."[22] Flinn ties women to "a realm in which rhythms, music, and poetry relay meaning, while logic, narrative, and language do not," and sees the dissonant sound track as part of what destabilizes the masculine, "visually oriented" signification of the film.[23]

In only two instances does a female character exhibit visual erotic appeal along traditional femme fatale lines. Of course, these very sequences make it into the trailer promoting the film, using the attraction of the classic femme fatale to lure spectators into the movie theater — in effect, making a promise the film will not keep. In one case, Friday (Marian Carr), the sister of a mobster, attempts to seduce Hammer. Her cool surface beauty and cryptic yet explicit dialogue seem like a throwback to an earlier stage of film noir, one that might have featured Lauren Bacall or Lizabeth Scott. But Friday's screen time is brief, less than four minutes; once Hammer uses her to get to her brother, she never appears again.[24]

In another scene, Velda (Maxine Cooper), Hammer's secretary, investigator, and girlfriend, attempts to arouse his interest. Dressed in a form-fitting black gown, she suggests that she is alive — unlike Christina, the object of Hammer's obsession — and tries to join him on the couch. Hammer rebuffs her, telling her to get to work seducing another character and soliciting information from him. Velda is liminally a femme attrapée seeking to domesticate Hammer, but her investigative competence and willingness to seduce men for information make her a femme fatale as well. In all her other scenes, Velda appears less than appealing, sweating through her workout or greasy faced in bed (Figure 6.1). No heterosexual seductions are successful in this film. Men respond to each other, prizefights, fast cars, and the lure of incredible wealth or incredible destructive power, but not to women.

However, by portraying women, for the most part, as other than spectacle, *Kiss Me Deadly* allows for an "active, investigative look, but one that [is] also associated with the feminine."[25] If the female character is not strictly the bearer of the look, then she may herself look, and in *Kiss Me Deadly* the female characters are associated with investigation and curiosity. All are also femmes fatales: they will suffer and die for their desire to know. Christina has somehow (we do not know how or why) pieced together the secret of the "great whatsit"; she knows about and fears its power, and she dies because of her knowledge. Velda does most of Hammer's investigating for him and realizes the seriousness and deadliness of his obsession long before he does. It remains unclear whether or not she and Hammer die in the final sequence; it seems unlikely they could survive, given their proximity to a nuclear explosion.[26] Gabrielle's curiosity, her desire to see inside the box regardless of the cost, stands in for the price that classic film noir always requires active, desiring women to pay. Mulvey suggests that if "Pandora's gesture may be interpreted as a self-reflexive look at a misogynist fantasy of femininity, [then] the box represents the association between the feminine and horror or evil."[27] *Kiss Me Deadly* both makes this association and leaves it open to question by not emphasizing the erotic allure of the female characters. Thomson asserts, "This is a wildly sexy film about a selfconscious [*sic*] stud who is terrified of doing it."[28] According to Thomson, "That big blast takes a woman whose curiosity overcomes fear or ownership."[29] He goes on to suggest that the "men crave the box but are desperate to keep it shut; [Gabrielle] longs to air it out."[30] Gabrielle opens the box, and "its attendant horrors" destroy her.[31]

Kiss Me Deadly denies certain spectator pleasures by deemphasizing the surface beauty of the female characters. Instead of exhibiting "to-be-looked-at-ness," the women in the film actively seek knowledge and understanding, often more successfully than the male characters. In this way, *Kiss Me Deadly* disrupts the usual classic film noir narrative gratification in favor of a more intriguing pleasure, one that forces a reassessment of gender roles. As I noted above, the film continues to draw the attention of critics and scholars. The misanthropy of the narrative leaves no one out; it hates men as much as it despises women, seeing men as responsible for and women as implicated in the evils of society. Yet perhaps because of its overt focus on male homoerotics, *Kiss Me Deadly* does something with female characters that few films noirs had previously done: it allows the female characters to be more than stylized, sexualized surfaces. Female

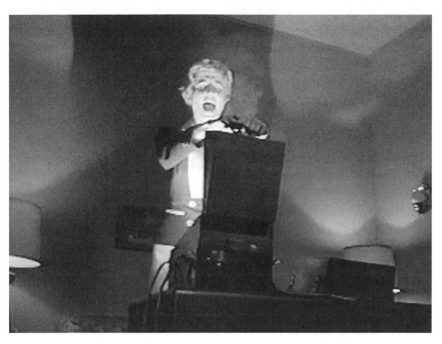

Figure 6.5. The femme fatale destroyed by her transgressive desire to see inside the box (*Kiss Me Deadly*, 1955)

characters look, not distractedly through a haze of cigarette smoke, but with intelligence and curiosity directly at what the male protagonist cannot decipher.

Nuclear retro-noir *Mulholland Falls* also lets the woman investigate, but it cannot resist the thrill of packaging her, of making her cosmetic appeal to heterosexual-male visual pleasure obscure her own intelligence and curiosity as well as the threat it contains. In both narratives, homoerotic undercurrents lurk just beneath the surface heterosexuality, and in both, women get murdered or nuked for their boldness, but in *Kiss Me Deadly* at least she gets to open the box. The more revisionary neo-noirs do not insist upon the same punishment for successfully curious women as do classic noir and retro-noir. But before discussing neo-noir, I return to 1942 and draw a parallel between the famous non-noir *Casablanca* and *L.A. Confidential,* a 1997 retro-noir that fulfills a remarkably similar ideological agenda.

PART 3

RETURN OF THE REPRESSED IN RETRO-NOIR

L.A. CONFIDENTIAL (1997) AND CASABLANCA (1942): DOES ANYTHING CHANGE AS TIME GOES BY?

Casablanca is a cult movie precisely because all the archetypes are there, because each actor repeats a part played on other occasions, and because the
characters live not the "real" life of human beings, but a life as stereotypically
portrayed by previous films. . . .

Casablanca has succeeded in becoming a cult movie because it is not *one*
movie. It is 'the movies.' . . .

When all the archetypes burst in shamelessly, we reach Homeric depths.
Two clichés make us laugh, but a hundred clichés move us because we sense
dimly that the clichés are talking among themselves and celebrating a reunion.

UMBERTO ECO, "Casablanca: Cult Movies and Intertextual Collage"

Hollywood has always told and retold the same tales, enhancing the appeal
of certain stories by dressing them up in different clothing while providing
cinema spectators with the dual pleasures of visual variety and narrative consis-
tency. I suggest that retro-noirs tell primarily reactionary, nostalgic tales about
gender and race, stories that confirm white male supremacy while marginalizing
women and nonwhites. Here, two texts demonstrate that point, one the famous
non-noir *Casablanca* (1942), the other the retro-noir *L.A. Confidential* (1997).
These two films tell remarkably similar stories about masculinity and femininity,

about whiteness, and about class. Although the women's movement, feminism, and the civil-rights movement have clearly altered the landscape of gendered and raced relationships in U.S. culture, most retro-noirs continue to provide film-goers with representations of men, women, and race that speak to a need to deny those changes.

Retro-noirs have far more in common with non-noir films from the classic period than with classic film noir. As I have shown, classic noir often featured men who, although strong and somewhat smart, might not be intelligent enough to outwit the femme fatale. Unlike classic noir, retro-noir now provides an ideo-logically safe site for the portrayal of reactionary representations of gender; of muscular, violent, and successful white masculinity; and of passive and objec-tified femininity. Class in these films conflates with race: nonwhites comprise the underclasses, whites the upper classes. Nonwhites in retro-noir serve only to confirm white male supremacy.

In *Dangerous Dames,* I note that whereas most female characters created by Hollywood in the noir years "accepted responsibility for the social disruptions of the postwar period," the femme fatale remained a glaring exception.[1] Femmes fatales do not perform like characters such as Ilse (Ingrid Bergman) in *Casa-blanca,* who functions almost solely as a beautiful object around which the nar-rative circles and who passively affects the plot by her mere presence. Femmes fatales such as Kitty in *The Killers* and Kathie in *Out of the Past* refuse the blame other non-noir women accept. For example, Rosalind Russell's character in *The Guilt of Janet Ames* (1947) takes full responsibility for most of the ills of postwar society.[2] One sure reason for the femme fatale's often violent recontainment in classic films noirs has to do with her glaring and enticing refusal to play a socially acceptable postwar female role.

Retro-noirs, however, almost never feature real femmes fatales; pastiche femmes fatales tend to take their places. Sixty years after the first film noir (*The Maltese Falcon,* 1941), retro-noirs ameliorate the threat of a powerful woman by erasing her entirely from most narratives, thereby eliminating one of the most potent pleasures of film noir itself. When a femme fatale does appear, she need not do much to earn eradication; she is quickly eliminated. Today, retro-noirs fulfill a cultural function once left to the non-noir filmic narratives of the forties and fifties: they seek to repress all impulses but those that confirm white male subjectivity. The homme fatal of classic film noir usually desired illegal economic gains and a dangerous dame, but male protagonists in retro-noir for the most part uphold the capitalist patriarchy. Occasionally, men who might be labeled queer do not make it to the final reel, but most men survive the retro-noir narra-tive, rewarded for upholding the dominant ideology. Through a reading of femi-ninities, masculinities, and raced representations offered to film spectators in the non-noir 1942 film *Casablanca* and in the 1997 retro-noir *L.A. Confidential,* I seek to answer the question, does anything change as time goes by?

Most movie aficionados can recite the story of *Casablanca,* including classic lines, without hesitation. Directed by Jewish immigrant Michael Curtiz, who also directed the significant film noir *Mildred Pierce* (1945), and starring quintessential noir protagonist Humphrey Bogart and a cast of European refugees from the Nazis, *Casablanca* remains a favorite romance and war, or prewar, film. But it is not a film noir. According to Robert Ray in *A Certain Tendency in the Hollywood Cinema, 1930–1980, Casablanca*'s "ideological project . . . [was] the overcoming of its audience's latent anxiety about American intervention in World War II," and it fulfilled this project without ambiguity.[3] *Casablanca* portrays a far less subversive moral and visual world than the one found in a typical noir film. In addition, the female protagonist serves as an antithesis to the powerful agency of the femme fatale, instead representing the kind of palatable femininity exhibited by most female characters in Hollywood productions other than films noirs in the forties and fifties.

As a movie aficionada, I still love to watch *Casablanca,* but the feminist and cultural critic in me chafes against and seeks to analyze the source of my pleasure in a film that thoroughly denigrates and objectifies female characters, and marginalizes nonwhites. *Casablanca,* like *L.A. Confidential,* appears to focus on a romance between a white man and woman, but the narrative really concerns intimate relationships between white men.

Often billed as the greatest (and here we read, heterosexual) love story ever told, *Casablanca* glorifies homosocial behavior between men. As Eve Kosofsky Sedgwick comments in *Between Men: English Literature and Male Homosocial Desire,* the word *homosocial* "describes social bonds between persons of the same sex" and "is a neologism obviously formed by an analogy with 'homosexual' and just as obviously meant to be distinguished from 'homosexual.' "[4] Sedgwick goes on to note that homosocial bonding, although not always rigidly set apart from homosexuality — she uses the examples of Greek culture — has in our culture been "characterized by intense homophobia, fear and hatred of homosexuality."[5] Residual traces of homosexuality, as well as the hatred and fear of it, surface in *Casablanca* and gain screen time in *L.A. Confidential.*

In the highly successful film noir *The Maltese Falcon* (1941), made just one year before *Casablanca,* Peter Lorre plays the role of Joel Cairo with "mincing menace," a characterization clearly intended as gay (Figure 7.1).[6] In *Casablanca,* Lorre reprises that role with the character of Ugarte (Figure 7.2). Ugarte, though not as clearly labeled homosexual, uses enough of the same mannerisms to be read as queer, especially for spectators familiar with the gardenia-scented Cairo from the previous film. Although Rick (Bogart) apparently has nothing but disdain for

Figure 7.1. Peter Lorre as Cairo in
The Maltese Falcon (1941)

Figure 7.2. Lorre as Ugarte in
Casablanca (1942)

Ugarte, Ugarte seems quite concerned with gaining Rick's respect and manages to briefly do so through his involvement in a bold act of thievery and murder. The character, eventually killed in jail, never arouses much sympathy or empathy from any of the other characters in the film, or from spectators. With a few telling variations, an analogous fate befalls a similar character in *L.A. Confidential*.

The homosocial bonding in *L.A. Confidential* is similar to that in *Casablanca*. Rick's beautiful friendships exist and develop not with the alluring female protagonist, Ilse (Bergman), but with her husband, Victor Laszlo (Paul Henreid), the black piano player, Sam (Dooley Wilson), and with Captain Renault (Claude Rains). Rick exhibits the tough guy persona of the hard-boiled detective and other hommes fatals, but his desires for wealth and women remain safely reined in, and he renounces even those tame desires at the end of the film. Ilse also survives since she does not function as a femme fatale: she does not decide her own fate or engineer her own demise. My use of the term *femme fatale* in classic film noir assumes her death or imprisonment, "which she orchestrates through her rebellion against ideological female roles as clearly as she victimizes any male characters."[7] As I mentioned earlier, the term *femme attrapée,* or "trapped woman," denotes the opposing female character in film noir, one who accepts her position in the patriarchal structure. Ilse, although often identified as a femme fatale, functions only as a femme attrapée, turning over any agency she might have possessed to the male protagonist, telling Rick, "You have to think for both of us." Early in the film, Renault chides Rick for sending away an attractive woman, saying, "How extravagant you are, throwing away women like that. Someday they may be scarce." Rick and Laszlo's exchange of Ilse at the end of the film, although more subtle, makes it clear that *Casablanca* tells the story of relationships between men; women are mere objects of trade.

Women are not the only objects of trade. In *Casablanca,* the North African setting provides local color and an exotic backdrop against which the white characters engage one another. *Casablanca* affords the spectator layers of otherness. Like many films of the period, it conflates race with class. Whites make up the upper classes; nonwhite refugees serve as a liminal middle class; and the colonized North Africans comprise the lower, working class. In interior environments the local culture provides servants and lower-level workers, and in the exterior sequences, a vibrant, polyglot hotbed of commercial enterprise. Members of the diverse European culture exist as both customers and higher-level workers in the interiors and as refugees or shoppers in the exteriors.

The struggle of good and evil is a struggle between white men and white cultures. The evil of the Nazis as represented in *Casablanca* has more to do with boundless colonizing than with Aryan purity, a representation that allows whiteness to retain its primacy in the ideological work of the film. Sam, Rick's black piano player and apparent friend, has obviously had a long relationship with Rick, yet remains much more a servant than a partner, even calling Rick "Boss." And although Rick tells fellow nightclub owner Ferrari, "I don't buy or sell human beings," he does exchange them—at the end of the film handing over Sam to Ferrari and Ilse to her husband. Nonwhites and women in *Casablanca* either are objects of exchange or function as narratively unimportant but visually interesting backdrops against which the homosocial white males engage in action.

The same can be said of retro-noir *L.A. Confidential.* Based on a novel by James Ellroy, *L.A. Confidential* takes place on the fringes of 1950s Hollywood and follows four white denizens of a police station as they seek to commit, cover-up, control, or solve various crimes. Aside from this quartet of cops, each with his own separate agenda, the other characters include a tabloid journalist played by Danny DeVito, female prostitutes enhanced (sometimes surgically) to resemble movie stars (Kim Basinger plays Veronica Lake look-alike Lynn Bracken), a nefarious financier who pulls strings in the background, a male prostitute, and various politicos. The film depicts racial prejudice, but the story focuses on crimes and cover-ups among the white characters.[8] Male members of the Hispanic and black culture serve as a criminal, economically and socially marginalized backdrop against which the more important and profitable white male criminality takes place.

As a retro-noir, produced in the nineties but set in the forties and fifties, *L.A. Confidential* appeases audience expectations on a number of levels. The cars, the clothing, the dialogue, the evocation of Los Angeles in the fifties—all promise a unique kind of nostalgic visual and narrative pleasure. Retro-noirs usually feature strong male protagonists, just as films noirs, according to Philip Green,

Figure 7.3. Bud attacking Lynn
(*L.A. Confidential,* 1997)

Figure 7.4. Lynn responding to Bud's blows
(*L.A. Confidential,* 1997)

"were usually movies about strong men," men with a " 'masculinity' worthy of respect even in defeat."[9] Even though, for me, films noirs are usually movies about strong women, I agree with Green about the sort of respectable masculinity represented by noir protagonists Humphrey Bogart and Robert Mitchum and see it reflected in this retro-noir as well. In *L.A. Confidential,* police detective Bud White, played by burly Australian actor Russell Crowe (who has since gained a great deal of fame), displays exactly this sort of manliness. Like Bogart's character in *The Maltese Falcon,* Bud upholds the law and survives this narrative, unlike the homme fatal Jeff (Mitchum) in *Out of the Past.* Bud's whiteness, made explicit in his name, and his sympathetic masculinity are both enhanced by the character's particular aversion to violence against women. But no spectator, male or female, can escape the uncomfortable knowledge that Bud's abhorrence of violence against women does not prevent him from punching his lover, Lynn (Kim Basinger), when confronted with her apparent betrayal (Figures 7.3, 7.4).

In a film noir—in the forties and fifties and before the women's movement—a man might hit a woman who had pushed him too far and still emerge with his respectable masculinity intact. In retro-noir, the situation changes. Public discourse on physically abusive relationships, discourse that exists largely because of the activism of second-wave feminism, dictates that no man should ever hit a woman and that if he does so once, he is likely to do so again. This leaves spectators of *L.A. Confidential* in an uncomfortable position.

Identification in the cinema does not necessarily follow gender lines; I glean as much pleasure from *wanting to be* Bogie as from *wanting* Bogie. Yet gendered spectator positions to *L.A. Confidential* exist. Identifying with Bud might allow a male spectator to fantasize about feeling tough, strong, heroic, noble, and battered, and about having Lynn (or Kim Basinger) as a lover and, later, a wife. But he must also identify as a woman-beater. A female spectator might want to be Lynn (or look like Kim Basinger) and to desire the physicality and masculinity of Bud, but she has to recognize the object of her desires as a potential abuser.

None of the reviews of *L.A. Confidential* mention Bud's physical abuse of Lynn or speculate on their diegetic future together. The synopsis of the film in *Sight and Sound* mentions that Bud attacks the man with whom Lynn supposedly betrays him, but neglects to mention that Bud attacks Lynn first.[10] *Commonweal* devotes a paragraph to Bud, calling him a "psychopathic Galahad" and detailing his brutality in shooting an unarmed rapist.[11] It, too, ignores the fact that he punches Lynn. I cannot believe that a review of a film set in the 1990s or 2000 could ignore that detail. Like the film itself, the reviews focus more on the male characters and ignore the beating of a female character.[12]

In "Russell Crowe's Special Brand of Masculinity," an essay in the *New York Times* published after *Gladiator*'s (2001) release, Mahohla Dargis does mention that Bud "pounds a wife-beater and, later, his own lover into the ground."[13] Dargis sees a trend in Crowe's films much like the one I identify in retro-noir. According to Dargis, Crowe is "a guy who's deadly serious about being a man. . . . Think of it as the return of the repressed: the resurrection of the angry white man."[14] As we shall see, *Fight Club* (1999) continues this resurrection.

In "Advertising and the Construction of Violent White Masculinity," Jackson Katz notes that movies serve as "a key source of constructions of dominant masculinity."[15] He goes on to note that in "late 20th century U.S. culture," media images have "the difficult task of stressing gender difference in an era characterized by a loosening of rigid gender distinction."[16] To do this, Katz speculates, images differentiate between femininity and masculinity by equating "masculinity with violence (and femininity with passivity)."[17] Indeed, this seems to be precisely what *L.A. Confidential* and other retro-noirs do. Bud, a desirable version of masculinity linked with muscularity and violence, becomes acceptable in the context of the past—a past that simultaneously evokes the masculinity of film noir while erasing the femme fatale's powerful brand of femininity once represented there.

Katz cites a similar example from television advertising, an example that again avoids controversy "by depicting the scene as historical."[18] A cruise line advertisement represents male pirates "swords drawn . . . simultaneously . . . fighting with each other while a couple of them are carrying off women."[19] Rape, depicted as an enjoyable part of an escapist adventure, evades censure when placed in a quasi-historical context. So does abuse.

The retro context of *L.A. Confidential* also allows the film to tell the same kind of story about gender as *Casablanca* does. Like *Casablanca*'s, *L.A. Confidential*'s narrative concerns itself primarily with relationships between white men, in this case a trio of police detectives and their boss. The detectives include Bud White and Ed Exley, played by Guy Pearce, who, like Crowe, has since become much better known. Here he struts very different stuff than he does in *The Adventures of Priscilla, Queen of the Desert* (1994), and has more professional ambition than the memory-challenged character in the bleak *Memento* (2000). Jack Vincennes, played by Kevin Spacey, also graces the screen. James Cromwell, who plays the captain of the police force, dances here to a tune radically altered from the one in *Babe* (1995). Curtis Hanson, the director of *L.A. Confidential,* told *Sight and Sound*'s Amy Taubin that he intentionally cast Crowe and Pearce to play Bud and Ed, respectively, because he sought actors with whom "the public had no prior emotional history, so that the audience could discover the characters."[20] For Hanson, Jack "was a moviestar among cops, and could be played by Kevin Spacey, who has moviestar charisma."[21]

Bud, Ed, and Jack could not be more disparate in their backgrounds or goals as police detectives. Jack thrives on the fame and fortune of Hollywood; Ed's mammoth ambition languishes behind wire-rimmed glasses and an aspiration to go by the book; and Bud believes in using any means necessary, including illegal means, to prevent criminals from acting again. But as the film proceeds, these three men begin to work together, despite their initial enmity, to root out the greatest source of evil in the film, a criminality personified by the figure of the fatherly chief of police, Captain Smith. In "Play It Again, Sigmund: Psychoanalysis and the Classical Hollywood Text," Krin Gabbard and Glen O. Gabbard suggest the father figure in *Casablanca* is split into "the benevolent Laszlo . . . and the sadistic Major Strasser."[22] In *L.A. Confidential,* no split separates the benevolent father figure from the sadistic. Both reside quite comfortably (for him) in Captain Smith, and he is central to the narrative.

Just as *Casablanca* provides spectators with a colorful background against which the drama of the white characters is performed, in *L. A. Confidential* blacks and Hispanics represent a lower-class criminality that the white characters use to cover up their more financially viable criminality. When dealing with non-white characters, Bud, Ed, Jack, and Smith treat them as criminals or manipulate them as potentially useful informants. *L. A. Confidential* ignores the possibility of black or Hispanic culture except as represented by Hispanic men jailed and beaten up in an early scene, black male rapists jailed and beaten because they are suspects in the murder of whites (a murder actually committed by Smith and his henchmen), or an Hispanic rape victim who sees to it that her black rapists are punished by implicating them in the murder of whites.

This ugly picture of race and race relations in Los Angeles does not get a reverse shot, a representation of neighborhood, such as spectators enjoy in the golden-hued suburbia of black private eye Easy Rawlins (Denzel Washington) in *Devil in a Blue Dress* (1995). A retro-noir, *Devil in a Blue Dress,* directed by a black man, starring black actors, and based on a novel by a black writer, represents race differently from the standard Hollywood product. As I have shown, classic film noir regularly represents black culture as lively, sophisticated, and not necessarily criminal, although it may be. Often in classic film noir the white male protagonist engages with that black culture, a move that may enhance his character.

In retro-noir *L.A. Confidential,* black and Hispanic men remain peripheral—none of the white male characters have real relationships with them. The stereotype of the jazz club is replaced with the stereotype of ethnic criminality. Bud does rescue the Hispanic woman by shooting an unarmed black rapist dead, but this act is motivated by his hatred of violence against women, and seems unconnected with her race. Certainly, Bud's burly masculinity seems as though it could measure up against any man's, white or black, but retro-noir never puts white masculinity into situations where such a measure might be taken. Instead, black and Hispanic males gain screen time only as powerless pawns in a criminal world controlled by white males. White masculinity reigns supreme.

White females are also peripheral, although Lynn (Basinger) does provide a sexy, pastiche femme fatale for spectators. As *Newsweek* reviewer David Anson notes, the actress "brings a touching, bruised sultriness to her good-bad-girl role."[23] John Simon, writing for *National Review,* suggests that Basinger's beauty, "now beginning to fade, is just right for the disenchanted Lynn."[24] I do not think Basinger's beauty has in any way faded, and the camera work allows her age (forty-four at the time the film was made) to enhance her portrayal of Lynn.[25] Terry Lawson of Knight-Ridder describes Basinger's role as that of "a glamorous call girl who ensnares three hotshot L.A. detectives in her web."[26]

Yet, like Ilse in *Casablanca,* Lynn remains incidental to the homosocial masculine narrative of the film. Lawson has seen enough noirs to know what a femme fatale should be doing (ensnaring men), and he therefore projects those actions onto Lynn. Stuart Klawans, reviewing the film for the *Nation,* seems to agree with me, noting that "despite its protestations of outrage over Womanhood Defiled, *L.A. Confidential* is itself content to use and discard Basinger."[27] Similarly, David Thomas, in a review for *Esquire,* asserts that although "this may be the best noir storytelling since *Chinatown,*" *L.A. Confidential* never "match[es] the earlier movie's tragedy—essentially because the women characters here never become as compelling as the men."[28] These reviewers in the popular press provide a careful and valid critique of this film's representation of gender.

In *L.A. Confidential* Lynn functions as a pastiche femme fatale on multiple levels (Figure 7.5). Within the narrative of the film, Lynn appears to her clients as a stand-in for Veronica Lake, the "sultry, provocative glamour star" with a "cool,

Figure 7.5. Lynn as pastiche femme fatale (*L.A. Confidential*, 1997)

determined" personality who ignited the film noir screens in the 1940s.[29] Just as she represents Veronica Lake, Lynn also represents the femme fatale of film noir. She walks the walk, talks the talk, and certainly dresses the part. But unlike the dangerous dames of film noir, she in no way drives the narrative or influences the outcome of events. Lynn operates at the behest of her pimp, Pierce Patchett (David Strathairn). Her one act of agency, one she may not have engineered, is to have sex with Ed. She tells Bud she thought it would help him, but instead it earns her a punch in the face.

In a brief scene following Lynn's beating by Bud, Ed goes to see her at the police station, sure that she holds the key to the source of the criminal activity. For an instant the spectator thinks she might know something too, but again Lynn functions merely as an object of desire or abuse, not a source of information. Her brief exercise in subjectivity has been brutally punished, and when Ed asks her about the identity of a murderer, she simply answers she has never heard of him. Ed believes her, and so does the audience. Her beauty and desirability remain separate from and less important than the masculine narrative. Lynn looks like but does not function as a femme fatale.

At the end of *L.A. Confidential*, Lynn drives off to rural Arizona with severely injured Bud. Like Ilse in *Casablanca*, Lynn's ultimate survival has direct ties to her lack of agency. The femme fatale almost always engineers her own demise— her dangerous agency cannot be allowed to remain unchecked. Lynn's brief moment of possible agency receives ample punishment: she gets a punch in the face but can survive the narrative. Lynn has also implied a desire to take her place in the domestic economy of small-town USA, asserting that she wants to return to rural Arizona, marry Bud, and open a dress shop. Unlike the classic noirs discussed previously, in retro-noir the dream of middle-class domestic existence remains idealized. In *L.A. Confidential,* the homemade pillow and kitsch Arizona decorations in Lynn's private bedroom represent the dream and signify her essential decency, despite her profession. In addition, her acceptance of and continued affection for Bud, who has been so seriously injured that he cannot speak or move as he sits in the backseat of a car, a man who might now be less than able-bodied, helps ensure her longevity.[30] Nevertheless, white male homosocial bonding remains more important than any heterosexual union.

Just as *Casablanca* ends with Strasser dead, shot by Rick with Renault's complicity, *L.A. Confidential* ends with Ed shooting Smith after Bud and Ed have joined together to overcome the captain. A brief comparison of the male characters in both films makes the parallel masculinities apparent. Strasser and Smith represent evil in their respective narratives. As usual, a psychoanalytic reading of both men, older than the other male protagonists, enables them to stand in as father figures, albeit figures who must be eliminated rather than obeyed in order to make the world right. Both Rick and Bud function as the tough-guy centers of their particular films, epitomizing American white male strength and independence, and each acts according to his own moral code. Renault and Jack both blow with the prevailing winds in order to ensure their own well-being, and both eventually succumb to the dominant morality of their narratives. Renault finally protects Rick from prosecution for Strasser's murder, walking off into the wet and foggy future with him, both men apparently determined to fight for the cause. Jack agrees to help Ed determine who is ultimately responsible for the evil in *L.A. Confidential* and dies for his trouble. Like Laszlo, Ed seeks to follow and profit by the rules of engagement, but also longs to possess Lynn. Or perhaps, he longs to possess Bud. Just before Lynn and Ed have sex, Lynn assures Ed that fucking her and fucking Bud White aren't the same thing; it is apparent to Lynn that Ed may actually be more interested in Bud than he is in her.

Of course, at the end of *Casablanca,* Laszlo leaves with Ilse, whereas at the end of *L.A. Confidential,* Ed can only watch Bud leave with Lynn. I have thought about why, given the narrative similarities between *Casablanca* and *L.A. Confidential,* the two films end as they do. Spectators still see the obligatory Hollywood heterosexual union during the final minutes of both films. I speculate that the reactionary impulse that informs *L.A. Confidential,* allowing Bud to punch Lynn and still remain the hero, might also prevent a homosocial couple from walking off into the future together in the 1990s movie.

Psychoanalytic theories make it increasingly difficult to read the end of *Casablanca* as anything but queer. In 1975, Harvey Greenberg noted that "it is fitting that Rick and Renault should stride together into the night, because it is Renault that Rick has secretly loved."[31] Likewise, earlier in the film Greenberg sees Renault expressing "repressed homosexual longings for the very man [Rick] he has been competing with."[32] The average spectator in the 1940s might have a chance of reading Renault and Rick's beautiful friendship as just that. But by the late 1990s, the implication of two men walking off together has become a risk that the reactionary *L.A. Confidential* cannot afford to take.

In some ways, however, *L.A. Confidential* deals somewhat more humanely with homosexuality than *Casablanca.* As I mentioned earlier, a character marginally marked as homosexual in *Casablanca,* Ugarte (Lorre), dies, apparently murdered, without arousing the sympathy of either the other characters in the narrative or the audience. In *L.A. Confidential,* homosexuality gets a somewhat more progressive response. Throughout the film, the characters use the idea of homosexuality as a method of intimidating suspects and as a possible angle for a publicity-stunt police bust. Nevertheless, unless the homosexuality can be of public use, as in the above situations, the private attitude of the characters toward homosexuality and homosexuals seems disinterested or accepting.

Approximately halfway through the film, Jack takes pity on a young male prostitute who has agreed to seduce an older male politician. The young man is not identified as strictly homosexual; he has apparently agreed to the seduction out of economic necessity. Jack seeks to interrupt the arranged tryst between the two men, bursting into a seedy hotel room saying, "Kid, Matt, come on, kid, you don't have to do this." Jack finds the male prostitute murdered, but his sympathy for the young man's situation humanizes, and functions to queer, his character. Perhaps Ugarte in *Casablanca,* the young man Matt, and even Jack in *L.A. Confidential* are hommes fatals, doomed by their apparently excessive desires, desires that resist the patriarchy, as surely as any femme fatale. But another gay character survives in this retro-noir. Narratively, Matt's murder serves to place Jack on the road to assisting Ed and Bud in their quest. But the corrupt homosexual politician whom the young prostitute was supposed to have seduced remains in power at the end of *L.A. Confidential,* a situation that would have been untenable during the noir years. Male brutality, male bonding, male powermongering, even some male homosexuality—all these versions of masculinity thrive or, at the very least, survive in the retro-noir world that disavows female power.

Umberto Eco finds "a hint of Socratic [male] love" between Rick and Laszlo in

Figure 7.6. Heterosexual relationships in *Casablanca* (1942)

Figure 7.7. Homosocial relationships in *L.A. Confidential* (1997)

Casablanca.[33] Eco views Laszlo as "ambiguously attracted by . . . Rick, and it seems that . . . each of the two plays out a duel of self-sacrifice to please the other."[34] According to Eco, "the woman is an intermediary between the two men. . . . She does not herself bear any positive value (except, obviously, beauty): the whole story is a virile affair, a dance of seduction between Male Heroes."[35] Although Eco is describing *Casablanca,* the description fits *L.A. Confidential* equally well. At the end of *Casablanca,* before Ilse ensures her longevity by going off with Laszlo, Rick and Ilse exchange the same sort of intense, meaningful final looks that Bud and Ed do at the end of *L.A. Confidential* (Figures 7.6, 7.7). Each film's concluding sequences include a similar series of shots and reverse shots.

In *Casablanca,* the exchange of looks signifies the relationship between the heterosexual couple, Rick and Ilse, and their renunciation of that relationship in light of a larger ideal (Figures 7.8 and 7.9). In *L.A. Confidential,* the meaningful final looks between Bud and Ed also occur as they, like Rick and Ilse, separate for a final time (Figures 7.10 and 7.11). Certainly the emotional or physical suffering the characters endured together partly explains the fervor of their gazes. But in *L.A. Confidential,* for an instant, the rigidly heterosexual, homosocial Hollywood narrative permits an intensity of feeling between men that also implies homoeroticism. *L.A. Confidential* repeats the clichés of *Casablanca,* with a few telling differences. Nevertheless, as Eco notes in the opening epigraph, "each actor represents a part played on other occasions . . . a life as stereotypically portrayed by previous films."[36]

Retro-noirs assume a reactionary function in light of the feminist and racial critique of contemporary society. In the postwar noir years, when most films portrayed female characters willing to accept a certain lack of masculinity, the femme fatale remained a glaring, enticing, and dangerous alternative who, there-

Figure 7.8. Rick gazing intently at Ilsa (*Casablanca*, 1942)

Figure 7.9. Ilsa looking back (*Casablanca*, 1942)

fore, had to be contained. At worst she is tortured and murdered; at best, she might be contained in marriage. In retro-noir, as *L.A. Confidential* demonstrates, and as an examination of *Mulholland Falls* and *Fight Club* will confirm, white male characters exhibit a kind of ultraviolent masculinity that, in the end, supports the capitalist patriarchy. And the female characters, pastiche femmes fatales, accept or ignore male lack, just as they did in non-noir narratives in the 1940s and '50s.

Retro-noir may, in fact, be reverse noir. Film noir represented a postwar crisis in masculinity and, whether intentionally or not, also explored the potential of female power and agency, but retro-noir seeks to ameliorate any threat of female power by presenting a fantasy that never existed in the fantasy of film noir. In nostalgic retro-noir, white men are men, and women are beautiful. True, the alluring representation of a woman remains, but the fascinating content provided by the powerful film noir femme fatale is almost totally absent. Whereas once noir provided spectators with strong women, today's retro-noir presents audiences with weak or passive women, with visions of white male brutality and female powerlessness and objectification. Retro-noirs offer a toned-down, bland, and domesticated version of femininity; film noir narratives offered intense visual and narrative pleasures surrounding a powerful female character. In a way, retro-noirs have been effeminated.

As I have shown, retro-noir also depicts race and class in less ambiguous, more obvious ways than classic noir once did, in part by conflating race with class. Both the non-noir *Casablanca* and the retro-noir *L.A. Confidential* make a clear distinction between the white upper classes and the underclass populated by nonwhites. This distinction might have been ideologically forgivable in 1942, but retro-noirs use the retro setting to avoid portraying the complexities

Figure 7.10. Ed gazing intently at Bud
(*L.A. Confidential,* 1997)

Figure 7.11. Bud looking back
(*L.A. Confidential,* 1997)

of race and class in the United States. Instead, white male supremacy remains unquestioned. In retro-noir, the varied pleasures of the classic noir text are replaced by a reactionary nostalgia for a fantasized past that simplifies and purifies complex questions of gender, class, and race. Retro-noir presents white masculinity as rightfully dominant, white femininity as passively peripheral, an idealized middle class, and the racial other as an unimportant backdrop. And, as we shall see, this retro fantasy is a burgeoning and regressive trend.

CHAPTER 8

MULHOLLAND FALLS (1996): NUCLEAR NOIR AS NUMBSKULL NOIR

The best film noirs take corruption as their starting—not ending—point. They assume the world is vile and then demonstrate just how vile. The people who made [*Mulholland Falls*] may not even be hip to all the rottenness on screen. I mean, what are we to make of the hearty sentimentality shown for a bunch of autonomous, head-bashing, pre-Miranda white L.A. cops?

PETER RAINER, "Nothing under Its Hats," *Los Angeles Magazine*

Mulholland Falls (1996) fits into the postclassic noir canon as a nuclear noir. A retro-noir starring a number of big names, big men, and a beautiful woman whose death initiates a search for the nuclear secret, *Mulholland Falls* has not been well received by most critics in the popular press, who have classified it as "numbskull noir" or "*Chinatown* for chowderheads."[1] Of course, the classic nuclear noir *Kiss Me Deadly* was not received well by critics either. As Naremore points out, when *Kiss Me Deadly* was first released, "*The New York Times* did not review it, the Legion of Decency condemned it, the British banned it altogether, and United Artists had difficulty advertising it in midwestern and southern towns."[2] Naremore notes that the film, a "quintessential example of how a supposedly 'cheap' artifact can acquire aura . . . is universally regarded as a masterpiece of noir."[3] Is it possible that *Mulholland Falls* might become the *Kiss Me Deadly* of the next generation? I doubt it.

Yet *Mulholland Falls* works well as a quintessential retro-noir in my taxonomy. With its obvious yet efficient editing, its shiny and clean cinematography, and its shallow yet beautiful characters, *Mulholland Falls* makes my arguments about retro-noir and serves them up in a narrative where an ideology of power, race, the middle class, masculinity, and femininity is rendered unambiguously. In *Mulholland Falls,* race is invisible; muscular white masculinity equates with power and violence. An alluring femme fatale appears, briefly engages in an act of agency, and is murdered. Here, femininity equates with physical beauty and powerlessness. Domestic life, presented ambiguously in classic noir, is in this film lovely and pastel, although threatened. In *Mulholland Falls,* as in *L.A. Confidential,* homosocial relationships matter most, but in *Mulholland Falls* homosexuality must be despised, punished, and violently eliminated.

A few reviewers in the popular press sought to praise the film, but most seemed to enjoy the ample opportunities it supplies for witty criticisms, focused primarily on *Mulholland Falls*'s well-dressed, muscular masculinity. In his review for the *New Statesman,* Boyd Tonkin suggests that "*Mulholland Falls* . . . achieves neither depth of field nor breadth of understanding. The crater formed by an H-bomb test yields no more meaning than the cut of a double-breasted jacket."[4] Tonkin refers here to the natty jackets worn by the "Hat Squad," a supposedly elite group of tough-guy L.A. cops working together outside the law to keep crime in check (Figure 8.1).

In *More Than Night,* Naremore devotes only half a paragraph to the film, noting that it draws heavily on *Chinatown* (1974) and that "aside from administering vigilante justice, the chief function of these four tough guys is to light cigarettes with Zippos and model a peacock collection of suits and accessories."[5] The male protagonists played by the physically imposing actors Nick Nolte, Chris Penn, Michael Madsen, and Chazz Palminteri, do impose themselves physically on all sorts of characters, their highly valued hats signifying the tip of their phallic masculinity in no uncertain terms. But the sleek surface of the film causes Tonkin to complain that "feeling, even identity, atrophies as the wardrobe's role expands to fill the void."[6] John Wrathall, writing for *Sight and Sound,* appears to agree, noting that "having established the idea of a tight-knit four-man squad . . . and [having] cast four heavyweight actors in the roles, the film then gives [two of them] nothing to do."[7] Interestingly, the two with nothing to do are Michael Madsen and Chris Penn, Mr. Blonde and Nice Guy Eddie from *Reservoir Dogs* (1992), actors who are capable of so much more.

They actually have *almost* nothing to do in *Mulholland Falls.* As Wrathall notes, they do "fail to protect Jimmy Fields," the gay character portrayed by Andrew McCarthy.[8] Jimmy, the best friend of Allison Ponds (Jennifer Connelly), the voluptuous woman whose corpse sets the story in motion, seeks police protection from Max Hoover (Nolte), the head of the Hat Squad. Jimmy considers Hoover responsible for Allison's death and taunts him repeatedly, asking, "Do I

Figure 8.1. Empty but imposing well-dressed masculinity (*Mulholland Falls*, 1996)

make you nervous?" and kissing Hoover as Hoover attempts to interrogate him (Figure 8.2). Jimmy, called the fruit, or fruitcake, by the squad, eventually gets police protection in the surly and unsympathetic forms of Eddie (Madsen) and Arthur (Penn). Of course, on asserting his hatred for and indifference to the gay Jimmy, Eddie also asserts his bond with Max Hoover, telling Jimmy, "Don't push your luck, Fields; the only reason we're here is because of Max." Fields disappears during a shoot-out, later washing up dead on the beach, having apparently been tortured and then shot through the mouth.

Like Ugarte in *Casablanca*, as well as Jack and Matt in *L.A. Confidential*, Fields's queerness makes him an homme fatal; he must be contained and he is, just as violently as the femme fatale. Hoover and Eddie's response to Jimmy exemplifies, in cruel form, the intense homophobia sometimes circulating around homosocial relationships in retro-noir. *L.A. Confidential*, in keeping with its more sophisticated, although still conservative, ideology, allows two possibly gay characters to die and another to stay in his position of power. Some of the characters in *L.A. Confidential* express extreme homophobia, yet others express attitudes of disinterest or sympathy. In *Mulholland Falls*, though, no one likes the gay man, Jimmy, except for the beautiful Allison (Figure 8.3).

Jimmy's home movies of his friend Allison point to her possible murderer and

Figure 8.2. A forbidden kiss, arousing anger and violence (*Mulholland Falls*, 1996)

allow the film spectator various titillating views of Allison herself. Allison does seem like a caricature—prompting one reviewer to insist, "yes, Virginia, there is a Jessica Rabbit."[9] In retro-noir, women who exhibit agency, however slight, will earn punishment. In Allison's case, her one act of agency is to film radiation-poisoned men in a hospital ward on a military base. Given the difficulty Hoover has in gaining entry to the ward later in the plot, the spectator wonders how Allison manages this act of subversion as well as what she intends by it. But as most of the reviewers note, no answers to logical questions of that depth are offered by the film.

Although Allison plays a version of the stock character "the hooker with the heart of gold," Kathleen Murphy, writing for *Film Comment,* sees her as "oddly moral."[10] Murphy also erroneously reads Allison as a fully empowered classic femme fatale, identifying her as "the hooker who will be [Hoover's] downfall."[11] Allison, because of her one possibly subversive act, is somewhat more of a femme fatale than Lynn in *L.A. Confidential.* With the exception of the instance described above, however, Allison remains a pastiche femme fatale. She does not drive the narrative through her actions; instead, her death motivates the film's action. Rather than Hoover, it is Allison who takes the big fall, both literally and figuratively: she is thrown from an airplane, and her corpse turns up pressed into

Figure 8.3. Femme fatale Allison, who dies for daring to investigate
(*Mulholland Falls*, 1996)

the dirt of an L.A. construction site. Hoover, her former lover, takes on the task
of seeking her murderer.

The other female character in the narrative is Katherine, Hoover's wife, played
by the consistently feminine Melanie Griffith. The spectator first meets Katherine
in a nightclub, where she waits for and meets her husband. The singer in the
club, a black man, serves as one of two instances where a black man appears on
screen. Unlike similar club scenes in *Out of the Past* or *Kiss Me Deadly*, the club in
Mulholland Falls has only white patrons, and no interaction occurs between the
black entertainer and the protagonist. The singer's beautiful falsetto and osten-
tatious beauty mark ensure that he presents no masculine threat. Unlike *Kiss Me
Deadly* or *Out of the Past*, *Mulholland Falls* contains no subversive hint of any
culture other than white culture. Even the black and Hispanic criminal cultures
that serve as a backdrop for *L.A. Confidential* disappear from the film, which
whitewashes L.A. almost completely.

Retro-noir, however, cannot afford to ignore the female archetypes. *Mulholland Falls* features both of the female characters of noir narratives: an apparent femme fatale, although I undermine that reading, and a femme attrapée,
Katherine. The camera takes the spectator inside the Hoovers' suburban bun-
galow and reveals a dream of pastel peach blankets, cleanliness, and sunlight or

Figure 8.4. The glorification of the dream of middle-class suburbia
(*Mulholland Falls,* 1996)

soft light (Figure 8.4). Katherine always looks beautiful, whether stretched out on the living room couch, reading in an easy chair, or wearing a nightgown that causes Murphy to see "the robust, heated sexuality of Harlow."[12] Most reviewers who mention the character at all agree with Stanley Kauffmann, who identifies Katherine as "little more than another patiently waiting, loyal wife, a happy concubine for the marvelously male figure."[13]

Although the other side of the domestic story—the female labor, money worries, and dreariness so often lurking at the edges of the mise-en-scène in a classic noir such as *The Killers*—does not appear in *Mulholland Falls,* the narrative does present a powerful and successful threat to the middle-class domesticity. The classic noir *The Big Heat* (1953) presented an idyllic married life that was destroyed violently and irrevocably when the wife was blown up.[14] Katherine survives the destruction of her home, first by a shattering but ostensibly legal FBI search of her home and then by filmic proof of Hoover's affair with Allison. Violated by both events, Katherine has had enough: she apparently ends her marriage with Hoover. Instead of hinting that the threat to the femme attrapée might be intrinsic to her existence in the domestic economy of the home, as many classic noirs imply, *Mulholland Falls* blames only exterior forces for the devastation of that ideal realm. The destruction of Katherine's wifely idyll occurs because of her husband's adultery and his connection to violence and criminality. Neverthe-less, if any of the characters walk away better off than they were at the beginning of the film, perhaps it is Katherine.

Hoover, although marginally marked as an homme fatal by his affair with Allison, renounces her and survives the narrative as well. His quest to solve her murder leads him to another of Allison's lovers, General Thomas Timms (John Malkovich), the head of the nascent Atomic Energy Commission. According to Ty Burr, in an article for *Entertainment Weekly,* Timms is "responsible for the *eeee*vil nuclear goings-on," although he is "so serene he nearly subverts *Fall*'s good guy/bad guy moral order."[15] Timms articulates a value system in which cer-tain people are allowed, even expected, to subvert the law in search of a greater good. Timms then parallels his murder and maiming of soldiers in nuclear ex-periments with Hoover's brand of lawless justice.

And although Burr might assert otherwise, *Mulholland Falls* has no good guy–bad guy moral order: most guys are good, although the military man respon-sible for Allison's death is overzealous. Timms establishes his moral right to do what he does and insists that Hoover exercises the same right; Hoover, and the narrative itself, tacitly accepts Timms's assessment. Spectators see a homosocial bond between two powerful white men, both of whom feel justified in their abuse of humanity. Hoover's strength lies in his physical strength and muscularity as well as his position as the right hand of law and order. Timms's strength lies in his knowledge of the ultimate form of muscularity, the destructive potential of nuclear weapons, and in his position as the right hand of military power. Allison's death — the death of a beautiful, pliable sexual toy — at least arouses remorse in both men, but the nuclear secret barely arouses anything.

Allison engineers her death through the minor and apparently altruistic act of filming radiation-sickened men. Relative to the greed, duplicity, and murderous actions of classic femmes fatales, Allison's activities seem pastiche indeed. Her murder is revenged, however. Hoover throws the man responsible for Allison's death from a military plane, mirroring her murder, and then survives the plane's crash into the desert with his partner, Ellery (Palminteri). As Wrathall notes, the characters have been told "that another A-bomb test is scheduled . . . so when they survive the crash in the desert, you're expecting they will now be blown to oblivion à la *Kiss Me Deadly*."[16]

Instead, Ellery dies from gunshot wounds (a fight precedes Allison's murderer being thrown from the plane), cradled awkwardly in Hoover's arms (Figure 8.5). The shot seems to cry out for a closer embrace and perhaps even a kiss — the cam-era even pauses to look for it — but the kiss, like the atomic explosion, is withheld. Foster Hirsch, in *Detours and Lost Highways: A Map of Neo-Noir,* reads this scene as redemptive for Hoover, "a male 'love' scene in which he cradles his dying part-

Figure 8.5. A kiss . . . withheld (*Mulholland Falls*, 1996)

ner."[17] Like the gay Jimmy, perhaps Ellery dies because of his exploration of his feminine side, a plot point that provides a running gag throughout the film as the character tries to get his burly buddies to practice the relationship-building methods his female psychoanalyst recommends.

The film closes with Ellery's burial and Katherine's decision to leave Hoover. In no way does the film imply that the larger crime, the hundreds of soldiers sick and dying because of nuclear testing, remains an issue. Hirsch tries to assert that "Hoover is on the trail of something much weightier than a precious objet d'art or a misbehaving heiress" and that "what is potentially at stake is nothing less than the fate of the earth," but this assertion is overstatement, if not pure hyperbole.[18] Neither Hoover nor any of the other characters in the film give any indication that they realize the implication of the nuclear secret the narrative investigates and then completely drops. In *Mulholland Falls,* a noir narrative comes up totally empty.

In perhaps the most damning of critiques, Tonkin claims that *Mulholland Falls* exemplifies postmodernism, perpetuating a negative view of that descriptor. Tonkin suggests that those seeking the distinction between modernism and postmodernism in art "watch *Chinatown* and *Mulholland Falls* back to back. QED."[19] While I am reluctant to consign postmodernism to such a negative position, Tonkin's analogy makes sense. *Mulholland Falls* does exemplify what many consider postmodern characteristics: it glorifies surface over depth, accessibility over complexity, and the past as digestible confection over the past as indecipherable problem.

Mulholland Falls is a dud; directed by New Zealander Lee Tamahori (who also directed *Once Were Warriors* [1994]), starring capable actors, and drawing on a rich noir canon, it still falls flat. Its representations of gender imply a nostalgic and reactionary return of the repressed—a powerful, violent white homosocial masculinity, as well as the sexual objectification and social subjugation of white femininity. In addition, the film fails to provide those small but intriguing hints that other narratives—of nonwhites or of other types of gender relationships or of less-than-ideal domestic situations—even exist. By erasing the gaps and fissures almost always included in classic noir, *Mulholland Falls* becomes a flat, unreflective surface. If *Kiss Me Deadly* suffers from overexposure to critical discussion, it is because it opens itself up to interpretation by spectators and scholars. *Mulholland Falls* stops interpretation short; audiences and, I suspect, scholars respond accordingly, with boredom and inattention.

One might hope that retro-noir, as a genre, has exhausted itself and its audience with the reactionary impulse that informs its narratives. Yet *Fight Club* manages to manifest many of the same tendencies, without the retro surface. Paradoxically, the retro-noir narrative finds its way into the future.

CHAPTER 9

FIGHT CLUB (1999): RETRO-NOIR MASQUERADES AS NEO-NOIR

Fight Club [is] the new guy-fi epic in which Brad Pitt arouses the animal within the postmodern man—and plays it to the hilt. While [the] film reminds us that there's a direct link between male resentment and fascism, it also can be enjoyed as a spectacle of feminized guys recovering their primal energies in the timeless area of the fight. . . . It's Nietzsche meets Orwell, except that this time Big Sister is Watching You. "We're a generation of men raised by women," Pitt tells his querulous alter ego, "and I'm not sure another woman is what we need."

RICHARD GOLDSTEIN, "Mr. Natural: Is Masculinity a Cultural Construction or a Biological Fact? Science (and Sci-Fi) Enter the Gender Fray," *Village Voice*

The first time I went to see *Fight Club* (1999), I walked out of the theater right as the narrator and Tyler Durden went to steal fat from the liposuction clinic. I knew this was what they were heading to do because I had insisted on hearing a detailed narration of the plot before seeing *Fight Club,* a device I often use to help me get through movies that I ought to see but do not desire to see. I did not leave because of the disturbing nature of the film, although it does contain heavy-handed violence and misogyny. Aside from my equally middle-aged brother and me, the only other people in the audience on Sunday afternoon in Salt Lake City were two young white boys, probably in their midteens.

The reason I left (taking my brother with me) had to do with the rapt attention and obvious enjoyment on the faces of these young men as they partook of

Fight Club's catalogue of increasingly violent fighting, fucking, and pop psychology. In retrospect, I wish I had stuck it out and—like Siegfried Kracauer with the little shopgirls—made the responses of those young men the object of my study; indirectly, perhaps I have.[1] While *Mulholland Falls* represents retro-noir at its most blatant and uninspired, *Fight Club* represents the impulses of retro-noir packaged in a seductive, sophisticated, and intriguing film. *Mulholland Falls* can be remembered (or forgotten) as "numbskull noir"; *Fight Club* requires more serious analysis.

Even a cursory look at *Fight Club* locates it in the realm of noir, which is why I knew I ought to see the film. Like many of the classic noirs, it features a subjective voice-over narration by a white male protagonist, an erotic triangle, a female object of desire who is both like the narrator and dangerous to him, a male antagonist who is both attractive to the narrator and dangerous to him, and an urban, crumbling, criminal milieu in which the plot of the film unfolds. *Fight Club* seems unlike the other films I discuss as retro-noir in its relatively contemporaneous setting. Therefore, according to my taxonomy the film should operate as neo-noir. But *Fight Club* only masquerades as neo-noir. Instead, its ideological project aligns it much more with retro-noir. *Fight Club* attempts to pose as revisionary, but the weight of the film's visual and narrative punches, like those of other retro-noirs, comes down firmly and overwhelmingly on the side of white male prowess and the reestablishment of a most pernicious white supremacist capitalist patriarchy.

Fight Club has ignited a great deal of critical and scholarly discussion, in part because the film simultaneously revels in and satirizes many culturally current issues of the late nineties. The plot revolves around the sleep-deprived white yuppie narrator (Edward Norton), who finds some relief from his ennui by attending support groups for people with fatal illnesses or other major health problems, such as testicular cancer. *Fight Club* focuses on upper-middle-class white masculinity rather than featuring the lower-middle- or working-class protagonists of many classic films noirs. As in classic noir, all of the significant characters are white.

The delicate balance the narrator has achieved in his unhappy life is upset by the arrival of another tourist at the group sessions (at the testicular-cancer group in particular): the cigarette-smoking, supposed femme fatale Marla (Helena Bonham Carter). The narrator's trouble with Marla breathes life into Tyler Durden (Brad Pitt), an anarchic, anticapitalist stud who appears to be everything the narrator is not. The narrator and Tyler set up housekeeping in a decaying mansion. Domesticity exists only between men in the film.

The two men start Fight Club, where other men come to indulge in their animal maleness by beating each other bloody.[2] Tyler begins a rough, orgiastic sexual relationship with Marla. Tyler and the narrator start to franchise Fight Club; Tyler dumps Marla. The fight clubs become part of Project Mayhem, an anticapitalist terrorist group bent on wiping out credit-card debt. Tyler serves as the group's absolute commander.

The dénouement of the film reveals the narrator's psychosis: Tyler is the narrator. In the final sequence, after he (the Ed Norton character) has managed to eliminate Tyler or become Tyler, he and Marla watch as the city crumbles around them. Project Mayhem has come to fruition. The images in *Fight Club*'s concluding sequence, which features skyscrapers collapsing against the backdrop of a night sky, seem eerily prophetic in the wake of September 11, 2001, and add to the film's ongoing critical capital.

Reviewers often mention the film in conjunction with *American Beauty* (2000), *Crash* (1996), and, in the case of those who are associated with *Fight Club*, *The Graduate* (1967). Many, including Chuck Palahniuk, the author of the book on which *Fight Club* was based, see the film as a version of Susan Faludi's *Stiffed: The Betrayal of the American Male*. According to Joel Stein, writing for *Time*, Palahniuk read Faludi's book after he wrote *Fight Club* but nevertheless calls his book "the fictionalized version of *Stiffed*."[3] And Faludi, according to Stein, calls *Fight Club* "*Stiffed* on speed."[4] Faludi, a writer often associated with conservative and reactionary postfeminism, also likens *Fight Club* to *Thelma and Louise* (1991), calling the film a "consciousness-raising buddy movie" and "an incisive gender drama."[5] But like other retro-noirs, *Fight Club* only functions as incisive gender drama for the male characters. The female characters, despite the fear and loathing the narrative reserves for them, remain passively peripheral to the drama presented by the film.

Marla, like Lynn (Basinger) in *L.A. Confidential,* looks exactly like a femme fatale when she makes her entrance into the narrator's life. Mysterious, wearing big black sunglasses and a hat, she shows up at the testicular-cancer support group just as the men engage in one-on-one embraces. The narrator, pressed cozily into the hormonally enlarged breasts of Bob (Meatloaf), instantly intuits the threat Marla represents to his existence. The first close-up of Marla shows her expertly lighting a cigarette, her large black hat blocking her face from view in the slightly high angle shot. In the second close-up, the straight-on camera angle moves in slow motion from a medium close-up to a close-up as Marla seductively exhales smoke from voluptuous red lips. Her sunglasses, hat, and dress add to the initial femme fatale characterization (Figure 9.1). After this sequence, however, Marla never again looks as if she belongs in a classic film noir; her thrift store glamor looks more like heroin chic. But the message seems clear: she is the source of all the problems for the narrator. In typical retro-noir fashion, this is not due to her actions or agency, just her presence.

Figure 9.1. Marla, another pastiche femme fatale (*Fight Club*, 1999)

The narrator, obsessed and disturbed by Marla's presence, confronts her as another self-help imposter, and they divide up the support groups so that they need not run into each other there. The narrator continues to do his job, a type of automobile-insurance adjustment that calculates the cost of safety recalls versus the cost of paying off injured individuals or bereaved relatives, an especially poignant occupation given the simultaneous eruption of the Firestone tire scandal in 2000. And then, right on cue and in direct response to Marla's intrusion at the groups, Tyler Durden shows up, sitting next to the narrator on one of his innumerable cross-country flights. The narrator, like the Everyman of some films noirs, gets sucked into a criminal and dangerous world by a beautiful femme fatale.

The plot deftly presents Marla simultaneously as the cause of the narrator's problems — in order to deal with the sexual tension she arouses, Tyler appears — and as nonessential to the film. In "Private Satisfactions and Public Disorders: *Fight Club*, Patriarchy, and the Politics of Masculine Violence," Henry Giroux describes Marla's effect on the narrator: "Once again, repressed white masculinity is thrown into a crisis by the eruption of an ultra-conservative version of post-1960s femininity that signifies the antithesis of domestic security, comfort and sexual passivity."[6] Marla does not exactly fit into any of the categories delineated by Sarah Projansky in *Watching Rape: Film and Television in Postfeminist Culture*.[7] Projansky uses the term *postfeminism* to describe both the reactionary and revisionary strands of current feminism and provides a detailed catalogue of those movements.[8] Although Marla certainly exhibits what Projansky calls (hetero)sex-positive characteristics, this brand of postfeminism is usually linked to "commodities that call for and support constant body maintenance (femininity)."[9] Marla's commodities come from someone else's laundry or the thrift store. In a sense, she transgresses both through her sexual appetites and her flaunting of the consumption-oriented conventions of femininity.

Unlike Giroux, many viewers seem blind to Marla's role as the cause of the narrator's psychic disruption. Raphael Shargel, writing for the *New Leader*, reads her character exclusively as "[Tyler] Durden's sexual playmate; their trysts together seem inserted solely to convince us Durden is straight."[10] Brian Johnson, in *Maclean's*, asserts that in *Fight Club* women "barely exist" and that Marla "is just a blip in the narrator's peripheral vision."[11] Stanley Kauffmann calls her "a druggie slut who winds up in the lives of both men, principally because the film needs a woman and the two men need a chance to display their sexual prowess or lack of it."[12] Marla never actually uses drugs recreationally on the screen, unless that includes her attempt to kill herself with sleeping pills, or more slowly with cigarettes, and we never see her intimate with anyone but the two male protagonists whom she considers to be one man. Maybe Kauffmann sees her as a druggie because of her fashion choices and a slut because of the big dildo on her bureau, her sexual history (which she details briefly for Tyler), and her vociferous enjoyment of sex. She assures Tyler that the dildo is not a threat; perhaps the assurance rings hollow for Kauffmann.

The narrative consciously makes Marla and the sexual threat she represents central to the male identity crisis in *Fight Club*, although as I have shown, many spectators fail to read or understand her as such. Marla's quandary throughout the film actually matches that of the spectator. She is necessary but peripheral as she watches the narrative unfold, never exactly sure what is happening. The running commentary on the DVD version of the film provides insight into how the men involved in the film see the character and Bonham Carter. Pitt describes the actor as "tasty," and her cheekbones, hair, and amazing eyes receive high praise from Norton, Pitt, and director David Fincher. Marla has been so objectified, so completely marginalized once she has fulfilled her function in bringing on the superstud Tyler Durden, that she almost disappears.

One reviewer, writing for *Time*, accuses feminism (!) of marginalizing the character, instead of the film itself, a perfect instance of backlash postfeminism. Richard Schickel suggests that Marla serves as a "gnarly representation of feminism's failures to create a more sympathetic female."[13] I see the character of Marla

Figure 9.2. Chloe's longing for intimacy, supposedly funny, definitely deadly
(*Fight Club*, 1999)

and the comments of Schickel as a failure as well: not as a failure of feminism, but as a sure sign that everything and nothing has changed in a supposedly post-feminist age. Women continue to be simultaneously completely objectified and completely guilty. As Projansky notes, backlash postfeminism "appeals to a nostalgia for a prefeminist past as an ideal that feminism has supposedly destroyed . . . [and] represent[s] feminism in a particularly negative light."[14]

Right after Marla clomps into the narrator's support groups, the film introduces two other female characters: one is a female support-group leader and the other is Chloe, a woman dying of cancer (Figure 9.2). According to the narrator, Chloe looks "the way Meryl Streep's skeleton would look if you made it smile and walk around the party being extra nice to everybody."[15] She is obviously dying, and not in a "Tibetan philosophy, Sylvia Plath sense," and makes an unsuccessful plea to her support group for someone to have sex with her. I do not discount the pleasures available in the nasty and intelligent humor of *Fight Club*. In the running commentary for the Chloe sequence on the DVD version of the film, Fincher insists that he wanted someone funny to deliver her lines as she offers a host of enticements to potential partners. Yet, the amusement comes at the expense of a female character who desperately wants sexual intimacy. Such a character often winds up taking the fall in Hollywood films; she wants more than

Figure 9.3. Gendering the critique: placing the blame on women (*Fight Club*, 1999)

Figure 9.4. A visually inventive, ultimately empty critique of capitalism (*Fight Club*, 1999)

a good woman should. *Fight Club* also has her dying of an incurable disease and, nevertheless, expects the spectator to get the joke in a sly but brutally misogynistic guise. Although the Chloe sequence described above takes place early in the film, news of Chloe's death reaches the narrator and the film spectator long after he has stopped attending the support groups, via Marla. It barely registers.

Other misogynistic turns occur periodically throughout the film, making it clear which gender should be blamed for the crisis in masculinity presented by the narrative. In a sequence mentioned earlier, the narrator and Tyler steal fat from a liposuction clinic. This fat, a female bodily fluid, provides them with a source of disgust and income. They render the fat, make soap, and sell the product at a department-store cosmetic counter for twenty dollars a bar (Figure 9.3). According to the narrator, "It was beautiful. We were selling rich women their own fat asses back to them." They also get the ingredients for explosives, which come in handy as Project Mayhem gets underway.

Fight Club expresses a critique of consumerism most overtly early in the film, through the glorious floating Ikea catalog of the narrator's apartment furnishings (Figure 9.4). The liposuction sequence genders the critique of capitalism and consumer culture — men with money, such as the narrator, arouse the spectator's sympathy or at least interest. Even the narrator's boss is humanized more than these faceless, despised, fat-assed rich women. Rich women arouse only ridicule and contempt and seem to stand in for the capitalist venture — ironically, a venture dominated by white males.

The same displaced contempt infuses Tyler's version of the problem with his generation: "We're a generation of men raised by women. I'm wondering if another woman is really what we need." Women, wholly and physically absent from the narrative except for Marla and Chloe, nevertheless carry the blame for society's masculine malaise. Not only is each individual woman guilty, women in general constitute the problem against which the male characters of the film must do battle. Giroux agrees, suggesting that "the film defines the violence of capitalism almost exclusively in terms of an attack on traditional . . . notions of masculinity, and in doing so reinscribes white heterosexuality within a dominant logic of stylized brutality and male bonding that appears to be predicated on the need to denigrate, and to wage war against, all that is feminine."[16]

Tyler certainly serves as a love object much more effectively than Marla, despite the heterocentrism of the conclusion of the film. Tyler, played by a buff and tough Brad Pitt, dresses like Marla in thrift-store chic, but with, according to Kaplan, the costume designer for *Fight Club,* a flashy look that is "the perfect example of how in the animal world the male creatures are always brighter."[17] Tyler really does the seducing in *Fight Club,* and although Brad Pitt usually plays powerfully to heterosexual female desire, here he turns his considerable charms on the men in the movie audience and on the narrator. Amy Taubin, in the *Village Voice,* suggests that the film has "a strong homoerotic undercurrent."[18] Some male spectators willingly talk about that appeal. Gregg Kilday, writing in the *Advocate,* takes note of Tyler's "breathtaking abs" and the suspense inherent in wondering "whether Tyler's low-slung pants will ever slide off his inviting bubble butt."[19]

Obviously, Bonham Carter as Marla does not provide the only instance of objectification, but the characterizations of Marla and Tyler differ in that Tyler drives the narrative. Marc Malkin, also in the *Advocate,* writes descriptively about the homoerotics of the film, calling it "a visual buffet of sweaty, dirty bodies, six pack abs, popping veins, and arms, and torsos intertwined in uninhibited bare-knuckled fighting."[20] Taubin describes the fight sequences as "shot in a wet-dream half-light that turns the men's bodies opalescent as they pound each other into the cement."[21]

Of course, the "uninhibited" fighting also serves as eroticized fantasy and male spectacle. As commentators writing about the film for *Sports Illustrated* note, "*Fight Club* is as romantic about fighting as *Pretty Woman* was about prostitution — Pitt and Norton never slur their words, and the teeth they lose are always molars, because movie stars can't afford to have NHL smiles."[22] Hockey-league smiles would certainly cut down on the surface appeal of the characters, if not the fights. David Rooney, in *Variety,* also sees pronounced homoerotic undercurrents, "on a surface level in the many toned bodies and especially in the way Pitt [Tyler] is costumed, and less superficially in themes of self-love, [and] in the narrator's magnetic attraction to Tyler."[23] In *Fight Club,* homosocial relationships offer exclusivity, violence, and erotic titillation to the male protagonist and the male spectator (Figure 9.5).

Figure 9.5. Tyler's overt appeal to the diegetic and nondiegetic male spectator (*Fight Club*, 1999)

Many male spectators feel intensely attracted to *Fight Club* although unable to articulate exactly why they respond this way. Peter Lehman perceptively notes in "Crying over the Melodramatic Penis: Melodrama and Male Nudity in Films of the '90s" that "images of men and the male body are caught within a polarity . . . [with] at one pole . . . the powerful, awesome spectacle of phallic masculinity, and at the other its vulnerable, pitiable, and frequently comic collapse."[24] *Fight Club* glorifies the former: Tyler splices images of erect penises into family films, and Fincher does the same in *Fight Club*. After all, as Lehman notes, "if the penis is going to be shown it had better be an impressive spectacle."[25] *Fight Club* participates in this "desperate attempt to collapse the distinction between the penis and the phallus" and thereby provides particularly potent pleasures for some male spectators.[26]

Fight Club is a dick flick, concerned above all with promoting the penis as impressive spectacle. In *Cinema and Spectatorship*, Judith Mayne provides another possible explanation for male fascination with *Fight Club*. According to Mayne, the cinema offers a " 'safe zone' in which homosexual as well as heterosexual desires can be fantasized and acted out."[27] Many films offer such "safe zones," but retro-noir makes these pleasures particularly gratifying for certain male spectators by interpolating the spectator into a world that glorifies male homosocial, violent, and erotic experience without overtly implying homosexuality at the level of denotation.

The movie spectator is not the only one for whom these pleasures exist. As Taubin notes, *Fight Club*'s director, Fincher, "doesn't pull back from the homo-eroticism, maybe because he seems not to be conscious that it exists."[28] Taubin quotes Fincher, who insists that "it's beyond sexuality" and further asserts that "the way the narrator looks up to Tyler and wants to please him and get all of his attention doesn't seem to me to have anything to do with sex."[29] Taking sex out of the male homosocial relationship at the level of denotation, however strongly sexuality resonates at the level of connotation, apparently enables not only some male spectators but also the male director and actors to enjoy a male alliance they might otherwise feel obligated to reject. *Fight Club* combines narrative pleasures with visual images that stress the penis as powerful and the actual embodiment of phallic masculinity in Tyler: a virtual inventory of hypermasculinity.

In typical Hollywood retro-noir fashion, *Fight Club* seeks in the final reel to defuse the sexism portrayed throughout the film, through the reestablishment and reassertion of heterocentrism and the reintegration of exiled and despised femininity into male life. Retro-noir *Mulholland Falls* focuses on male bonding, haberdashery, and the physically violent side of police work, and uses Melanie Griffith and Jennifer Connelly to deflect male fears of homoeroticism. Similarly, but with more delicacy, *L.A. Confidential* focuses on the intellectual rigors of crime solving while also featuring Bud White's physical prowess and male char-acters who take and deal out beatings. In *L.A. Confidential,* Kim Basinger keeps male fear at bay. In *Fight Club,* multinational capitalism and consumerism serve as the overt enemy in a narrative that implies male bonding, male physicality, and male violence spring forth as the natural result of a feminization of culture. Of course, Helena Bonham Carter's character arrives just in time to ensure "that the happy ending is a distinctly heterosexual one."[30] Hollywood expertly delivers and then recontains male homoerotic desire in retro-noir. Women, as signifiers of heterosexuality and as guilty objects, serve a crucial function.

Men are not to blame in *Fight Club.* At least white men are not to blame. As I note above, nonwhite characters have no significant roles in the narrative. Only one man in the film is apparently at fault for how his life has turned out. In this brief and distressing sequence, called "Human Sacrifice" on the DVD chapter breakdown of the film, Tyler terrorizes an Asian liquor store clerk named Ray-mond (Joon B. Kim), as the narrator looks on. As I mention in Chapter Two, representations of race in noir have much more to do with the white protagonist and the stability of whiteness than with any other discourse of race. Gregg Kil-day sees Tyler as "yet another embodiment of Norman Mailer's 'white Negro,'" yet unlike the protagonists of classic noir, and like those of retro-noir, Tyler does

Figure 9.6. Terrorizing the racial other (*Fight Club,* 1999)

not establish his credentials for hipness through his familiarity with and acceptance into black culture.[31] Even Kilday suggests that Tyler gains hipness primarily through " '70's pimp threads," that is, through his clothing.[32]

Fight Club may be ambivalent about or blind to blackness, perhaps unwilling to measure white against black masculinity, but its contempt for Asians gains screen time. In the "Human Sacrifice" sequence, Tyler holds a gun to the hysterically frightened Asian man's head and insists that he go back to school to pursue a veterinarian's degree, a career path the clerk had once embraced but given up because it required "too much school" (Figure 9.6). Once Tyler threatens the sobbing Raymond with surveillance to ensure that he pursues his scholastic goals, Tyler tells Raymond to "run on home." Brian Johnson, writing for *Maclean's,* notes that the sequence has "nasty racial overtones," but no one on the film's DVD commentary track, which includes remarks from Fincher, Pitt, Norton, and author Palahniuk, even mentions the race of the clerk.[33] Giroux's assessment of the sequence suggests that "class does not operate as a critical category in this film."[34] Giroux goes on to critique Tyler's view that "choice . . . appears to be an exclusively individual act, a simple matter of personal will that functions outside of existing relations of power, resources, and social formations."[35]

A white clerk would have, presumably, served the same function. Or would he have? Author Palahniuk remarks that most spectators and readers sympathize with the terrorizer, not the clerk (in the film, Tyler holds the gun and does the terrorizing; in the book the narrator performs this human sacrifice). Asian men, stereotypically hardworking survivors in the gritty urban milieu, here become the infantilized object of white male racial frustration and derision. Tyler stands in for the white father, urging the less capable racial other to make something of himself. Unlike the guilty women in *Fight Club,* the Asian man, by virtue of his maleness, is worth recuperating. The narrative asks the spectator to believe that being terrorized by Tyler will cause Raymond to pursue a profession instead of working as a clerk, and even implies that he will thank his oppressors. According to Tyler, Raymond's breakfast tomorrow will taste "better than any meal you and I have ever tasted." Giroux makes his own inferences, insisting that Tyler tells the narrator tomorrow "will be the most important day in Raymond's life because he will have to address what it means to do something about his future."[36]

Raymond presumably survives the narrative of *Fight Club* and goes on to live a full life as a veterinarian, but another man, Bob, does not survive. Some see Bob, a testicular-cancer survivor with breasts caused by his hormonal imbalance, as a feminized male, a character who recuperates the film from overwhelming misogyny. Because of his voluptuousness and the seeming gentleness of his personality, Bob does receive some of the satirical treatment reserved for women in the narrative, but in the end he gains acceptance into the club because he is already a member. When Bob dies during a Project Mayhem attack on a corporate target, the outpouring of sorrow from the narrator and the members of Project Mayhem are immediate and heartfelt—they rage in grief. Chloe's death barely registers with the narrator; Bob's death causes him to wake up from his existential malaise to the dangers of Tyler's grand anarchic design. Bob, despite his "bitch tits," is a man, and therefore his death affects the outcome of events in the narrative.

Faludi sees *Fight Club* as renouncing "even the violence its lead character is drawn to, and . . . the adolescent fraternity that so much of men's media seems unable to escape."[37] She further suggests that "when [the narrator] sends the boys away in the final scene, and throws his lot in with the defiant, if deviant, women . . . he seems poised finally to begin life as an adult man."[38] She even calls the film a "quasi-feminist tale, seen through masculine eyes."[39] Here, Faludi subscribes in part to the reactionary discourse that suggests "men turn out to be *better* feminists than are women."[40]

Where Faludi sees renunciation of violence, a quasi-feminist outcome, and male potential, I see a Hollywood ending, designed to do what Hollywood endings have always done and in the most reactionary of ways. I have never been able to read the inevitable containment of the femme fatale in the final min-

Figure 9.7. The destruction of skyscrapers and an obligatory heterosexual union (*Fight Club*, 1999)

utes of every classic film noir as entirely convincing. The energy and enthusiasm that powerful female characters had for achieving their goals provided so much pleasure that part of me always ignored the ending. Many of the most potent pleasures Hollywood has to offer are forbidden as well, and *Fight Club* plays to similar but more ominous desires. Whereas the femme fatale wants more than she should, which often but not always includes the man of her desires, what the men in and of *Fight Club* really want is a world without women. *Fight Club* attempts to tidy up its orgy of male violence and racism, male homosocial and erotic couplings, and misogyny in the last five minutes of the film into a neat heterosexual union between the narrator and Marla (Figure 9.7). Just as the re-containment of the femme fatale rings false, this facile recontainment of male anger and hostility toward women and nonwhite men seems frighteningly hollow. As reviewer David Sterritt notes, "the irony of *Fight Club* is that it embodies the very symptoms it calls attention to."[41]

The ideas hinted at in *Fight Club* are worth exploring. Tyler, to a certain degree, functions as an homme fatal, and the narrator as an homme attrapé. Tyler seeks to exist outside of the capitalist enterprise and, like other hommes fatals, dies at the end of the film. The narrator survives, having acquiesced in the demands of the white supremacist capitalist patriarchy. Ironically, this highly successful and profitable film suggests that consumption-driven late-market capitalism does not offer redemption, or even happiness; it only feeds itself. Likewise, *Fight Club* suggests that changing gender roles cause rifts and revisions in how the culture understands itself and that cults of white masculinity have dangerous, misogynist, conformist, and racist potential. It proves that homoeroticism is part of the pleasure Hollywood has to offer all spectators.

But *Fight Club*—perhaps because it is too much of the culture it hopes to critique—comes up empty-handed, managing primarily to arouse the appetites it promises to interrogate. The film's representation of race and gender aligns it closely with other retro-noirs. *Fight Club*'s vision of gender roles seems diametrically opposed to the vision provided by postclassic neo-noirs, which allow their female protagonists to survive, thrive, and commit or solve crimes, with and without male companionship or assistance. When neo-noirs end with a heterosexual coupling, the relationship seems more organic than in retro-noirs such as *Fight Club*.

If film noir and postclassic noir represent the history of ideas, the ideas about gender and race circulating in *Fight Club* and other retro-noirs seek to redeem reactionary, misogynistic, violent, and often racist white masculinity. The ideas driving neo-noir seem to offer refreshing, revisionary, and liberating notions of masculinity and femininity without abandoning the excitement that has always infused the concept of noir. Unfortunately, this revisionary appropriation of gender representation in neo-noir does not extend equally to race; in fact, these films often remain reactionary in portraying race. But even with regard to this issue, neo-noir is less easily categorized.

PART 4

REVISION OF THE REPRESSED IN NEO-NOIR

CHAPTER 10

TWILIGHT (1998): AGE, BEAUTY, AND STAR
POWER—SURVIVAL OF THE FITTEST

Very much befitting its title, *Twilight* is an autumnal murder mystery awash in rueful intimations of mortality. [It] plays like a riff on Phillip Marlowe in old age, complete with jaundiced observations on L.A. lifestyles, lower-class probing into upper-class corruption, and moneyed privilege removing celebrities from moral and legal accountability. Coloring everything is the pronounced feeling on the part of the three male characters . . . that they are nearing the end of the road.

TODD MCCARTHY, *"Twilight," Variety*

Twilight (1998), starring Paul Newman (73), Gene Hackman (67), Susan Sarandon (52), James Garner (70), and Stockard Channing (54), has enough mature star power to earn the moniker geriatric or (less fondly) geezer noir by virtue of the male protagonists alone.[1] *Twilight*'s director, Robert Benton, worked with Newman in the frigid but lovely *Nobody's Fool* (1994), another film in which the male protagonist gets to act Newman's age. *Nobody's Fool* takes place in the squeaky cold of a small northern town in winter; *Twilight* revels in the warmer California haunts of classic film noir, modern California architecture (and not postmodern architecture), a complex story line, clipped dialogue with an utter lack of hipness, and, to quote Newman himself, "good old-fashioned acting."[2]

Good old-fashioned noir turns up, too, in the location shooting, the lighting, the voice-over narration of the male detective, the erotic triangles, and the interest and attention the film devotes to gender and class—all with a neo-noir twist

117

that does not rely solely on the nongeneric vintage of the actors. Unfortunately, the representation of nonwhites does not reflect revision; instead, this postclassic neo-noir exhibits a reactionary nostalgia for racial stereotypes, including the glorification of whiteness and the maligning of nonwhites. As in *Fight Club, Mulholland Falls,* and *L.A. Confidential,* all of the significant characters are white.

Twilight sets up yet another erotic triangle, this time between Harry (Newman), a former cop, detective, and alcoholic, and a famously successful but aging Hollywood couple, Catherine (Sarandon) and Jack (Hackman). Unlike paramours in the classic films noirs discussed here, all the members of the triangle survive at the end of *Twilight.* As Raphael Shargel aptly notes, "Fear of the big sleep is never far from the thoughts of the characters in a film noir, but most of them generally worry that their lives will be snuffed out prematurely," as do most of the members of the erotic triangles in *The Killers* and *Out of the Past.*[3] Shargel goes on to assert that the "principals in *Twilight* face a slower, no less terrifying prospect," one written into the wrinkles on their skin: the specter of imminent death by natural causes that haunts the entire film.[4]

Plenty of people do die of unnatural causes in the course of *Twilight.* Indeed, the plot of the film hinges on the mysterious death and disappearance of Catherine's first husband, Billy, twenty years ago, right around the time she and Jack fell in love. After an opening sequence in Mexico, during which Harry retrieves a young woman from the arms of her lover and winds up shot in the groin, the narrative reopens in classic noir style. The scene in Mexico provides the only moment in which the spectator really sees Harry's rugged, wrinkled face, or any face, in full sun. From then on, careful framing, half-light, low light, or high-key lighting serves to keep all of the aging actors looking almost as fine as if they were being coddled by the soft-focus photography of Hollywood's classic years.

After the opening scene, a police interview in a small, poorly lit room begins, as does Harry's narration, commenting upon the fact that the world does not lose its power to seduce and introducing the object of his desire, Catherine. This sequence simultaneously implies that Harry has lost his sexual potency; the cops think the shot in the groin he took in Mexico took care of that. In a smart segue from the Mexico sequence to the past introduced by Harry's voice-over, both scenes begin with a woman swimming, underwater, in the dappled blue of a pool. In the Mexico sequence, the figure is that of Mel (Reese Witherspoon), Catherine and Jack's daughter. The next time, it is Catherine herself. The daughter replaced by the mother, youth by maturity, and Catherine does not suffer from the comparison.

Catherine, the femme fatale around whom the mysteries of the narrative circulate, shares responsibility for a number of the murders that take place in the course of *Twilight.* Twenty years before the start of the film, her first husband—

angry, drunk, and determined to confront her lover, Jack—winds up dead and buried on the property of Jack's unfinished beach house. Raymond (James Garner) actually carefully orchestrated this disappearance, presumed a suicide at the time. A studio guard and former cop, Raymond steps in to help Jack and Catherine "clean things up." It is Raymond, a friend of Jack and Harry's, who sets Harry up with the Mexico caper—a job Harry bungles, leaving him injured (presumably emasculated) and living above the garage at Jack and Catherine's palatial home.

The murders that occur in the film all take place because people seek to reawaken a past Catherine prefers be left alone, especially since Jack, sick with cancer, has only a year to live. Harry, seeking to help Catherine and Jack buy off potential blackmailers, becomes the link that leads the police, including Harry's former police partner, Verna (Stockard Channing), right to the star couple and the mysterious disappearance of Catherine's husband twenty years earlier. As it turns out, Raymond actually commits all the murders, the more recent ones with a great deal of effort to ensure Harry's survival. Raymond also murdered Catherine's first husband, who was injured but not dead after confronting Jack. In the end, Harry's rekindled investigative skills lead him to Raymond, and Harry kills him. Harry is unable to walk away from all the blood shed on Catherine's behalf.

Catherine, an actress who has starred in such films as *The Last Rebel* and *The End of Desire,* seems as though she might have almost as impressive a filmography as that of Susan Sarandon, who plays the character. Sarandon, known for her intelligence, beauty, social consciousness, and, perhaps most of all, her role in *Thelma and Louise* (1991), imbues Catherine with many of the qualities spectators associate with Sarandon herself.[5]

In "Articulating Stardom," Barry King distinguishes between personification and impersonation in acting styles.[6] King notes that with personification "the range of the actor is limited to parts consistent with his or her personality," and with impersonation "the 'real' personality of the actor should disappear into the part."[7] Of course, impersonation implies greater acting skills; personification implies a well-developed star discourse that provides or imbues the star with personality. Sarandon seems capable of both acting styles, and the intertextuality of her public and star personae often enhances her portrayals of various characters.

In her discussion of *Thelma and Louise,* Sharon Willis notes that one of the pleasures that film offers is how at "the fantasmatic level, the film pries gender away from sexuality, pries feminine masquerade loose from the effects of glamour and sexual seduction, makes the body into its own costume."[8] Although she might be discussing the deglamorization of the female characters in *Kiss Me Deadly,* Willis refers, of course, to Thelma and Louise's external transformation.

Figure 10.1. Susan Sarandon as femme fatale Catherine (*Twilight*, 1998)

In *Twilight*, Catherine is older than many femmes fatales, but she epitomizes gender as sexuality, and feminine masquerade as glamor and sexual seduction (Figure 10.1).

Yet in our memories, traces of Sarandon in her other roles, and as a public persona, still exist. Traces of Paul Newman's roles reside in Harry. Garner's roles, especially as television's Jim Rockford in *The Rockford Files,* give Raymond a past. One of Hackman's films actually stands in for one of Jack's movies. The interplay of filmic, star, and public personae within the characters developed in *Twilight* provide a pleasing postmodern depth to the noir narrative, especially in a film whose featured stars have so much Hollywood history on which to draw.

Femme fatale Catherine determines the outcome of events in the film without leaving her home or doing anything more than dialing the phone to share her worries with Raymond. Raymond does the rest, and this allows Catherine to deny responsibility. As she tells Harry, "I never asked him to kill anybody." Harry responds, "Yeah, but you knew he would." The film tries to set Catherine up as the fall guy, just like Kitty in *The Killers* and Kathie in *Out of the Past,* but Catherine does not take the fall, and though Harry may be over her by the end of the film, the spectator is not. Or perhaps I should say this spectator is not.

Janet Maslin calls the character "vain, conniving and glossy."[9] Richard Alleva, writing for *Commonweal,* insists that even "such a woman is capable of her own version of fidelity."[10] Jonathan Romney sees her as "snappy, snake-eyed, [and] acerbic."[11] Todd McCarthy, however, suggests that "Catherine has a . . . charming, as well as honest, way of stating her case and achieving her ends," and John Simon sees her as "earthily feminine but with a hint of hidden fragility—infinitely desirable."[12] The reviewer for the *Army Times* sees Catherine as "chilly, confident, and impeccable in a Nancy Reagan sort of way."[13]

The variety of interpretations of Catherine's character speaks both to Sarandon's abilities and to the impossibility of enforcing a spectator's position. Catherine has been the woman in a number of erotic triangles: between her first husband and Jack, between Harry and Jack, and, by implication, between Raymond and Jack long before Harry shows up on the scene. But the apex of every triangle, for Catherine, has always been Jack. She might use her sexuality to achieve her goals, but her love for Jack remains unswerving and boundless. In the end, the spectator can only marvel at, and perhaps envy, that devotion, even though overt eroticism no longer enters into the connection between Jack and Catherine.

That lack in Jack and Catherine's relationship mirrors the relationships in the erotic triangles of classic film noir. In *Out of the Past,* the sexually charged nature of Kathie's relationship with Jeff gains screen time, but her relationship with Whit—the man with a prior claim to her allegiance, at least in his mind—is desexualized. In *The Killers,* the powerful effect of Kitty's sensuality on Swede becomes immediately apparent; Kitty and her husband never exchange a desiring look. Similarly, in *Twilight,* Catherine makes love to Harry, perhaps to gain his support in her efforts to keep the past from resurfacing. Even here, the camera work and lighting carefully maintain an aesthetic distance from the actors.

Amy Taubin, writing for the *Village Voice,* finds this fanciful cinematography grating. According to Taubin, "What's the point of having a senior citizen sex scene if you're going to frame him from the collarbone up, thereby keeping the tired flesh out of the *picture?*"[14] Taubin seems, however, to be missing the point: despite the age of the lovers, in *Twilight,* as in the classic noirs, the erotics of the triangle are focused upon the femme fatale and the other man. But unlike the ambiguous motivations that spice up classic noirs, Catherine's allegiance is never in doubt; she loves her husband (Figure 10.2).

At one point in *Twilight,* Jack responds with a violence and virility that belie his illness. Having just had a heart attack, Jack lies on the floor, the concerned faces of his wife and her lover hovering above him as Catherine puts the oxygen mask to his face. The camera takes Jack's eye view as he puts together the clues. Catherine wears only Harry's shirt, a pink one that Harry wore earlier in the day. Jack thrashes out, knocking Catherine away. Bud White, caught in an apparently similar situation, beats up Lynn Bracken in *L.A. Confidential.* In *Twilight,* Jack

Figure 10.2. Catherine and Jack (*Twilight*, 1998)

responds with frustrated action to the incontrovertible evidence that he is being cuckolded even as he dies. Gene Hackman never looks sick — the lighting and camera work portray him as glowing, healthy, and handsome, just as it does the other aging actors in the film — but we know that Jack is dying. Jack, who apparently played countless tough guys on film, guys capable of shooting "twelve guys with a six-shot revolver," has nearly reached the end of his life. His frustration and anger with his situation lend his response validity.

Although Catherine's relationship with Jack seems central to the narrative, other spectators understand the film differently. For Alleva, writing for *Commonweal*, "Newman [Harry] and Garner [Raymond] inhabit the emotional center of the movie."[15] Alleva sees "star chemistry" between the two and notes that the actors engage "in a friendly duel called Let's See Who Can Underact the Other off the Screen."[16] Despite the strength of the scenes between Harry and Raymond, that homosocial bond does not survive (Figure 10.3). Unlike *Casablanca,* for example, *Twilight* brings to the screen the ending of a beautiful friendship. Harry shoots Raymond, even though Raymond was protecting Jack and Catherine. The homosocial bonds between men in this neo-noir are not invested with the vitality or eroticism of the homosocial relationships in retro-noir. Jack and Harry are

Figure 10.3. A doomed homosocial relationship (*Twilight,* 1998)

friends, but Jack and Catherine's connection drives the narrative. Harry and Raymond are friends, but Harry's moral code cannot be derailed by that friendship.

And finally, like most Hollywood films, the end of *Twilight* stresses heterosexual rather than homosocial relationships. Jack and Catherine make their way to the end of his life, and Harry and Verna head off for a tryst in Catalina. Verna, a smart police investigator who, unlike her male colleagues, guesses the level of Catherine's involvement in the murders, also verifies for herself that Harry is still tryst-worthy. In retro-noirs such as *Fight Club,* the threat to masculinity remains repressed; in neo-noir, the threat makes its presence felt, although Verna confirms for all of us that Jack still has it. And, as Romney notes, in "a further tender twist, the beautiful people turn out at the end to be motivated by an unfathomably tough unconditional love."[17]

Twilight, like classic noir, considers questions of class while keeping a focus on white heterosexual relationships. In many classic films noir, the femme fatale and homme fatal often seek more than a working-class existence. Swede, homme fatale in *The Killers,* suffers from the same fatal desire as many femmes fatales. In *Twilight,* both Harry and Raymond view themselves as other than, or outside the circle of, the beautiful people to which Jack and Catherine belong. When

Catherine complains to Harry that she and Jack are broke, he corrects her, saying, "No, I'm broke. You and Jack are overextended; I'll explain the difference to you sometime, so you'll understand." This real economic difference between Harry and Catherine causes Harry to regret the violent deaths of the various small-time blackmailers who try to make a profit off of Catherine and Jack's past.

Those blackmailers include "a couple of lowlife lovers, Jeff and Gloria, played with endearing rudeness by Liev Schreiber and Margo Martindale."[18] These two might have been the main characters, a femme and an homme fatal, in a different neo-noir. Both end up dead, and "tacky, mean and devoted, they provide one of the movie's most complicated moments of sadness."[19] Jeff and Gloria do resemble many of the desperate couples in classic noir; Roy (Humphrey Bogart) and Marie (Ida Lupino) in *High Sierra* (1941), and Davy (Jamie Smith) and Gloria (Irene Kane) in *Killer's Kiss* (1955). In *Twilight,* Gloria elicits spectator sympathy as she dies of gunshot wounds, acknowledging to Harry her gift for loving losers, including Jeff, who has also been murdered. Harry understands that he has much more in common with these two blackmailers than he does his "beautiful people" employers. Neo-noir keeps its focus on its star characters but, like classic film noir, allows hints about other sorts of lives to enter into the narrative.

Raymond, the film's bad guy, has come to have more in common with Jack and Catherine than he does with the economically strapped Harry. Although he once lived just like Harry does, Raymond has bartered his usefulness to Jack and Catherine into a spectacular home overlooking the city and a life of well-heeled leisure. Raymond is an homme fatal with materially more to lose than almost any character in *Twilight,* and therefore he perpetrates all the violence. Catherine seeks to hold together her life so that her husband can die in peace; Raymond seeks to hold together Catherine's life so that he can continue to live the plush lifestyle he can no longer do without. At the end of the narrative, like the hommes fatals in other noirs, Raymond will die for his desires. For Raymond, those desires include his house.

Peter Plagens, writing for *Newsweek,* goes so far as to suggest that it is not homosocial or heterosexual relationships that are the focus of the film, asserting "the real central characters in 'Twilight' are the classic modern houses used as locations for a story set in the present."[20] The remarkable California architecture does take center screen a number of times. Plagens provides details, noting that "Jack and Catherine's house was built around 1930 by Cedric Gibbons (who designed the Oscar statuette) for Dolores Del Rio[;] their desert hideaway is an unfinished Frank Lloyd Wright project, abandoned in 1946[,] and Garner's [Raymond's] hillside nest is a John Lautner spaceship from the late '40s."[21]

The film also takes us into less famous but nevertheless ubiquitous examples of classic California architecture, including two run-down California bungalows that once signified, however ambiguously, the 1950s American dream of suburban domesticity. These bungalows now house low-rent blackmailers and sickly retired cops, but they once housed Mildred Pierce, and detective Dave Bannion in *The Big Heat.* Romney calls *Twilight* "an eloquent essay on west coast ranch modernism," yet the narrative seems to imbue these fine examples of American architecture with a sense of loss and regret.[22] The dreams embodied by the glorious and mundane architecture of the 1930s, '40s, and '50s seem even more remote than they did in the classic noirs. And how is it possible that a Frank Lloyd Wright house today remains unfinished in Malibu? The film's treatment of race also arouses regret.

While *Twilight* pays careful attention to economic class, it plays the race card in a way that ultimately undermines its class consciousness. As I have shown, film noir has always been about whiteness—white masculinity and femininity, with racial others relegated to specific roles within those narratives. As Naremore notes, most "films noirs of the 1940s are staged in artificially white settings, with occasional black figures as extras in the backgrounds," although there were "occasional attempts to give brief speaking roles to black people, and a conscious effort was made to avoid depicting them as the minstrelshow caricatures or comic illiterates of the 1930s."[23]

In classic noir the white protagonist's association with black culture and individuals often serves to enhance his "aura of 'cool.' "[24] In *Twilight,* the only ethnic character, with the exception of extras or bit parts in the police milieu, Ruben (Giancarlo Esposito), seems to have more to do with caricature and comedic effect than any attempt to infuse Harry with coolness. Even Ruben's potential threat (as a younger, more virile man) to Harry's (aged) white masculinity is rendered impotent by the characterization of Ruben as childlike and foolish (Figure 10.4). Harry, and the spectator identifying with Harry, sympathizes with the low-class white blackmailers, but he ridicules the Hispanic Ruben, a bumbling, wannabe private detective. In his review of the film, Romney suggests that the character "is awkward comic relief, as bogus a genre throwback as Charlie Chan's number one son."[25] McCarthy also dislikes this characterization, asserting that Ruben, "utterly implausibly, aspires to be Harry's partner and seems willing to do all manner of flunky work to that end; the role is strictly a structural convenience, with no human credibility."[26] I agree with these reviewers and suspect many spectators, while enjoying these fine white actors, must have felt a similar discomfort at the racist portrayal of nonwhites in *Twilight.*

Twilight, a neo-noir, presents revisions in the representations of gender and gendered relationships, yet is reactionary in terms of representations of race. *Twi-*

Figure 10.4. The stereotype of the ethnic sidekick (*Twilight*, 1998)

light continues noir's focus on issues of class, and it empathizes with the choices poor white people make in order to achieve the American dream that Jack and Catherine appear to possess. But though the narrative displays sympathy for poor whites, it makes a similarly struggling person of color into a joke. Perhaps those responsible for the production of these films currently feel more social and material pressure to revise their understanding of gender than they do of race. Late-1990s retro-noir exhibits reactionary versions of gender and gendered relationships, but neo-noir has a different and more complex project. In *Twilight*, Catherine proves a formidable femme fatale, a character whose triumph is tinged with regret but who seems on some level to deserve what she gets, the opportunity to live out the rest of her life together with her husband, in peace.

I have made a case for the femme fatale as fatal to herself, but at least part of the narrative pleasure of the postclassic neo-noir comes from the femme fatale's survival. The neo-noir femme fatale can be fatal to others if necessary to achieve her goals, but she often survives and sometimes thrives. The narrative trajectory of classic film noir insisted on the femme fatale's death; her agency could not remain unchecked. In postclassic noir, the femme fatale may cause death and destruction, but the film allows her to actively drive, as well as survive, the narrative. The aged male protagonist, Harry, an homme attrapé unwilling to work outside the law for economic gain, also survives, walking off into the sunset with a younger woman on his arm. In the neo-noir *Fargo*, the investigator, a pregnant woman, also triumphs. *Fargo* continues the neo-noir appropriation of noir's gender and class issues and deals somewhat more ambiguously than *Twilight* with the representation of race.

CHAPTER 11

FARGO (1996): A WOMAN WHO IS NOT HERSELF MEAN—SNOW-SWEPT HIGHWAYS AND MARGIE

Enter Marge Gunderson . . . the town's clodhopper police chief. Outfitted in a floppy hat and ballooning parka, she also happens to be seven months pregnant and vomits, therefore, not because of a grisly crime scene but from morning sickness. Throughout the investigation, she maintains both equilibrium (waddling slightly) and a promethean appetite (eating for two). As the detective ratiocinator, Margey pretty much defies every Raymond Chandler cliché— no cynicism, no witticisms, no eroticism. The closest she comes to a gruff retort is, "You have no call to get snippy with me."

THOMAS DOHERTY, *"Fargo," Cineaste*

In the neo-noir *Fargo* (1996), all the dark and shadowy excesses of classic noir get inverted, whitewashed in the snowy environs of northern Minnesota and, briefly, North Dakota in winter.[1] The Coen brothers, Joel, who wrote and directed, and Ethan, who wrote and produced the movie, grew up in Minnesota.[2] *Fargo* has a lot more going for it than a frozen 1987 setting that includes exaggerated Minnesota accents, a new tan Ciera car, a smorgasbord, blizzards, and lots of people in well-padded parkas with hoods. Despite the attractions of the bizarre crime-gone-wrong story line, the setting, and the eccentric cast, the real pleasure of *Fargo* resides in the character of Brainerd police chief Marge Gunderson (Frances McDormand), a woman who competently, though not always calmly, solves the crime and brings in the most murderous criminal by the end of the movie. Seven months pregnant, always hungry, wide-eyed, and smart, Marge does not exactly fit into the mold of the hard-boiled detective of classic noir, yet her familiarity with the mean snow-swept highways (as opposed to the hard-boiled detective's mean streets) and her sleuthing abilities hint at another side of her wholesome persona. *Fargo* provides spectators with an admirable and oddly intriguing white middle-class female protagonist surrounded by all sorts of middle- and lower-class men: criminal, murderous, selfish, scheming, dumb, and sweet. With her Minnesota accent, her brown, pregnancy-modified cop uniform, and her hat with earflaps, Marge ought to be a caricature. Instead, she provides the film with a warm center.

The narrative begins with a suburban criminal bumbler and car salesman, Jerry Lundegaard (William H. Macy), who seeks to alleviate his mysterious and tremendous debt by hiring two low-life criminals, the talkative Carl Showalter (Steve Buscemi) and the impassive and murderous Gaear Grimsrud (Peter Stormare), to kidnap his wife, Jean (Kristin Ruedrud). Jerry's plan includes a million-dollar ransom extorted from his wealthy and callous father-in-law, Wade (Harve Presnell), a small portion of which will pay off the kidnappers. This plan goes immediately wrong. Jerry never tells the kidnappers not to hurt his wife; Gaear eventually kills her. Gaear also kills three other people, including a highway patrol officer, while he and Carl make their getaway with Jerry's wife on the back floorboard of their new tan Cutlass Ciera (part of their payoff for the kidnapping). These murders, taking place outside of Brainerd, fall into Marge's jurisdiction, and she begins her investigation.

Meanwhile, Jerry's father-in-law, Wade, a controlling and successful businessman, insists on paying the ransom himself, foiling Jerry's grift and leading to Wade's murder by the talkative kidnapper, Carl. Carl takes the million-dollar ransom, buries a portion of it along a fence line on a deserted, snowy highway, and returns to the hideout to split the rest with Gaear, who has by now killed their captive. Unfortunately, Carl argues with Gaear about splitting the Ciera and winds up as another of Gaear's victims: Gaear murders him with an axe and seeks to destroy the evidence using a wood chipper. Marge, by chance, sees the tan Ciera parked outside the cabin hideout and catches Gaear during this act. She takes Gaear into custody after shooting him in the leg as he attempts to escape across a frozen lake. The film ends with Marge and her husband Norm bundled up in bed, looking forward to the birth of their child in two months.

Supposedly, the narrative is based in truth. The film opens with gentle piano music and the typewritten, full-screen assertion that, "This is a true story. The events depicted in this film took place in Minnesota in 1987. At the request of the survivors, the names have been changed. Out of respect for the dead, the rest has been told exactly as it occurred." The black screen then fades to a bluish white. As the credits play, a black bird becomes visible, flying erratically but somewhat from left to right across the screen. Then a power pole and car headlights come into view. As the car draws closer to the camera, the music swells, and it becomes apparent that the car is pulling a trailer; Jerry is on his way to Fargo, North Dakota—this is the only scene in the film that takes place in Fargo—to deliver the new car to Carl and Gaear as part of their kidnapping payoff. According to Josh Levine in *The Coen Brothers: The Story of Two American Filmmakers*, composer Carter Burwell "drew on an old Scandinavian hymn, 'The Last Sheep,' which he arranged more grandly for orchestra" for the atmospheric music.[3] This theme recurs throughout the film and seems to imbue the events on the screen with an almost mythic dimension, even an event as seemingly ordinary as a big American car pulling another big car on a trailer down a deserted highway in winter.[4]

Of course, the rural setting of *Fargo* is not totally anomalous to noir narratives. Classic films noirs occasionally stray into nonurban environments. In *Out of the Past,* Jeff seeks to escape his past in the rural Sierra town of Bridgeport. The setting accentuates the difference between the worlds—one natural, the other artificial and urban—Jeff inhabits. It simultaneously suggests, from a gendered perspective, that although the rural environment appears to offer the male protagonist a measure of safety, the femme attrapée Ann struggles to find fulfillment there. Despite her relative blandness, she is bored and stifled by her rural milieu. In *The Killers,* Swede also manages to briefly escape his destiny by hiding out in a small town, although, as in *Out of the Past,* the security of the setting proves an illusion. In *Gun Crazy* (1950), the criminal lovers both come from rural environments, and the relative safety and dullness of that milieu seem to be precisely what drives them to crime. One sequence in *Gun Crazy* even has the lovers deciding on one final caper as they hide out from the police in a ramshackle shack during a blizzard; the severity and cold of the setting add to their desperate desire for something else.[5]

Fargo revives small-town noir and, like classic noir, does not seek to portray small-town life as wholly safe and secure, or as particularly exciting, despite the criminality that abounds in the narrative. In *Fargo,* low-key Minnesota pastimes such as ice fishing, shoveling slush, and dining out at an all-you-can-eat smorgasbord replace the fly-fishing and sitting out by the creek in *Out of the Past* and relaxing at the small diner in *The Killers.* But the implications of the activities remain the same: excitement and small town life do not go together.[6]

Neo-noirs are not the only films to rediscover rural settings. As Paul Arthur notes in "Let Us Now Praise Famous Yokels: *Dadetown* and Other Retreats," "low-budget independent films" have revived small-town America in an "attempt to relocate a socially-redemptive dynamic of family and community."[7] *Fargo* does this, but without the overt focus Arthur sees in most of these films on a "rehabilitative or recuperative function . . . in the representation of an 'endangered' white masculinity."[8] Speaking of films such as *Heavy* (1996), *Sling Blade* (1996), and *Nobody's Fool* (1996), Arthur claims the rural settings create "a safe haven and an ethical mandate for success-challenged male losers" in the nonurban realm.[9] *Fargo* does portray the nonurban setting as a place where some men can be safe even if they are not exactly stereotypically successful, but it also shows how success-challenged criminals face a problem in Marge. Through her, and the criminality she fights against, Marge represents one facet of what Arthur sees as typical of the recent spate of nonurban films, the portrayal of the "nonurban as an atavistic zone not completely immune from intractable problems of urban life but cushioned by an ongoing connection to old-fashioned humanistic values."[10]

Certainly the film's insistence on the truth of the story seems like an old-fashioned opening gambit. Particular events do come together to make the plot whole. For example, according to Levine, "the brothers mentioned in an interview reading a newspaper account of a man in Connecticut who put his wife in a woodchipper."[11] Levine also notes that "the character of Jerry Lundegaard, the car salesman, came in part from a real salesman Ethan [Coen] had encountered while buying a car" and that "the infuriating conversation with a couple about TruCoat [a rust-proofing that adds substantially to the cost of their new car] . . . was taken almost verbatim from his encounter."[12] The characters of Jerry and Marge share a sort of Midwest ordinariness. Levine quotes Joel Coen, who insists that "Marge and Jerry are both very banal, like the interiors and the landscape."[13] Coen goes on to say, "she is banal in a good way, a good person where he is evil."[14]

The character of Marge was written for Frances McDormand, who won an Academy Award for best actress for the role. McDormand's skill as an actor has more to do with impersonation that personification. She can be a femme fatale survivor (*Blood Simple,* 1985), a crazed football fan (*Lone Star,* 1995), a femme fatale in a retro-noir (*The Man Who Wasn't There,* 2001) or Marge Gunderson; each character seems wholly individual. Perhaps because McDormand's life has remained less public than Susan Sarandon's, the spectator does not carry a perception of her into the movie theater, allowing McDormand to occupy her characters almost without interference from intertextual influences. Marge is, however, no femme fatale. Nevertheless, McDormand sees "something scary about Marge that's hard to articulate."[15] McDormand sees the character of Marge as "simple and on-the-surface, but she's not naïve, and she's not innocent, because she's good at her job, which gives her contact with crime and murder."[16] She is a successful investigator and survives the film.

In his discussion of the movie, "Flare to White: *Fargo* and the Postmodern Turn," Steven Carter reads Marge as much the same as the murderous Gaear. According to Carter, "psychopath Gaear Grimsrud is indifferent to the plight of his victims, but so is Chief Marge Gunderson."[17] For Carter, the film "isn't a crime film." Instead, he makes a case for the film being a "critique of a certain contemporary, or postmodern response to the crime of murder" and insists that "no one in the film has an iota of respect for the dead."[18] Carter makes some astute observations about *Fargo,* including discussions of the centrality of television to the stories the film has to tell, but he dramatically misreads Marge. Carter quotes Marge's observations about the murdered highway patrol officer as she describes the body to her partner, Lou (Bruce Bohne): "Well, he's got his gun on his hip there, and he looked like a nice enough fella."[19] Carter insists that "uncaring . . . dwells beneath the lexical surface" of the character's speech, and goes on to assert that Marge "can only respond esthetically, not emotionally, to suffering and death."[20] Carter both misquotes and misreads Marge in this sequence. The character actually says, "Well, he's got his gun on his hip there and he looks like a nice enough guy. It's a real shame," with a genuine tone of regret in her voice.[21]

Marge's sympathy and humanity are revealed on a smaller scale, as well, but Carter has no skill in reading those either. Just after Marge laments the death of the highway patrol officer, she and Lou discuss the trooper's last entry in his citation book—he had stopped a tan Ciera with plates that read DLR. Lou figures the officer got shot before he could finish writing up the citation, but Marge gently suggests the plates are probably dealer tags. As the long-faced Lou sits next to her in the patrol car looking especially sheepish, Marge immediately launches into an old joke Lou obviously already knows. She seeks to minimize his error instead of focusing on it.

Marge's relationship with her husband adds to the gentleness of her characterization, although Carter also reads that relationship as cold and calls her husband Norm (stage actor John Carroll Lynch) "zombie-like."[22] Ronald Bergan, in *The Coen Brothers,* notes that "the marriage between Marge and the non-demonstrative, well-named Norm, dull and habitual as it may be, rings true."[23] Norm certainly does not qualify as successful by stereotypical standards. He apparently works at home, painting pictures of wildlife, especially birds, for use on postage stamps. He supports Marge by making her eggs early in the morning when she gets called out to investigate a triple homicide. She supports him by stopping to pick up the night crawlers for his ice-fishing expedition and by telling him how proud she is of him when his art gets accepted for a three-cent

Figure 11.1. Sleuth Marge's glamorous introduction (*Fargo*, 1996)

stamp. A spectator might wonder how Marge wound up with Norm, who does not seem to share her intellect, but the tenderness and hominess of their scenes together emphasize their mutual devotion.

Many of the sequences in *Fargo* function as wonderful information-packed moments, full of the minutiae that convince a film audience to suspend disbelief and become immersed in the lives presented on the screen. Marge and Norm do not spring onto the screen fully clothed in broad daylight. Instead, a camera slowly surveys a golden-hued but crowded interior full of stuffed birds, including a mallard and a loon, and the materials and books of an artist and bird lover as the theme music described above plays mournfully. Just as the camera pans to a bed containing a couple sleeping under a mountain of blankets, the woman lying facing the phone and the camera, the phone rings and Marge's eyes pop wide open. A third of the way into the film, the female protagonist finally gets her unglamorous introduction. As she talks on the telephone, a man's arm, clad in flannel pajamas, falls heavily over her body (Figure 11.1). Both Norm and Marge sit up, and he insists, after clearing his phlegm in a glaringly realistic moment, on making her some breakfast. They get out of bed, and Marge's pregnancy becomes apparent.[24] The improbable neo-noir sleuth is on the case, once Norm feeds her some eggs and gives the prowler (police car) a jump.[25]

Marge's crime-solving skills hint at a facet of her personality at odds with her apparent wide-eyed Midwest innocence, and another sequence in *Fargo* infuses her relationship with Norm with just the slightest hint of a question. Nighttime phone calls seem fairly common for Marge and Norm, in part at least because they appear to go to bed early, a common phenomenon in a region where, in winter, night falls around 4 P.M. In this sequence, which takes place soon after Marge has started her investigation, the phone again awakens her in the dark, but this time it is an old high school chum from the Twin Cities, Mike Yanagita (Steve Park), who has apparently seen her on television talking about the murder case. Although the plans are made off-screen, she apparently decides to see this old friend again, and combines the trip with some investigative work as well. During a colossal lunch at a smorgasbord restaurant, Marge tells Norm and an officer who has just given her some Twin Cities' leads that she thinks she'll "take a drive down there then." They both look surprised: the police officer says, "Oh yeah?" and Norm, roused from his somnambulistic chewing, looks at her curiously and reiterates, "Oh yeah?" The narrative does not pursue Norm's curiosity but does follow Marge to the Twin Cities, where she meets Mike in a bar at the Radisson.

Before she meets Mike, however, Marge encounters one other nonwhite character, Shep Proudfoot (Steven Reevis), a Native American car mechanic who apparently hooks Jerry up with the kidnappers, Carl and Gaear. Like *Twilight*, *Fargo* concerns itself primarily with whiteness. Unlike *Twilight*, *Fargo* treats its nonwhite characters as something more than demeaning ethnic stereotypes; the nonwhite characters shown here defy facile interpretation. Shep, a physically imposing and tight-lipped man on parole for various entanglements with the law, endures a brief interview with Marge about phone calls he received from Carl, in which she does most of the talking (Figure 11.2).

Shep then finds Carl and brutally beats him. In his discussion of the film in *Cineaste,* Thomas Doherty notes, "the inscrutable Indian mechanic Shep Proudfoot . . . would be very out of place in a Kevin Costner film."[26] For Krin Gabbard, in *Black Magic: White Hollywood and African American Culture,* Shep *is* a "racial stereotype" and a "malignant and savage force of nature . . . the true face of American toughness."[27] Yet the film at least implies that Shep's criminality, anger, and brutality are to a certain extent the result of his background and economic situation. Gaear, played by Swedish actor Peter Stomare, seems equally closemouthed and even more brutal, but without any understandable motivation. Whiteness does not imply better, less criminal, smarter, or higher class in this film.

The Coen brothers, as auteurs, thrive on presenting audiences with bizarre and inexplicable characters and story lines that seem at once too odd to be true

Figure 11.2. Shep endures Marge's questioning (*Fargo*, 1996)

and too odd to be anything but true.[28] *Fargo* fits into this tradition. Nevertheless, the sequence between Mike Yanagita and Marge remains almost indecipherable in terms of narrative continuity. Mike, an Asian American with the same powerful Minnesota accent as Marge, meets his hugely pregnant high school friend in a Radisson Hotel bar and immediately comes on to her; he tries to sit next to her and put his arm around her but is gently rebuffed (Figure 11.3). He then claims he has a successful job with Honeywell, and that his wife, who also attended their high school, has died of leukemia. He breaks down in tears while Marge looks on, uncomfortable, sad, and shocked. Marge finds out in a subsequent phone call to another high school friend that Mike never married, has psychological problems, and lives at home with his parents.

Levine identifies Mike as Korean American. According to Levine, "this seemingly unnecessary strand heightens Marge's sense of her good fortune in life and gives her a further glimpse into the bizarre complexities of the human personality."[29] Levine also reports that Ethan Coen "claimed the subplot was part of their 'experimenting with naturalism.'"[30] Carter calls the appearance of Yanagita "a brilliant stroke" and claims that the character, "a mentally-disturbed Japanese-American who speaks with a Minnesota accent . . . the quintessence of disparity in *Fargo*'s quirky universe: a walking raise en scene."[31] Bergan also calls Mike a

Figure 11.3. Marge and Mike at the Radisson (*Fargo,* 1996)

Japanese Minnesotan and suggests that the sequence is meant to emphasize or subvert the point "that there is something Japanese about the way the natives of Minnesota refuse to express emotion," an assertion that seems to revel in multiple stereotypes.[32] For Gabbard, Mike follows a tradition of racist depictions of Asians on screen, "another weak Asian man aspiring unsuccessfully to connect with a white woman."[33] Doherty does not mention Mike's ethnicity and suggests that the sequence is "not a red herring, just a moment in time, underscoring Marge's fidelity to husband and friends and the weirdness in everyday life, homicides aside."[34]

Marge is so dramatically unhip that enhancing her character through her contact with nonwhite culture, as occurs in classic film noir, seems impossible. Certainly her empathetic yet firm response to Mike underscores her human decency. Marge might have hoped for some fun conversation with her old school friend; when he reveals his supposed tragedy, she responds sympathetically and even follows up by checking on him with another friend. Perhaps, as Carter hints, the sequence touches on the difficulties of being outside the cultural norm, as the Jewish Coen brothers themselves may have been growing up in Minnesota. Mike's psychological problems, expressed in his intense desire for all-American success at the most basic level of job and family, may well be the result of his otherness. As with *Fight Club*, the use of an Asian male character to comment on male success and achievement might have more to do with different kinds of white masculinity than with Asian masculinity. Perhaps Mike, like Raymond in *Fight Club*, bears the burden of failure in the capitalist patriarchy that cannot as easily be placed on a white male character.

White male characters do, however, fail spectacularly in *Fargo*. Jerry Lundegaard functions as a reverse image of Marge, as unlikable as she is likeable, as stupid and inflexible as she is smart and intellectually nimble. Levine quotes William H. Macy, the superb, elastic-faced actor who plays Jerry, on the character:

> The thing I loved most about Jerry is the fact that he never gives up. He sets the plan, he is sure it will work, and despite all the information to the contrary, he never deviates from it. Up to the very last scene in the movie, he's still fighting to make it work. You just gotta love somebody that has this kind of faith. On the other hand, he's as dumb as a bag of rocks, and I liked that too.[35]

For Levine, Jerry is the "real engine of the film."[36] Janet Maslin sees Jerry as "a milquetoast of a villain, what with the golf toys and matching pencils adorning his office, or the galoshes and grocery bags that accompany him to a crime scene" (Figure 11.4).[37]

Maslin does not mention that two of the golf toys adorning Jerry's office are figurines that portray a black golfer and caddy. As Gabbard notes, this follows the tradition of the "lawn jockeys [that have] disappeared from middle-class homes or were simply painted white."[38] Perhaps Jerry is oblivious to his own racism, just as many spectators are probably oblivious to the inclusion of the figurines in the mise-en-scène. Kim Newman, writing for *Sight and Sound*, calls Jerry "likeable but clearly doomed."[39] Homme fatal Jerry seems far from likeable, and his ridiculous plan actually dooms his wife, his father-in-law, various parking lot attendants, a couple of innocent passers-by, a highway patrol officer, and some criminals. He probably survives, although in prison. Jerry looks like an homme attrapé, but his desires for financial gain far beyond his economic station in life doom him; he is an homme fatal, fatal to himself. The film never provides any information about how Jerry acquired the tremendous debt that inspires his disastrous plan. Spectators can build a life for Marge and Norm from the details of the mise-en-scène and tidbits of diegesis. Jerry's life remains a mystery; he will not reveal his motivations to Carl and Gaear in the opening sequence, telling them "it's personal," and the film, as it unfolds, keeps them a secret.

Similarly, Gaear's murderous criminality also lacks understandable motiva-

Figure 11.4. The grocery-carrying villain at the scene of the crime (*Fargo,* 1996)

tion. According the Bergan, the giant Paul Bunyan statue that welcomes drivers to Brainerd has "madly staring eyes so that he looks like an axe murderer" and resembles kidnapper Gaear, "who buries an axe in his partner's neck and then chops him up."[40] Gaear's partner Carl (Buscemi) certainly talks more and exhibits more emotion that Gaear, making his character less of an enigma. Carter, unable to understand Marge, sees Carl as "easily the film's most sympathetic character."[41] Carter even suggests that Carl "expresses more human feeling . . . than do his victims."[42]

Once again, my reading of the film directly opposes Carter's. In one particularly unsympathetic sequence, Carl watches with pleasure as kidnap victim Jean, her head covered with a black hood, tries blindly to escape her captors outside their hideaway. As Gaear stands impassively next to him, Carl giggles and laughs outright as Jean stumbles blindly and falls onto the snow-covered ground. In a later scene, the talkative Carl ironically gets shot in the mouth by Wade, Jean's father. Carl responds by shouting vociferously and shooting Wade dead. Carter sees Carl's response as "much more normal" than Wade's, who simply falls dead to the ground.[43] It makes sense that a character would respond more quietly to being shot numerous times in the chest than to a nonlethal, though painful, gunshot wound to the face. Carter also sees kidnap victim Jean's "barely audible whimpers" as insufficient expressions of emotion compared to Carl's shouts of

Figure 11.5. Marge on the snow-swept highway (*Fargo*, 1996)

displeasure and pain.[44] Jean has been kidnapped, beaten up, threatened, blind-folded, and transported by people who have no concern for her well being; perhaps a whimper is all the character could muster.

Jean, kidnapped and eventually murdered by Gaear, gets embroiled in the plot because of her husband's stupidity. When introduced early in the film, she seems like a caricature of a suburban Minnesota housewife: cooking dinner, concerned about her son's grades, coddling her father and husband, and oblivious to or ignoring the tension between the two men. Jean's middle-class life, as in many classic films noirs, is totally undermined by the criminality that her husband invites into their home. After her kidnapping, dressed in pink sweats, wearing a pink sweater, with a hood over her head, she disappears, all but physically, from the story. She sits breathing frost-covered breaths through the hood, as Gaear emotionlessly watches her or the television. Jean's son worries about her, but Jerry and her father both seem more concerned about money than Jean's safety. Her body winds up on the floor of the cabin, and even her son disappears from the narrative. Jerry, crying and screaming during his capture in a rural motel room, proves to be the last the audience sees of the Lundegaard family.

White masculinity and femininity in *Fargo* emphatically do not get star treatment. Marge and Norm, the film's ideal couple, could hardly portray less excitement and sensuality. Marge, despite looking, according to McDormand, "like a huge turd out there in the snow, waddling around," proves to be a tenacious, brave, and wholly admirable crime fighter (Figure 11.5).[45] Like the protagonists in classic noir, Marge is a middle-class hero. She does not struggle against that existence, nor is it glorified.

The other female characters—prostitutes, waitresses, secretaries, and wives— seem equally middle or lower class. They are amusing but less interesting than Marge. The overt linkage between criminality and masculinity does not exist between criminality and femininity in the film. Men—Jerry, Carl, Gaear, Shep, and even Wade—bear all the responsibility for the evils that occur. Other men—like Norm, Marge's coworkers, mechanics, and shovelers of slush—seem more like dull but funny local color than Hollywood enticements. One of the most powerful pleasures of the cinema is having our expectations foiled; *Fargo* fulfills the desire for a well-wrought story with a strong female character without lapsing into the glossy sameness of most Hollywood productions. And it portrays non-white characters more ambiguously than does *Twilight*. *Fargo*'s attention focuses on white landscapes and white characters, but the film does not resort strictly to reactionary cliché in its representation of nonwhite characters. Instead *Fargo* serves up an apparently bland but delicious neo-noir film in shades of white and gray.[46] Neo-noir *Jackie Brown* (1997) does even more to revise race, gender, and class in noir.

CHAPTER 12

JACKIE BROWN (1997): GENDER, RACE, CLASS, AND GENRE

Pam Grier was one of the first important female action heroes. She was able to both exploit the male libido and assert [physical] power over men.

DARIUS JAMES, *That's Blaxploitation!*

I knew I needed a great-looking 44-year-old who looks like she can handle anything but is actually very vulnerable. Sounds like Pam Grier to me.

QUENTIN TARANTINO, QUOTED IN JILL GERSTON,
"Pam Grier Finally Escapes the 1970s," *New York Times*

Neo-noir *Jackie Brown* (1997) has it all: a gorgeous black femme fatale, a glib black criminal, a host of other peripheral characters, a low-key white male protagonist who never seeks the limelight, a pair of cocky but unsuccessful white cops, and a triple-cross complex enough to rival the plot of classic noir *The Big Sleep. Jackie Brown* reflects noir influences in the characters, the plot, and the working-class milieu that serves as the film's setting.[1] It also features a densely layered, information-packed mise-en-scène that rewards repeated viewing. A middle-aged, underpaid airline stewardess, Jackie Brown, played stunningly by Pam Grier, winds up backed into a corner by a gun dealer, Ordell (Samuel L. Jackson), the police, and an ATF (Bureau of Alcohol, Tobacco and Firearms) officer. Jackie embodies allure, intelligence, vulnerability, and strength. Despite her

Figure 12.1. A woman at the wheel: the triumph of a neo-noir femme fatale (*Jackie Brown*, 1997)

considerable powers, she survives the narrative of the film, driving off alone in the final scene to a life of leisure abroad (Figure 12.1).

Jackie Brown allows the "bad guys" some time to develop—actors such as Samuel L. Jackson and Robert De Niro should not languish in bit parts. The lawmen, like the insurance investigator Riordan in *The Killers,* are peripheral but necessary to Jackie's plans, and bumbling as well. Jackie enlists the assistance of Max Cherry (Robert Forster), an homme attrapé working within the capitalist system—but at its fringes—as a bail bondsman. Max instantly falls for Jackie. Like Sam in *The Killers,* Max functions as kind of a liminal character, moving through the criminal and noncriminal realms with a sort of detachment and acceptance. Jackie, meanwhile, uses her considerable acumen and appeal to double cross both Ordell and the law and drive off with half a million dollars.

I like Pam Grier's portrayal of a middle-aged (and gorgeous) black woman who decides to risk it all for the chance to escape the economic prison of her life. Jackie seems at once fearful (and justifiably so, since she knows Ordell's propensity for violence) and bold, desperate and methodical. According to Jill Gerston, writing for the *New York Times,* Pam Grier "always portrayed strong, resourceful women, no matter how skimpy her clothing or awful her dialogue" in the blaxploitation films of the seventies.[2] Grier sees the characters she played in those

Figure 12.2. Pam Grier shining as Jackie Brown (*Jackie Brown,* 1997)

movies as "heroines of the women's movement. . . . They showed women how to be assertive and self-sufficient, not passive victims."[3] Jackie Brown does much the same thing, but with a late-1990s neo-noir flair that does not insist she kill every man in her path or be killed in the final reel.

Some reviewers familiar with Grier's earlier roles evidently cannot bear to see Grier older, and not scantily clad. Richard Corliss, writing for *Time,* claims that Grier "is given little chance to shine; you never even glimpse her magnificent shoulders."[4] Jackie Brown represents a new type of female character for noir narratives, but Corliss can apparently only envision an old characterization as successful. And he must have dozed off during the powerful scene in which Jackie, in a sleeveless, short red sheath, gives Ordell a verbal dressing-down out on his patio (Figure 12.2).

Although I have never invested much theoretical capital in thinking about authorship or intentionality, I persistently read texts as a heterosexual white female spectator, and my own intentions influence those readings. Philip Green, in *Cracks in the Pedestal: Ideology and Gender in Hollywood,* identifies himself as a male spectator and points out, quite accurately, that most of the output of Hollywood is the creation of men.[5] According to Green, "men create dominant visual culture: that's why it's dominant."[6] Quentin Tarantino, director of *Jackie*

Brown, which he based on the novel *Rum Punch* by Elmore Leonard, certainly feels as if he created and owns Jackie. Tarantino, in an interview by Eric Bauer, insists, "I like the idea of following a female lead character. I think I have an extremely unfair rap from people who say, 'Ah, but can he write women?' . . . It's funny, but I do feel that Jackie Brown is mine. She's the same character as in the book, but making her black affects her because her life experiences are different and her dialogue is different."[7]

Although she remains all but invisible, a black woman also occupies the center of one of the narrative threads in *Pulp Fiction* (1994). In "The Bonnie Situation," Tarantino writes himself into a narrative as Jimmy, the white husband of Bonnie, a black woman whom no one wants to risk displeasing. Writing prior to the release of *Jackie Brown,* bell hooks does not approve of what she calls Tarantino's "'white cool': a hard-core cynical vision that would have everyone see racism, sexism, homophobia but behave as though none of that shit really matters."[8] In Tarantino's films, hooks goes on to insist, "domination is always and only patriarchal—a dick thing."[9] But hooks also understands Bonnie to be different, suggesting that the only one who would protest against the "white supremacist capitalist patriarchy" that even the black men want in on is "the black woman who has no face—Jimmy's wife in *Pulp Fiction.*"[10] In *Cool Men and the Second Sex,* Susan Fraiman discusses Tarantino's "coolness" and his "white-Negro persona."[11] For Fraiman, *Jackie Brown* marks a departure from *Pulp Fiction*'s use of violence to nullify "the ordinary and intimate . . . along with the women who represent it."[12]

Women represent more than the ordinary and intimate in *Jackie Brown.* The visibility and success of Jackie almost seems like a response to hooks's critique of the representation of black femininity in *Pulp Fiction.* The black woman in *Jackie Brown* has a powerful personality, and a face as well.[13] The film opens with a shot lasting just over a minute, featuring Jackie primarily in a medium shot (from the waist up) in a blue stewardess jacket, backed by a blue, brown, and gray tile wall treatment, standing tall as she rides an airport walkway to her job on a cut-rate airline (Figure 12.3).

Jackie moves into the shot, standing still on the walkway; the changes in the wall treatment behind her indicate her movement although she does not advance from the right side of the screen until the very end of the shot. The nondiegetic music, "Across 110th Street" by Bobby Womack, helps situate Jackie, obviously not as the third brother of five, but as a person "doing whatever I had to do to survive" and knowing "there was a better way of life I was just trying to find." The shot gives the spectator plenty of time to take in Grier's statuesque beauty and her zaftig figure—we are immediately captivated.

Tarantino's and my own pleasure in seeing Grier on screen seems to tap into a

Figure 12.3. Jackie, getting nowhere (*Jackie Brown,* 1997)

white desire to be or have black femininity. Eric Lott discusses the white male will to blackness in "Racial Cross-Dressing and the Construction of American Whiteness," but does not begin to theorize female desire. Black masculinity is certainly stereotypically associated with sexual potency, and black femininity seems similarly invested, yet Jackie Brown and Bonnie in *Pulp Fiction* represent more than that as well. Both characters drive their respective narratives with the force of their intelligence and personality, rather than their sexuality. Of course, physicality is still part of the equation with Jackie Brown. As Kent Jones notes, writing for *Film Comment, Jackie Brown* "begins in a state of rapturous absorption as Pam Grier travels down the moving sidewalk."[14] But this opening sequence also places the character on a treadmill, and suggests she might be ready to seek a way out.

Max Cherry also takes about a minute to be smitten by Jackie. He falls hard and fast as he bails her out of jail late at night; she has been picked up transporting money and drugs out of Mexico for Ordell. Just watching Jackie walk from the half-lit jail yard onto the street seems to be all it takes. Again, the nondiegetic sound track supplements the sequence, which primarily features a close-up of Max's face as he watches her walk while Bloodstone sings "Why do I keep my mind on you all the time, when I don't even know you?" Max becomes increasingly impressed, especially after he discovers that Jackie has stolen his gun from his glove box during the trip to her house. Unlike most femmes fatales, Jackie lives in a home, not a glamorous or sleazy hotel room. She occupies a quiet, clean, yet poorly furnished apartment in a suburban neighborhood. The camera takes us inside her apartment numerous times, adding to both her appeal and the depth of her characterization as a woman struggling on the edge of financial ruin.

As noted above, when a domestic space does occur in a noir narrative, it often appears threatened. The threat to Jackie appears the instant she arrives home from jail. Ordell waits in his car, listening to Johnny Cash. He watches Max drop her off, puts on the gloves he wore while murdering one of his cohorts in an earlier scene, and walks to her front door. Once inside, he dims the lights and makes a bit of small talk while attempting to find out what Jackie might have told the cops, then proceeds to put his hands around her neck. Suddenly, another side of Jackie's character reveals itself. She disarms Ordell, having surreptitiously retrieved the gun she stole from Max from her purse. She threatens to shoot him in the dick if he does not "shut the fuck up" and goes on to tell him what they are going to do about their common problem.

Ordell is the only character who consistently notices and comments on race; in this case, he accuses the cops of pitting "black against black" and seeking to turn Jackie against him. Once Jackie handles this threat, at least temporarily, the sequence ends with her escorting Ordell to the door. After a brief cut to black, the next sequence opens with a transition shot showing her opening the same door to let Max in the following morning.

The domesticity of Jackie's home, despite the recent frightening intrusion of Ordell and the cheapness of her furnishings, makes the morning exchange between Jackie and Max especially moving. Jackie, dressed in a fluffy, off-white robe, returns Max's gun to him, makes him coffee, and puts a Delfonics record on the stereo (Figure 12.4). (She keeps her record albums in a plastic milk crate.) They discuss growing old, being tired, and economic necessity. Jackie makes it clear to Max that just as she cannot afford to start over with her record collection by replacing them with CDs, neither can she afford to start over with her financial life. She is prepared to betray Ordell in order to avoid jail time and ensure her own survival. As Kent Jones succinctly puts it, "Jackie Brown knows that she has to either scam, live honorably and end up with nothing but a Social Security check, or die at 44."[15] Like many femmes fatales, she decides on the scam.

In classic film noir, the characters who decide on the scam have to pay the price for that decision, yet the choice of the attrapés, whether hommes or femmes, to live honorably is not presented as an easy, glamorous, or even enjoyable choice in films like *The Killers* or *Out of the Past*. In neo-noir, the choice remains similar, but the stakes have changed because of cultural and industrial changes. As

Figure 12.4. A rare glimpse inside the domestic space of a femme fatale
(*Jackie Brown*, 1997)

David Cook reports in *A Narrative History of Film*, the Production Code insisted that "all criminal activities within a given film were . . . punished" and "under no circumstances could a crime be shown to be justified."[16] Cook goes on to note that the code "was obviously restrictive and repressive" and may well have kept American films from "becoming as serious as they might have, and perhaps, should have, been."[17]

Of course, the Production Code may also have aided in providing some of the narrative depth in classic noir. Many noirs were low-budget B-movies; those involved in their production knew about life on a shoestring. Classic noirs could not show that crime pays, but they could treat the working-class protagonist with sympathy and understanding, making the slide into criminality less shocking and more understandable. With the constraints of the Production Code removed, Jackie can tell Ordell to "shut the fuck up," as well as commit a crime and get away with it, all with the audience's approval.

Jackie is not the only woman in the film to get away with it, although most do not fare as well as she does. Other female characters in *Jackie Brown* include women whom Ordell considers part of his stable. One woman, Sheronda (Lisa Gay Hamilton), sits in a darkened and apparently repugnant house in Compton. Another, Simone (Hattie Winston), lives in a house Ordell says he rents for her

Figure 12.5. Melanie and Louis in the mall parking lot, just before he shoots her (*Jackie Brown*, 1997)

in Compton. Simone takes off with $10,000 dollars when Ordell tries to make her a pawn in his games. Melanie (Bridget Fonda), Ordell's white "pot-smoking surfer chick" is shot by Ordell's underling Louis (De Niro) for mouthing off continuously (Figure 12.5).

Melanie had tried to convince Louis to steal the money from Ordell. She was unsuccessful, and like many aspiring femmes fatales, she dies. But before Melanie takes a bullet in her tanned belly, Jackie gives her a wad of money the police will later find stuffed down her shorts. In this neo-noir, a white femme fatale dies for attempting to rip off her boyfriend, but two black femmes fatales, Simone and Jackie, successfully make the same move. Black femmes fatales fare better than white ones. Although these female characters do not function as feminist paradigms, *Jackie Brown* does allow an intelligent, attractive, and duplicitous black woman to get the best of a number of white and black men while exhibiting some female solidarity.

Male solidarity fares less well in the film. Retro-noirs glorify male solidarity, but neo-noir *Jackie Brown* deals ironically with it. Ordell mercilessly murders both of his male colleagues, white Louis (De Niro) and black Beaumont (Chris Tucker), before Jackie engineers Ordell's death. The notion of male investigative dominance, under scrutiny even in classic noir, undergoes a revision that

Figure 12.6. The mall, a safe place for Jackie to transform herself (*Jackie Brown*, 1997)

does not allow for eventual primacy. Federal ATF agent Ray Nicolette (Michael Keaton) and cop Mark Dargus (Michael Bowen), both white, try to play the good cop–bad cop routine with Jackie, only to get played by her instead.[18] Keaton, as Ray, does a brilliant job of self-consciously occupying his masculinity, his obstreperous leather jacket, and even his pants. Ray obviously enjoys his perception of himself as a male investigator, as a man in a position of power, and as the writer of Jackie's script. Max recognizes and even understands Ray, telling Jackie, "He's just a young guy having fun being a cop." However, Jackie has in fact scripted Ray's part, and even purchased herself a power suit on his watch (Figure 12.6).

The mall where Jackie purchases her suit, and perpetrates the grift on Ordell and the law enforcement officials who try to use her to catch Ordell, serves as the site of much of the action of the film. Jackie meets Ordell there early in the film to show him what she plans. She appears to run into Max there after he has taken in a movie, and invites Max to assist her in her plan. She goes through a practice run for all involved that winds up as an opportunity for Simone to take off with $10,000, and finally she brings her plan to fruition at the mall.

In *Window Shopping*, Anne Friedberg notes that "the street is made safely distant inside the mall."[19] Jackie uses the mall, with its "blindness to a range of urban blights — the homeless, beggars, crime, traffic, even weather," to assure that she

Figure 12.7. Jackie, in her suit, looking on as Ray crouches over the dead Ordell
(*Jackie Brown,* 1997)

escapes forever the urban blight contiguous with her working-class life.[20] Friedberg suggests that the "shopping mall — and its apparatical extension, the shopping mall cinema — offers safe transit into other spaces, other times, other imaginaries."[21] Max seeks other imaginaries in the cinema, but Jackie seeks transit
to a real space of financial security, and she uses the well-lit benignancy of the
mall to mask her activities, even doing a bit of shopping as she pulls off her plan.
Friedberg notes that the "mall is an appropriate contemporary site for crises of
identify because it is also a space where identity can so easily be transformed."[22]

Jackie marks her attempted transformation with the purchase of a suit she has
"had her eye on," in a sense prefiguring her successful transit from the treadmill
of economic hardship to a life of plentitude. She wears the suit until Ordell is dead
and her success is confirmed. Jackie manipulates Ray into doing the shooting.
After Ray shoots Ordell, we see our final shot of the ATF officer, a wonderful dead
man's eye view of him as he crouches over Ordell, with Jackie in the background
(Figure 12.7). Ray may finally be figuring out that he has not been successful in
using Jackie.

Jackie does not, however, lie to or manipulate all men. At the end of the movie,
Jackie even asks Max, who has assisted her throughout the scam, to join her in
her life abroad. Although he does seem surprised at the depth of his attraction

to Jackie, Max chooses not to go with her to Europe. It is a good moment of both plot and character tension, for the extent to which Max has fallen for Jackie has been made completely clear in a beautiful, continuously shot sequence taking place inside Jackie's apartment early in their relationship and the film. The sequence opens with Jackie entering her apartment at 11 P.M., having spent the day and evening organizing her scam. The camera, stationed in her bedroom, only half watches her. More than anything else, it remains stationary as Jackie walks in and out of the shot, hitting the message button on her phone machine, hanging up her coat, getting a drink of orange juice and a cigarette. Throughout the continuous shot, Max's voice plays in the background, providing Jackie with his home number, his office number, and an impossibly long series of beeper numbers. This man does not want to risk Jackie not reaching him if she has the least inclination to do so.

Kent Jones, although taken with Jackie, admires Max too, describing him as "a guy who is fully conscious of how ordinary and unspectacular he is but who has a good modest sense of style (there's the faintest hint of late-Sixties–Playboy Club–Joe Namath about him) . . . who is well past the age when he thinks he's capable of remaking himself, suddenly ignited by this beautiful ex-con."[23] Although he looks sorely tempted, Max refuses Jackie's invitation at the end of the film. Jackie suggests he might be scared of her, and he admits he is "a little bit." Max, like the earlier homme attrapé Sam in *The Killers,* has seen it all, and chosen his path.

Max helps Jackie escape from the economic prison of her existence and takes a fee for doing so. Jackie invites him to go with her to Europe—and for a moment we anticipate he will say yes. Hollywood has firmly indoctrinated us to hope for heterosexual unions at the end of all movies, no matter how unlikely. Perhaps Max ensures his survival by refusing her offer. The homme fatal often wants more—more money, a more sexually and socially active woman—and these desires lead to his destruction. Max resists taking any more money than the amount he and Jackie agreed upon and also resists Jackie's considerable attractions. In the classic film noir *The Maltese Falcon,* Sam Spade (Humphrey Bogart) sends Brigid O'Shaughnessy (Mary Astor) to prison rather than worry about her eventual betrayal of him; Max just lets Jackie go. Jones suggests that Max does not go with her because "she's an ex-con" and "partly because she's black."[24] For Jones, Max's refusal "might be the saddest and most subtly tragic depiction of racism in movies."[25]

A different reading comes from bell hooks. In *Outlaw Culture: Resisting Representations,* hooks discusses *The Bodyguard* (1992) and *The Crying Game* (1992) as films that, "despite flaws . . . evoke much about issues of race and gender, about difference and identity."[26] For hooks, *The Bodyguard* "conservatively suggests that interracial relationships are doomed," while it also deems "black female life . . . valuable, worth protecting."[27] *Jackie Brown* makes a similar move. Yet I am not sure that race or Jackie's prison background have much to do with Max's refusal. Jackie is bigger, bolder, and smarter than Max. He knows this, and so does the spectator. Perhaps, just as Jackie suggests a new characterization of femininity—one that is smart, attractive, vulnerable, and powerful—Max suggests a new characterization of respectable masculinity—one that is smart, attractive, vulnerable, and conscious of the power of women.

In neo-noir many of the choices hinted at in classic film noir gain a voice and vision that was only suggested in the earlier films. Misogyny, expressed in the inevitable death or containment of the femme fatale in classic noir, appears in neo-noir: women are objectified mercilessly on the television screen in Melanie's apartment in *Jackie Brown,* and Melanie gets shot for talking too much. But a few women, including Jackie Brown, escape that generic treatment; they are free and (relatively) wealthy. In *Jackie Brown,* race is neither marginalized nor clearly readable. Certainly the black criminal, an homme fatal with excessive desires, takes the fall, along with a black and white associate, and a white man survives the narrative intact. A strict reading of race in the film might suggest that the white man comes out on top in the United States, especially since the black femme fatale leaves the country.

But the fact that Jackie, a black woman, winds up successful and free seems to infuse this late-1990s neo-noir with the same sort of spirit that once infused classic noir. In classic noir, spectators paid the price for the pleasure of watching the femme fatale drive the narrative by seeing her contained in the final reel. In *Jackie Brown* and other neo-noirs, the pleasures are less costly but no less intense. Jackie drives off to the airport, listening to the same song that played in the background as she was introduced in the opening sequence: Bobby Womack's "Across 110th Street." She sings the words, not admitting that what she did was okay, but that she did what she did to get by (Figure 12.1). *Jackie Brown* reinvigorates noir. Class struggles, gender dramas, and even race relations take on narrative prominence. And although postmodern, poststructuralist ambiguity remains, the white supremacist capitalist patriarchy does not reign unchecked.

DOING IT FOR bell: CULTURAL CRITICISM AND SOCIAL CHANGE

Radical postmodernist practice, most powerfully conceptualized as a "politics of difference," should incorporate the voices of displaced, marginalized, exploited, and oppressed (black) people.

bell hooks, "Postmodern Blackness"

A continuum connects classic noir and postclassic noir, the same continuum that connects feminism to third-wave feminism and postfeminism, and modernism to postmodernism. The endpoint is not the current "post" isms; these isms lead somewhere too. Modernist cultural critics Theodor Adorno and Max Horkheimer felt that film induced a dangerously passive state in spectators, one where imagination shut down in the face of the relentless consumption of the same old new product. In the mid-1940s, Horkheimer and Adorno collaborated on "The Culture Industry: Enlightenment as Mass Deception." They asserted that "the culture industry as a whole has moulded men as a type unfailingly reproduced in every product" and added that all "the agents in this process, from the producer to the women's clubs, take good care that the simple reproduction of this mental state is not nuanced or extended in any way."[1] In his 1936 essay "The Work of Art in the Age of Mechanical Reproduction," Walter Benjamin took a more optimistic view of film's potential. He suggests that the "progressive reaction [to art] is characterized by the direct, intimate fusion of visual and emotional enjoyment with the orientation of the expert."[2] For Benjamin, the expert

155

status of cinema spectators, as they engage in the mass consumption of a film, enables a progressive rather than reactionary response.

In the late 1990s and in the first decade of the twenty-first century, both reactionary and progressive noir texts appeared, and spectators consumed these texts with varying degrees of awareness. Adorno and Horkheimer give too little credit to the consumers of popular culture; Benjamin, perhaps too much. Nevertheless, Benjamin's remarks speak to my own desire to enable competent readers of cultural texts, to instruct progressive readers who may also become progressive artists. The expert in the audience might well become the moviemaker or the cultural critic. I cite the views of the popular and scholarly press to evoke various audiences, to gauge their responses to filmic texts. Postmodern cultural critic Edward Said, in "Opponents, Audiences, Constituencies, and Community," asks, "Who writes? For whom is the writing being done? In what circumstances?"[3] He goes on to suggest that these are "the questions whose answers provide us with the ingredients for making a politics of interpretation."[4] The film reviewer in the popular press who sees and critiques sexism and racism at the movies bodes well for changing movies. If those writers revel in misogyny and fantasies of white male supremacy, then producers will continue to make movies that fulfill those longings. My goal as a film theorist, scholar, and teacher is to consider the way we read and understand film history and films noirs and even perhaps to change the way film represents gender, race, and class by facilitating an understanding of those issues in various audiences. Activism is writing, thinking, speaking, and teaching in a way that encourages critical participation.

At my first Society for Cinema Studies conference in Denver in 2002, I excitedly attended a session on feminist film theory, the esteemed scholars of my graduate student days sitting on a panel at the front of the room.[5] After the session I talked with my peers, other scholars who had recently entered academic careers from graduate schools across the county. We all consider ourselves feminists; we talked about the rich and rewarding nature of our own intellectual work with its inclusion of queer theory, race theory, and masculinity studies. For us, the panel discussion we had witnessed, with its nostalgia for past feminisms, seemed limited in focus. Yes, seventies and eighties feminist film theory starts us off thinking critically and complexly about film; yes, Laura Mulvey's lucid and remarkably intelligent style serves as a fine model of academic film criticism; yes, I would and did start a syllabus for a feminist film theory course with "Visual Pleasure and Narrative Cinema."

From there, though, I moved to masculinity studies and bell hooks's *Reel to Real: Race, Sex, and Class at the Movies*. Feminist film theory is alive and well in my scholarship and in the thinking and writing of my students, who constitute the future of film production, film reception, and film spectatorship. But these students are also trained to think about heterocentrism, queer theory, and race, and are better equipped to read films and change film forms than I was at their intellectual age. My experience in 2002 forced me to become more aware of my own commitment to feminist theory. But that commitment has led to intellectual activism that includes feminist, queer, masculinity, and race theory as equally important issues.

Late-1990s retro-noir, like other genres in Hollywood today, exhibits both the conservative, reactionary reassertion of the patriarchy that is part of postmodernism and the condemnation of women and feminism that is part of reactionary postfeminism.[6] The stylish noir surface remains, but the ambiguous construction of gender, race, and class featured in classic noir disappears. In retro-noir, men are men and get to survive; women do not drive the narrative and may live or die; and the middle-class home and family offer an enticing rather than a stifling, dull, or loveless alternative to the criminal world. Retro-noir texts allow spectators to return to a cinematic past that is in many ways more reactionary than that of classic film noir. The male protagonists in retro-noir, such as Bud White in *L.A. Confidential,* Hoover in *Mulholland Falls,* and the narrator-Tyler in *Fight Club,* might struggle and suffer, but their struggles have almost nothing to do with the female characters.

The femmes fatales in nineties retro-noirs are almost all pastiche femmes fatales. Their reward, in two out of three films, is survival. Allison in *Mulholland Falls* has the audacity to investigate, and for that she is thrown from a plane. Despite their lack of agency, all these women look like and are read by critics as femmes fatales, seemingly out of habit or conditioned expectation. *Fight Club,* perhaps the newest incarnation of retro-noir, no longer marks itself as such by representing a past. *Fight Club* is the most menacing of these films, in part because it masquerades so effectively as something other than retro-noir while reveling in the same misogyny and homophobia exhibited in those texts. And *Fight Club,* like other retro-noirs, also deals in reactionary representations of race.

Whereas classic film noir once used the white male protagonist's friendship or familiarity with nonwhite culture as a way to underscore his liberal humanity, retro-noir does not bolster the muscular hypermasculinity of its white male characters with such a characterization. Instead, nonwhite characters are invisible (*Mulholland Falls*), represent a culture of criminality and subjection (*L.A. Confidential*), or provide the white male character an opportunity to display his superiority through the intimidation of a nonwhite character (*Fight Club*). Retro-noir is reactionary, allowing the return of repressed white masculinity in the most violent and emphatic of ways.

Neo-noir is often revisionary, although the appropriation of noir themes into new ways of understanding gender and class does not always extend to representations of race. Neo-noir might be reactionary with regard to race (as in *Twilight*), or somewhat ambiguous (*Fargo*), or potentially revisionary (*Jackie Brown*). But in representing gender and class, neo-noir celebrates women, revolts against tradition, and at least partially unmoors the patriarchy, revealing the more progressive side of third-wave feminism and postmodernism.[7]

Jackie Brown allows the female protagonist not just to survive but thrive. In *Twilight,* the femme fatale is also a devoted femme attrapée, and although Catherine may cause the deaths of a number of people, she also survives the narrative. In *Fargo,* the whole notion of a male investigator undergoes radical revision, resulting in intense narrative and visual pleasures that have nothing to do with the sexual objectification of women. Neo-noir also includes a notion of what it means to be financially strapped, to be a member of the lower or middle class — something classic noir always understood and represented, however surreptitiously. In a sense, then, neo-noir takes advantage of its genre and its time and place in film and cultural history to elaborate on questions of gender, class, and race that classic noir always seemed to hint at.

Postclassic noir continues to gain screen time. Films such as *Memento* (2000), *Mulholland Drive* (2001), and *Lantana* (2001) appear to be neo-noirs, and *The Man Who Wasn't There* (2001) follows the generic taxonomy for retro-noir. In *The Man Who Wasn't There,* racism and sexism appear, but do not drive the narrative; the film almost blankly represents racist asides as well as homophobic and sexist attitudes. Although not a retro-noir, the wonderful retro-melodrama *Far from Heaven* (2002) considers race, class, and gender screen time in a way that both acknowledges the past and represents it. In *Far from Heaven,* racism drives the narrative, as do gender relationships, heterocentrism, and class issues. The result is a much more nuanced and aware filmic text, one that even the Academy Awards recognized and rewarded (although not with an award, just with a nomination) as progressive. Perhaps the retro-melodrama *Far from Heaven* points the way for retro-noir in the twenty-first century. These films might gain a new vibrancy by appropriating the revisionary impulses of neo-noir and even classic noir, as well as other films that represent the past without reveling in reactionary nostalgia.

Postclassic noir allows all the disparate forces circulating in our culture to gain screen time. Retro-noir proves that the aims of feminism are far from satisfied. Neo-noir, although it allows female subjectivity somewhat more freedom, also benefits from a feminist reading. Both strands of postclassic noir reveal our culture's continuing struggles with class and race, including white privilege. As a cultural critic and a film aficionada, I wait anxiously to see what direction noir will take next. Scholarship can encourage change, and bell hooks's style of cultural criticism epitomizes this. In "Good Girls Look the Other Way," she commends Spike Lee for creating a film, *Girl 6,* that provides "a broader, more complex vision of womanhood in general, and black womanhood in particular."[8] Spike Lee may have made *Girl 6* in response to hooks's call for a change in his filmmaking.[9] Similarly, Quentin Tarantino may have made *Jackie Brown* in response to her criticism. In the introduction to *Reel to Real,* she notes that Tarantino values film criticism, and then, in "Artistic Integrity: Race and Accountability," accuses his movies of making "racism and sexism entertaining."[10] It is possible, therefore, that bell hooks changed the way these two male filmmakers think about and represent race and gender in their films.

My goal, as a teacher and scholar, is to affect future cultural critics, filmmakers, producers, and consumers of popular culture, twenty-three students at a time. These students are women and men equally capable of becoming producers of cultural texts. I mean for them to consider issues of gender, sexuality, class, and race as they write, think, watch, and read. I do not seek to replicate my theoretical background in these students; indeed, my whiteness and heterocentrism may be subject positions they can avoid. Their tastes and interests differ from mine, yet I trust their ability to critically read texts for sexism, heterosexism, and racism when they leave my classroom. Provided with the opportunity to engage in cultural production, they will produce more nuanced and aware representations of race, class, and gender. On the cultural continuum, then, the reactionary and nostalgic trends demonstrated by retro-noir may fade, be displaced, and finally be rejected. And the more revisionary plots and characterizations of neo-noir may become the aesthetic, commercial, and societal norm. That is the cinematic future I seek.

NOTES

Introduction

1. Marlowe almost seems afraid to engage in a verbal exchange with her, his intellect perhaps occupied with figuring out the impenetrable plot of Raymond Chandler's novel as brought to the big screen.

2. Marlowe winds up with Vivian Rutledge (Lauren Bacall), thanks to the force of spectator desire. Bogart and Bacall, recently married, had to end up together at the end of this film; moviegoers got what they most wanted to see.

3. William H. Chafe, *The Paradox of Change: American Women in the 20th Century* (Oxford: Oxford Univ. Press, 1991), 122.

4. Ibid., 123, 132.

5. Paula Rabinowitz, *Black and White and Noir: America's Pulp Modernism* (New York: Columbia Univ. Press, 2002), 22; bell hooks, *Black Looks: Race and Representation* (New York: Routledge, 1992) and *Outlaw Culture: Resisting Representation* (New York: Routledge, 1994), 197.

6. Philip Green, *Cracks in the Pedestal: Ideology and Gender in Hollywood* (Amherst: Univ. of Massachusetts Press, 1998), 6.

7. Jans B. Wager, *Dangerous Dames: Women and Representation in the Weimar Street Film and Film Noir* (Athens: Ohio Univ. Press, 1999).

8. Night was often simulated by shooting during the day and using a dark filter. When night-for-night photography is used, the sequence is actually shot at night or in low-light conditions, resulting in deep black shadows.

9. Classic film noir often ignores these generic characteristics, too; hence the difficulty of defining film noir as a genre, style, period, etc.

10. See Stephen Prince, *Classical Film Violence: Designing and Regulating Violence in Hollywood Cinema, 1930–1968* (New Brunswick, N.J.: Rutgers Univ. Press, 2003), for an in-depth discussion of how the Production Code influenced filmmaking in Hollywood.

11. Ibid., 293.

12. Eric Lott, "Whiteness: A Glossary," *Village Voice* (May 18, 1993): 38.

13. Eric Lott, "The Whiteness of Film Noir," *American Literary History* 9, no. 3 (Autumn 1997): 551.

14. Ibid., 545.

15. Rabinowitz, *Black and White,* 14.

16. Kate Stables, "The Postmodern Always Rings Twice: Constructing the *Femme Fatale*

in '90s Cinema," in *Women in Film Noir*, ed. E. Ann Kaplan, new ed. (London: British Film Institute, 1998), 170. Stables calls the female characters in her essay " '90s femme fatales"; I draw a distinction between these early-1990s sexual performers and the late-1990s female characters who still function as femmes fatales, but without the overt performance aspect of their sexuality. After the voracious early-1990s femmes, the late-1990s femmes return to sexual presence.

17. Ibid., 172–173.

18. Slavoj Zizek, *The Art of the Ridiculous Sublime: On David Lynch's "Lost Highway,"* Walter Chapin Simpson Center for the Humanities Short Studies (Seattle: Univ. of Washington Press, 2000), 12.

19. Laura Mulvey, "Visual Pleasure and Narrative Cinema," in *Visual and Other Pleasures* (Bloomington: Indiana Univ. Press, 1989).

20. Rabinowitz, *Black and White*, 18.

21. Teresa Amott and Julie Matthaei, *Race, Gender, and Work: A Multicultural Economic History of Women in the United States* (Boston: South End Press, 1991), 13.

22. Raymond Borde and Etienne Chaumeton, *A Panorama of American Film Noir, 1941–1953*, trans. Paul Hammond (San Francisco: City Lights Books, 2002). See James Naremore's fine discussion of the French critics in *More than Night: Film Noir in Its Contexts* (Berkeley and Los Angeles: Univ. of California Press, 1998).

23. Green, *Cracks in the Pedestal*, 6.

24. Of course, the femme fatale as sexual performer has not completely disappeared from the screen. One reason for the lack of success of *Femme Fatale* (2002) might be that the representation of the femme fatale as a porn star has outlived its cultural usefulness in the twenty-first century.

25. See Chapter 12 in Wager, *Dangerous Dames*, for a discussion of *The Last Seduction*, 130–134.

26. Green, *Cracks in the Pedestal*, 6.

Chapter 1

1. See the chapter on film noir in Steven Neale, *Genre and Hollywood* (London: Routledge, 2000), 151–177, for a succinct discussion of these ongoing debates; see also "Appendix C: Other Studies of Film Noir," in *Film Noir: An Encyclopedic Reference to the American Style*, 3rd ed., ed. Alain Silver and Elizabeth Ward, 327–385 (Woodstock, N.Y.: Overlook Press, 1992).

2. Low-key lighting uses little or no fill light, causing stark pools of light. Night-for-night photography is actually shot at night or in low-light situations rather than with a night-simulating filter. These techniques typify film noir lighting.

3. Richard Martin, *Mean Streets and Raging Bulls: The Legacy of Film Noir in Contemporary American Cinema* (Lanham, Md.: Scarecrow Press, 1999), 2.

4. Ibid., 4.

5. Ibid., 2.

6. Ibid., 3–4.

7. Neale, *Genre and Hollywood*, 171.

8. Ibid., 173–174.

9. Ibid., 174.

10. Naremore, *More than Night*, 11.

11. Ibid.

12. Rabinowitz, *Black and White*, 16.

13. Ibid.

14. Neale, *Genre and Hollywood*, 18.

15. Ihab Hassan, *The Postmodern Turn: Essays in Postmodern Theory and Culture* (Columbus: Ohio State Univ. Press, 1987), 92.

16. Ibid., 93.

17. *The Long Goodbye* is based on the 1953 novel by Raymond Chandler, but the film is set in the 1970s.

18. *Chinatown* is set in 1937.

19. Anne Friedberg, *Window Shopping: Cinema and the Postmodern* (Berkeley and Los Angeles: Univ. of California Press, 1993), 202.

20. Helene A. Shugart, Catherine Egley Waggoner, and D. Lynn O'Brien Holstein, "Mediating Third-Wave Feminism: Appropriation as Postmodern Media Practice,"

Critical Studies in Media Communication 11, no. 2 (2001): 197.

21. Fredric Jameson, "Postmodernism and Consumer Society," in *The Anti-Aesthetic: Essays on Postmodern Culture* (Seattle: Bay Press, 1983), 111–125; the quote is from 117.

22. Ibid.

23. Ibid.

24. Ibid.

25. Yvonne Tasker, *Working Girls: Gender and Sexuality in Popular Cinema* (London: Routledge, 1998), 135.

26. Friedberg, *Window Shopping*, 2.

27. Ibid.

28. Ibid.

29. Jameson, "Consumer Society," 118.

30. Friedberg, *Window Shopping*, 179.

Chapter 2

1. Janey Place, "Women in Film Noir," in Kaplan, *Women in Film Noir*, 61.

2. Carl Macek, "*Raw Deal*," in Silver and Ward, *Film Noir*, 238. This description seems much more lurid than the film. My reading of *Raw Deal* suggests that the woman, Ann, seeks to redeem the male character, seeing in him the potential for goodness more than the promise of sexual fulfillment beyond normal (?) bounds.

3. Chris Straayer, "*Femme Fatale* or Lesbian Femme: *Bound* in Sexual *Différance*," in Kaplan, *Women in Film Noir*, 155.

4. Tasker, *Working Girls*, 127.

5. Green, *Cracks in the Pedestal*, 204.

6. Straayer, "*Femme Fatale*," 155.

7. Ibid.

8. Ibid., 158.

9. Martin, *Mean Streets*, 27.

10. Ibid.

11. Ibid., 67.

12. Ibid., 115.

13. Ibid., 132.

14. Ibid., 90.

15. Ibid.

16. Ibid., 91.

17. Ibid.

18. Neale, *Genre and Hollywood*, 175.

19. Naremore, *More than Night*, 262.

20. Martin, *Mean Streets*, 90.

21. Tasker, *Working Girls*, 127.

22. Patrice Petro, *Joyless Streets: Women and Melodramatic Representation in Weimar Germany* (Princeton, N.J.: Princeton Univ. Press, 1989).

23. Ibid., 4.

24. Ibid., 8.

25. Friedberg, *Window Shopping*, 2.

26. Ibid., 201.

27. Ibid.

28. Brenda O'Neill, "What Do Women Think?" *Herizons: Women's News and Feminist Views* 16, no. 2 (2002): 20.

29. Amanda Lotz, "Communicating Third-Wave Feminism and New Social Movements: Challenges for the Next Century of Feminist Endeavor," *Women and Language* 26, no. 2 (2003): 2.

30. Ibid., 5.

31. This brief discussion of postfeminism and third-wave feminism hints at the ongoing debates about what each of these terms describes. Some scholars use postfeminism to indicate both the revisionary and reactionary versions, which Lotz groups under third-wave feminism. I follow those who use postfeminism to describe only conservative, reactionary movements, and third-wave feminism to identify progressive or revisionary movements.

32. Leslie Heywood and Jennifer Drake, introduction, *Third Wave Agenda: Being Feminist, Doing Feminism*, ed. Heywood and Drake (Minneapolis: Minnesota Univ. Press, 1997), 1.

33. Shugart, "Mediating Feminism," 206.

34. Ibid., 198.

35. Lotz, "Third-Wave Feminism," 7.

Chapter 3

1. Straayer, "*Femme Fatale*," 153.

2. David R. Roediger, *The Wages of Whiteness: Race and the Making of the American Working Class*, rev. ed. (London: Verso, 1999), 8.

3. Ibid., 12.

4. Thomas Cripps, *Hollywood's High*

Noon: Moviemaking and Society before Television, excerpted in *Movies and American Society,* ed. Steven J. Ross (Oxford: Blackwell, 2002), 181.

5. Ibid., 182.

6. Oscar Micheaux, "The Negro and the Photo Play," in Ross, *Movies and American Society,* 185.

7. Anna Everett, *Returning the Gaze: A Genealogy of Black Film Criticism, 1909–1949* (Durham, N.C.: Duke Univ. Press, 2001), 304.

8. Judith Mayne, *Cinema and Spectatorship* (London: Routledge, 1993), 148.

9. Manthia Diawara, "Noir by Noirs: Towards a New Realism in Black Cinema," in *Shades of Noir: A Reader,* ed. Joan Copjec (London: Verso, 1993), 262.

10. Ibid., 262.

11. Naremore, *More than Night,* 240.

12. Eric Lott, "Racial Cross-Dressing and the Construction of American Whiteness," in *The Cultural Studies Reader,* 2nd ed., ed. Simon During (London: Routledge, 1999), 243.

13. Ibid., 242.

14. Ibid., 248. I would add masculinity, implicit in Lott's essay.

15. Lott, "Whiteness of Film Noir," 550.

16. Ibid., 551.

17. Naremore, *More than Night,* 220.

18. Ibid., 225.

19. Ibid., 226–227.

20. Ibid., 229–231.

21. Ibid., 232.

22. Ibid., 235.

23. Ibid., 236.

24. Ibid., 237.

25. Everett, *Returning the Gaze,* 304.

26. See the following: Donald Bogle, *Toms, Coons, Mulattoes, Mammies, and Bucks: An Interpretive History of Blacks in American Films,* 4th ed. (New York: Continuum, 2001.); Thomas Cripps, *Making Movies Black: The Hollywood Message Movies from World War II to the Civil Rights Era* (New York: Oxford Univ. Press, 1993) and *Slow Fade to Black: The Negro in American Film, 1900–1942* (New York: Oxford Univ. Press,

1977); Ed Guerrero, *Framing Blackness: The African American Image in Film* (Philadelphia: Temple Univ. Press, 1993).

27. Bogle, *Mammies and Bucks,* 119.

28. Ibid., 121.

29. I also discuss *Devil in a Blue Dress,* directed by Carl Franklin, in *Dangerous Dames.*

30. Diawara, "Noir by Noirs," 263.

31. Ibid., 277.

32. Susan Fraiman, *Cool Men and the Second Sex* (New York: Columbia Univ. Press, 2003).

Chapter 4

1. Silver and Ward, *Film Noir,* 153.

2. Borde and Chaumeton, *Panorama of Noir,* ix–x, 10.

3. In the Hemingway short story, first published in 1927, both the white counterman and the white gunmen refer to Sam as "the nigger," an overt form of racism that is left out in 1946 for reasons touched on in Chapter Three and discussed fully in Everett's *Returning the Gaze.* The black audience had a public voice, and the white film industry needed to acknowledge that voice as well as the role of blacks in fighting for U.S. interests. The frightened demeanor of the cook does reflect his characterization in the short story. See Ernest Hemingway, "The Killers," in *The Short Stories of Ernest Hemingway* (New York: Scribners, 1938).

4. Oliver Harris, "Film Noir Fascination: Outside History, but Historically So," *Cinema Journal* 43, no. 1 (2003): 3–24.

5. As Neale notes in *Genre and Hollywood,* homodiegetic narration is connected to "characters who at some point appear on screen," as opposed to heterodiegetic "third-person" narration (176).

6. Lilly's name implies purity and innocence; Kitty evokes sexiness and risk.

7. Harris intriguingly notes that Lilly and Swede were supposed to have a date to go to the movies. According to Harris, "Swede's seduction into the world of crime and desire, his rendezvous with fate and fascination, takes place . . . because he breaks a date to

go to the cinema" ("Film Noir Fascination," 13). The implication, then, is "all the couples in the theater had kept *their* dates at the movies" (ibid.).

8. Unlike many femmes fatales, Kitty never reveals her background or motivations. Many scholars and critics remain blind to the provocation for the femme fatale's selfish and greedy actions, although she may articulate them clearly. In *Gun Crazy* (1950), femme fatale Annie Laurie Starr (Peggy Cummins) talks about her poor childhood and tells the male protagonist quite plainly, "I want things, lots of things." Similarly, in *The Big Heat* (1953) femme fatale Debbie (Gloria Grahame) explains her choice of a hoodlum boyfriend to detective Bannion (Glenn Ford), saying, "I've been rich, and I've been poor; believe me, rich is better." Kitty, in *The Killers,* never says what she wants, but her unstated desire to escape seems apparent, given the working-class context of the film.

9. Vivian Sobchack, "Lounge Time: Postwar Crises and the Chronotype of Film Noir," in *Refiguring American Film Genres: Theory and History,* ed. Nick Brown (Berkeley and Los Angeles: Univ. of California Press, 1998), 137.

10. Ibid., 146.

11. Ibid., 158.

12. See my discussion of the stakes involved for women in the domestic sphere in *Dangerous Dames.*

13. Sobchack, "Lounge Time," 144.

14. Robert Porfirio, "*The Killers:* Expressiveness of Sound and Image in *Film Noir,*" in *Film Noir Reader,* ed. Alain Silver and James Ursini (New York: Limelight Editions, 1996), 183.

15. Place, "Women in Film Noir," 50. See also my discussion of femmes fatales and femmes attrapées in Chapter One of *Dangerous Dames.*

16. Deborah Thomas, "How Hollywood Deals with the Deviant Male," in *The Movie Book of Film Noir,* ed. Ian Cameron (London: Studio Vista, 1992), 64.

17. Ann (Virginia Huston) in *Out of the Past* (1947) functions more as a femme attrapée, especially in her visual representation. In Chapter Five I discuss her character in more depth.

18. See an expanded discussion of *Gun Crazy* in *Dangerous Dames,* 92–102.

19. Julie Wosk, *Women and the Machine: Representations from the Spinning Wheel to the Electronic Age* (Baltimore: Johns Hopkins Univ. Press, 2001), 198.

20. Ibid.

21. Ibid.

22. Ibid.

23. Sobchack, "Lounge Time," 137–138.

24. Harris, "Film Noir Fascination," 14. Harris calls the character "Reardon." I use the spelling provided in Silver and Ward, *Film Noir.*

25. Paul Smith, "Eastwood Bound," in *Constructing Masculinity,* ed. Maurice Berger, Brian Wallis, and Simon Watson (New York: Routledge, 1995), 81.

26. Ibid.

27. Justine Elias, "Up, Out, and Away," *Village Voice,* May 3–9, 2000, 1. The room is in a boarding house, not a motel.

28. Ibid.

29. Harris, "Film Noir Fascination," 18–19.

30. Ibid., 19.

31. Ibid.

32. In my next project, tentatively titled "Jazz and Cocktails: Race and Noir," I plan to explore the production histories of many films noirs, in part to answer questions about whiteness in *The Killers* and in part to look at the casting and screenwriting decisions that inform the appearances of nonwhites in films noirs.

Chapter 5

1. Bosley Crowther, review of *Out of the Past,* in *The New York Times Film Reviews, 1913–1968,* vol. 4 (New York: New York Times and Arno, 1970), 2217.

2. Borde and Chaumeton, *Panorama of Noir,* 65.

3. Karen Burroughs Hannsberry, *Femme Noir: Bad Girls of Film* (Jefferson, N.C.: McFarland, 1998), 206.

4. Tom Flinn, "*Out of the Past*," in *The Big Book of Noir,* ed. Ed Gorman et al. (New York: Carroll and Graf, 1998), 74.

5. Ephraim Katz, *The Film Encyclopedia,* 2nd ed. (New York: HarperCollins, 1994), 953.

6. Tom Flinn, "Daniel Mainwaring: An Interview," in Gorman, *Big Book of Noir.* Flinn notes that Nick Musuraca, the cameraman for the film, "was not aware of any pot smoking on the set" (67–68).

7. Crowther, review of *Out of the Past,* 2216.

8. Katz, *Film Encyclopedia,* 953.

9. James Agee, *Agee on Film: Criticism and Comment on the Movies* (New York: Modern Library, 2000), 299.

10. Ibid., 372.

11. Katz, *Film Encyclopedia,* 953.

12. Nicholas Christopher, *Somewhere in the Night: Film Noir and the American City* (New York: Free Press, 1997), 7.

13. Naremore, *More than Night,* 240.

14. Ibid.

15. Flinn, "Mainwaring," 71.

16. Amott and Matthaei, *Race, Gender, and Work,* 173.

17. Rabinowitz, *Black and White,* 61.

18. Wosk, *Women and the Machine,* 206.

19. Naremore, *More than Night,* 230.

20. See Chapter Six.

21. Those of us who fish wonder about the test strength of the line the boy used.

22. Chris Peachment, "Past Imperfect," review of *Out of the Past, New Statesman,* Aug. 21, 1998, 40.

23. Ibid.

24. Blake Lucas, "*Out of the Past,*" in Silver and Ward, *Film Noir,* 219.

25. Naremore, *More than Night,* 182.

26. Ibid.

27. Place, "Women in Film Noir," 61.

28. John Harvey, "Out of the Light: An Analysis of Narrative in *Out of the Past,*" *Journal of American Studies* 18, no. 1 (1984): 78.

29. Ibid., 79. Coincidentally, when I first discovered *Out of the Past,* I was living in California, working as caretaker for a large estate on Lake Tahoe and taking weekly trips to the mountains around Bridgeport in search of Sierra spring ski mountaineering. When we were not skiing, we would wander around Bridgeport, which looks remarkably similar to the way it does in the film—the courthouse still features a wrought iron fence and stunning mountain scenery still surrounds a sleepy tourist town.

30. Flinn, "Mainwaring," 74.

31. Harvey, "Out of the Light," 86–87.

32. Ibid., 87.

Chapter 6

1. See R. Barton Palmer, *Hollywood's Dark Cinema: The American Film Noir* (New York: Twayne, 1994), 94–104, for a detailed plot synopsis and analysis of *Kiss Me Deadly.*

2. Prince, *Film Violence,* 185, 190.

3. Mark Osteen, "'The *Big* Secret,' Film Noir, and Nuclear Fear," *Journal of Popular Film and Television* 22, no. 2 (1994): 89.

4. Ibid.

5. Naremore, *More than Night,* 153.

6. Robin Wood, "Creativity and Evaluation: Two Film Noirs of the Fifties," in *Film Noir Reader 2,* ed. Alain Silver and James Ursini (New York: Limelight Editions, 1999), 104.

7. Robert Lang, *Masculine Interests: Homoerotics in Hollywood Film* (New York: Columbia Univ. Press, 2002), 125. Lang's discussion points out the vivid and apparent homoerotics of *Kiss Me Deadly.*

8. Ibid., 139.

9. Wood, "Creativity and Evaluation," 105.

10. Naremore, *More than Night,* 241.

11. Ibid.

12. Amott and Matthaei, *Race, Gender, and Work,* 174.

13. Ibid.

14. Laura Mulvey, "The Myth of Pandora: A Psychoanalytical Approach," in *Feminisms in the Cinema,* ed. Laura Pietropaolo and Ada Testaferri (Bloomington: Indiana Univ. Press, 1995), 6.

15. Ibid., 11.

16. Ibid.

17. Ibid., 15.

18. Ibid.

19. The male homoerotics of the film makes this desexualization of the feminine less strange.

20. David Thomson, "Dead Lily," *Film Comment* 33, no. 6 (1997): 18.

21. Mulvey, "Pandora," 15.

22. Caryl Flinn, "Sound, Woman, and the Bomb: Dismembering the 'Great Whatsit' in *Kiss Me Deadly*," *Screening the Past,* June 2000 <http://www.latrobe.edu.au/screeningthepast/reruns/rr0600/cfrr10b.htm>.

23. Flinn's analysis at times seems to equate a certain sort of knowledge with women.

24. Lang draws heavily on the Spillane novel in discussing the film, which enhances his ability to read the homoerotics of *Kiss Me Deadly.* Thanks to the Production Code, explicit sexual meaning in the literary inspirations for many films noirs became muddled in the translation into film. This translation problem makes the film version of *The Big Sleep* almost completely incomprehensible. The novel's plot is driven by a pornography ring, male homosexuality, and illegal drug use. The film uses visual style, a few murders, and Bogart and Bacall to keep the viewers watching, leaving only traces of its lurid literary antecedent.

25. Mulvey, "Pandora," 16.

26. As originally released in 1955, the film ends with the explosion. A 1997 release of the new video version of *Kiss Me Deadly* includes an additional eighty-two seconds of film showing Hammer and Velda in the surf, watching the explosion. According to David Poland, this ending is from director Aldrich's "personal print" ("Flash of Genius or Mistake? [The Final 82 Seconds of the Original Robert Aldrich Motion Picture *Kiss Me Deadly* are discovered by Glenn Erickson]," *Entertainment Weekly,* June 27, 1997, 129).

27. Mulvey, "Pandora," 18.

28. Thomson, "Dead Lily," 19.

29. Ibid.

30. Ibid.

31. Mulvey, "Pandora," 11.

Chapter 7

1. Wager, *Dangerous Dames,* 122.

2. See the discussion of this film in Kaja Silverman, *Male Subjectivity at the Margins* (New York: Routledge, 1992), ch. 2.

3. Robert B. Ray, *A Certain Tendency in the Hollywood Cinema, 1930–1980* (Princeton, N.J.: Princeton Univ. Press, 1985), 90.

4. Eve Kosofsky Sedgwick, *Between Men: English Literature and Male Homosocial Desire* (New York: Columbia Univ. Press, 1985), 1.

5. Ibid.

6. Silver and Ward, *Film Noir,* 182. Lorre, born in Hungary, was a major German film star in the 1930s; he went into exile when the Nazis came to power (Katz, *Film Encyclopedia,* 843).

7. Wager, *Dangerous Dames,* 15.

8. See discussion of race and *Devil in a Blue Dress* in *Dangerous Dames,* 124–127.

9. Green, *Cracks in the Pedestal,* 204.

10. John Wrathall, review of *L.A. Confidential, Sight and Sound,* Nov. 1997, 45.

11. Richard Alleva, "City of Angels," *Commonweal* 124, no. 18 (1997): 3.

12. As Dana Polan noted after screening the classic noir *In a Lonely Place* during the Point Blank conference in Tucson, 2000, reviewers of that film similarly ignored or marginalized the murder of a female character in 1950 (Dana Polan, address, Point Blank Conference, University of Arizona, Tucson, May 2000).

13. Manohla Dargis, "Russell Crowe's Special Brand of Masculinity," *New York Times* (March 4, 2001): 2A.1.

14. Ibid.

15. Jackson Katz, "Advertising and the Construction of White Male Masculinity," in *Rereading America: Cultural Contexts for Critical Thinking and Writing,* ed. Gary Colombo, Robert Cullen, and Bonnie Lisle, 4th ed. (Boston: Bedford, 1998), 460.

16. Ibid., 461.

17. Ibid.

18. Ibid., 463.

19. Ibid., 462–463.

20. Amy Taubin, "L.A. Lurid," *Sight and Sound*, Nov. 1997, 11. Of course, since 1997 both Crowe and Pearce have gained considerable fame.

21. Ibid.

22. Krin Gabbard and Glen O. Gabbard, "Play It Again, Sigmund: Psychoanalysis and the Classical Hollywood Text," *Journal of Popular Film and Television* 18, no. 1 (1990): 8.

23. David Ansen, review of *L.A. Confidential, Newsweek*, Oct. 27, 1997, 68–70.

24. John Simon, review of *L.A. Confidential, National Review*, Oct. 27, 1997, 56.

25. I am guessing that Lynn is supposed to be in her thirties.

26. Terry Lawson, "*L.A. Confidential* Star Retains Her Sultry Image after a Two-Year Break," Knight-Ridder/Tribune News Service, Sept. 15, 1997, 915.

27. Stuart Klawans, review of *L.A. Confidential, Nation*, Oct. 13, 1997, 34–35.

28. David Thomas, review of *L.A. Confidential, Esquire*, Oct. 1997, 50–51.

29. Katz, "White Masculinity," 776.

30. Those familiar with *The Best Years of Our Lives* (1946) will see the similarities between Lynn's response to Bud's injuries and the good woman's response to a returning veteran's disability. See Silverman, *Male Subjectivity at the Margins*.

31. Harvey Greenberg, *The Movies on Your Mind: Film Classics on the Couch from Fellini to Frankenstein* (New York: Dutton, 1975), 103.

32. Ibid., 89.

33. Umberto Eco, "Casablanca: Cult Movies and Intertextual Collage," *SubStance* 47 (1985): 10.

34. Ibid.

35. Ibid.

36. Ibid., 9.

Chapter 8

1. Ken Tucker, in his review of the film, calls *Mulholland Falls* "*Chinatown* for Chowderheads" (Ken Tucker, "You Can Leave Your Hat On: The Detectives Are Defective in Nolte's *Mulholland Falls*," *Entertainment Weekly*, May 3, 1996, 62). The reviewer in *L.A. Magazine* calls the film "numbskull noir" (Peter Rainer, "Nothing under Its Hats: *Mulholland Falls* Is Numbskull Noir Only a Dirty Harry Could Love," *Los Angeles Magazine*, May 1996, 141).

2. Naremore, *More than Night*, 155.

3. Ibid.

4. Boyd Tonkin, review of *Mulholland Falls, New Statesman*, Sept. 6, 1996, 43.

5. Naremore, *More than Night*, 212.

6. Tonkin, review of *Mulholland Falls*, 43.

7. John Wrathall, review of *Mulholland Falls, Sight and Sound*, Sept. 1996, 48.

8. Ibid.

9. Tucker, "Leave Your Hat On," 62.

10. Kathleen Murphy, "Totems and Taboos: Civilization and Its Discontents According to Lee Tamahori," *Film Comment* 33 (1997): 28.

11. Ibid.

12. Ibid.

13. Stanley Kauffmann, "Some Crime, Some Comedy," review of *Mulholland Falls, New Republic* 214, no. 22 (May 27, 1996), 28.

14. See my discussion of *The Big Heat* in *Dangerous Dames*, 103–113.

15. Ty Burr, "The Wizard of Odd," *Entertainment Weekly*, Aug. 23, 1996, 132.

16. Wrathall, review of *Mulholland Falls*, 48.

17. Foster Hirsch, *Detours and Lost Highways: A Map of Neo-Noir* (New York: Limelight Editions, 1999), 164.

18. Ibid.

19. Tonkin, review of *Mulholland Falls*, 43.

Chapter 9

1. I refer here to Weimar film critic Siegfried Kracauer's essay, "The Little Shopgirls Go to the Movies," in which Kracauer imagines the female spectator's emotional response to melodramatic movies (Siegfried Kracauer, "Die kleinen Ladenmädchen gehens in Kino," in *Das Ornament der Masse* [Frankfurt am Main: Suhrkamp, 1977]).

2. By 2004, the idea of a fight club had

become a joke. Two comedies, *Old School* and *Jackass: The Movie,* suggest a similar masculinity narrative, a narrative that excludes femininity except to prove heterosexuality and that promotes the pleasures of male physical pain.

3. Joel Stein, "The Emasculation Proclamation," *Time,* Oct. 25, 1999, 46.

4. Ibid.

5. Susan Faludi, "It's *Thelma and Louise* for Guys," *Newsweek,* Oct. 25, 1999, 89.

6. Henry A. Giroux, "Private Satisfactions and Public Disorders: *Fight Club,* Patriarchy, and the Politics of Masculine Violence," *JAC: A Journal of Composition Theory* 21, no. 1 (2001): 9.

7. Sarah Projansky, *Watching Rape: Film and Television in Postfeminist Culture* (New York: New York Univ. Press, 2002), 80.

8. As I note in Chapter Two, other scholars identify both the reactionary and the revisionary movement as third-wave feminism, or delineate the reactionary strand as postfeminist and the revisionary as third wave.

9. Projansky, *Watching Rape,* 80.

10. Raphael Shargel, "The Social Outrage Season," *New Leader,* Nov. 1999, 18

11. Brian Johnson, "Bare-Knuckled Knockout," *Maclean's,* Oct. 25, 1999, 86.

12. Stanley Kauffmann, "Primal Stuff," *New Republic* 221, no. 19 (Nov. 8, 1999), 64.

13. Richard Schickel, "The Conditional Knockout," *Time,* Nov. 11, 1999, 83.

14. Projansky, *Watching Rape,* 67.

15. All quotes taken from the film, unless otherwise noted.

16. Giroux, "Private Satisfactions," 5.

17. Dennis Hensley, "He's Sew Fine," *Advocate,* Nov. 23, 1999, 63.

18. Amy Taubin, "21st Century Boys," *Village Voice,* Nov. 19, 1999, 43.

19. Gregg Kilday, "Why I Hated *Fight Club,*" *Advocate,* Nov. 23, 1999, 63.

20. Marc S. Malkin, "Why I Loved *Fight Club,*" *Advocate,* Nov. 23, 1999, 66.

21. Taubin, "21st Century Boys," 43.

22. Kevin Cook and March Mravic, "Fight Cult," *Sports Illustrated,* Nov. 1, 1999, 31.

23. David Rooney, "*Fight Club:* An Adrenaline Rush of a Movie," *Variety,* Sept. 13, 1999, 47.

24. Peter Lehman, "Crying over the Melodramatic Penis: Melodrama and Male Nudity in Films of the '90s," in *Masculinity: Bodies, Movies, Culture,* ed. Peter Lehman (New York: Routledge, 2001), 26.

25. Ibid.

26. Ibid., 27.

27. Mayne, *Cinema and Spectatorship,* 97.

28. Taubin, "21st Century Boys," 43.

29. Ibid.

30. Mayne, *Cinema and Spectatorship,* 97.

31. Kilday, "Hated *Fight Club,*" 66.

32. Ibid.

33. Johnson, "Bare-Knuckled Knockout," 87.

34. Giroux, "Private Satisfactions," 13.

35. Ibid.

36. Ibid.

37. Faludi, "For Guys," 89.

38. Ibid.

39. Ibid.

40. Projansky, *Watching Rape,* 68.

41. David Sterritt, "Hollywood's Violence Club," *Christian Science Monitor,* Oct. 22, 1999, 15.

Chapter 10

1. I indicate the actors' ages at the time the film was released. The reviewer for *Entertainment Weekly* even renames *Twilight,* on the downside, *Grumpy Old Gumshoes* (Rebecca Ascher-Walsh et al., review of *Twilight, Entertainment Weekly,* Feb. 20–27, 1998, 52).

2. Chuck Arnold, "The Numbers Game," *People Weekly,* Feb. 23, 1998, 136.

3. Raphael Shargel, review of *Twilight, New Leader,* Mar. 9, 1998, 21.

4. Ibid.

5. *Thelma and Louise* provides one version of dames in the driver's seat, but then they drive off a cliff. The female protagonists who inspire my title survive their filmic narratives.

6. Barry King, "Articulating Stardom," *Screen* 26, no. 5 (1985): 27–50.

7. Ibid., 30.

8. Sharon Willis, "Hardware and Hard-bodies: What Do Women Want?" in *Film Theory Goes to the Movies,* ed. Jim Collins et al. (New York: Routledge, 1993), 127.

9. Janet Maslin, "*Twilight:* A Round of Championship Bantering, Senior Division," *New York Times on the Web,* Mar. 6, 1998, 2.

10. Richard Alleva, "Real Actors v. Real Slobs: *Twilight* and *The Big Lebowski,*" *Commonweal,* April 10, 1998, 22.

11. Jonathan Romney, "LA Lore," *New Statesman,* Dec. 4, 1998, 38.

12. Todd McCarthy, review of *Twilight, Variety,* March 2, 1998, 83. John Simon, review of *Twilight, National Review,* April 6, 1998, 58.

13. I cannot figure out if this is a positive or negative characterization. Given the source and the tone of the review, I suspect the reviewer is being complimentary (Pat Dowell, "Cast Helps Keep *Twilight* from Fading," *Army Times,* March 23, 1998, 42).

14. Amy Taubin, "The Old 'Hood,'" *Village Voice,* March 17, 1998, 64. Emphasis Taubin's.

15. Alleva, "Real Actors," 22.

16. Ibid., 23.

17. Romney, "LA Lore," 38.

18. Dowell, "Cast Helps *Twilight*," 42.

19. Ibid.

20. Peter Plagens, review of *Twilight, Newsweek,* Mar. 16, 1998, 72.

21. Ibid.

22. Romney, "LA Lore," 38.

23. Naremore, *More than Night,* 236, 240.

24. Ibid., 240.

25. Romney, "LA Lore," 38.

26. McCarthy, review of *Twilight,* 58.

Chapter 11

1. The title of this chapter refers to Raymond Chandler's essay "The Simple Art of Murder," in which Chandler describes his detective hero, suggesting that "down these mean streets a man must go who is not himself mean, who is neither tarnished nor afraid" (Raymond Chandler, "The Simple Art of Murder," in *The Simple Art of Murder* [New York: Random House, 1988], 18).

2. I grew up in Ely, Minnesota, population 4,500 or so at the time. Ely is farther north and more (yes!) rural than Brainerd, so the movie has ample geographic and colloquial pleasures, and even briefly revives an incipient Minnesota twang whenever I watch it. My Minnesota relatives insist that no one really talks as the actors do in *Fargo.*

3. Josh Levine, *The Coen Brothers: The Story of Two American Filmmakers* (Toronto: ECW Press, 2000), 131–132.

4. See Krin Gabbard's extended discussion of this music and composer Burwell in *Black Magic: White Hollywood and African American Culture* (New Brunswick, N.J.: Rutgers Univ. Press, 2004), 130–134.

5. See my discussion of *Gun Crazy* in *Dangerous Dames,* 92–102.

6. Of course, there is excitement in hooking a fish, whether ice fishing or fly-fishing. These films do not actually show that moment (except when Jeff's friend hooks and kills a criminal in *Out of the Past*), perhaps to mitigate the potential for excitement in the activity.

7. Paul Arthur, "Let Us Now Praise Famous Yokels: *Dadetown* and Other Retreats," *Cineaste* 23, no. 1 (1997): 30–33.

8. Ibid., 30.

9. Ibid.

10. Ibid.

11. Levine, *American Filmmakers,* 120.

12. Ibid., 121.

13. Ibid.

14. Ibid.

15. Ibid., 127.

16. Ibid.

17. Steven Carter, "Flare to White: *Fargo* and the Postmodern Turn," *Literature and Film Quarterly* 27, no. 7 (1999): 239.

18. Ibid.

19. Ibid.

20. Ibid.

21. Unless otherwise noted, all quotes are from the DVD version of the film.

22. Carter, "Flare to White," 240.

23. Ronald Bergan, *The Coen Brothers* (New York: Thunder's Mouth, 2000), 171.

24. As Mary Kate Goodwin-Kelly notes in a conference presentation, "on one hand we are encouraged to share the film's pleasure in this atypical figure who transcends the boundaries of social and generic expectations," but that pleasure is undercut "by the film's obsessive preoccupation with her [pregnancy]." Goodwin-Kelly makes a convincing case for the film's preoccupation with Marge's condition, pointing out that the morning sickness she suffers is unusual at seven months, that the camera work consistently accentuates her size, that her tremendous appetite renders her "gross and excessive." Of course, this textual ambivalence is not limited to Marge's character but extends to all the other characters as well. This may be why the focus on her pregnancy does not serve to undermine the pleasures of Marge as female crime solver. See Mary Kate Goodwin-Kelly, "Pregnant Body and/as Smoking Gun: Reviewing the 'Evidence' of *Fargo*" (paper presented at the Society for Cinema and Media Studies Conference, Atlanta, March 2004), 2, 9.

25. During Minnesota winters, people keep their cars plugged in to electricity at night to prevent the cold from freezing the battery. Sometimes even with that precaution, a jump is necessary.

26. Thomas Doherty, "*Fargo*," *Cineaste* 22, no. 7 (1996): 47.

27. Gabbard, *Black Magic,* 137.

28. Speaking of odd occurrences, the *Salt Lake Tribune* reported in December 2000 that a "Japanese woman seeking fictitious loot from movie 'Fargo' mysteriously dies" of exposure, adding that she mistakenly looked in Bismarck, North Dakota ("Japanese Woman Seeking Fictitious Loot From Movie 'Fargo' Mysteriously Dies," *Salt Lake Tribune,* Dec. 9, 2000, A21).

29. Levine, *American Filmmakers,* 123.

30. Ibid.

31. Carter, "Flare to White," 241.

32. Bergan, *Coen Brothers,* 39.

33. Gabbard, *Black Magic,* 135. Gabbard also points out that the only African American character to appear in *Fargo* is a black man whom Shep "knocks . . . unconscious by bouncing his head off the wall . . . and then returns to pummeling Carl" (128).

34. Doherty, "*Fargo*," 47.

35. Levine, *American Filmmakers,* 128.

36. Ibid., 127.

37. Janet Maslin, "*Fargo*," *New York Times on the Web,* March 8, 1996.

38. Gabbard, *Black Magic,* 128.

39. Kim Newman, "*Fargo*," *Sight and Sound* 6, no. 6 (1996): 40.

40. Bergan, *Coen Brothers,* 176.

41. Carter, "Flare to White," 244.

42. Ibid.

43. Ibid., 240.

44. Ibid.

45. Bergan, *Coen Brothers,* 171.

46. *The Man Who Wasn't There* (2001), also written by the Coen brothers and directed by Joel Coen, is a black-and-white homage to film noir that fits quite neatly into my taxonomy. The femme fatale, Doris (McDormand), who is also a femme attrapée married to the male protagonist, commits suicide in jail. She has been falsely accused of the murder of her lover, an act committed by her husband. As in all retro-noirs, Doris only appears to drive the narrative. She does, however, ensure her demise through her desire to escape the dull domesticity of her married life. Her husband and other male characters move the narrative forward.

Chapter 12

1. *Kill Bill: Vol. 2* (2004), directed by Tarantino, points to the director's enduring interest in noir. The film's opening sequence and closing credits clearly pay homage to classic film noir.

2. Jill Gerston, "Pam Grier Finally Escapes the 1970s," *New York Times,* Dec. 21, 1997, sec. 2, late edition (east coast).

3. Ibid.

4. Richard Corliss, "*Jackie Brown*," *Time,* Dec. 22, 1997, 80.

5. Green, *Cracks in the Pedestal.*

6. Ibid., 37.

7. Erik Bauer, "The Mouth and the Method," *Sight and Sound,* March 1998, 8.

8. bell hooks, "Cool Cynicism: Pulp Fiction," in *Reel to Real: Race, Sex, and Class at the Movies* (London: Routledge, 1996), 47.

9. Ibid., 48.

10. Ibid.

11. Fraiman, *Cool Men,* 1.

12. Ibid., 4.

13. For Fraiman, Jackie's blackness makes her more phallic, since in Tarantino's imaginary, "blackness . . . so strongly connotes masculinity" (*Cool Men,* 164, 165).

14. Kent Jones, "A Critic's Heart Is an Ocean of Longing," *Film Comment* 34 (March–April 1998): 24.

15. Ibid.

16. David Cook, *A History of Narrative Film, 1889–1979* (New York: Norton, 1981), 267.

17. Ibid.

18. In the classic noir *Touch of Evil* (1958), Charlton Heston plays Mike Vargas, a Mexican narcotics agent. In *Jackie Brown,* Dargas looks like Vargas without the brownface.

19. Friedberg, *Window Shopping,* 113.

20. Ibid.

21. Ibid., 121.

22. Ibid.

23. Jones, "Critic's Heart," 25.

24. Ibid.

25. Ibid.

26. bell hooks, *Outlaw Culture: Resisting Representations* (New York: Routledge, 1994), 62.

27. Ibid.

Conclusion

1. Theodor Adorno and Max Horkheimer, "The Culture Industry: Enlightenment as Mass Deception," in *Cultural Studies Reader,* ed. Simon During, 2nd ed. (London: Routledge, 1993), 35.

2. Walter Benjamin, "The Work of Art in the Age of Mechanical Reproduction," in *Illuminations: Essays and Reflections,* trans. Harry Zohn, ed. Hannah Arendt (New York: Schocken Books, 1968), 234. Adorno edited and introduced the first published collection of Benjamin's writing in Germany in 1955.

3. Edward Said "Opponents, Audiences, Constituencies, and Community," in *The Politics of Interpretation,* ed. W. J. T. Mitchell (Chicago: Univ. of Chicago Press, 1983), 7.

4. Ibid.

5. Petro discusses a similar experience at the 1999 Society for Cinema Studies conference in the last chapter of *Aftershocks.* Patrice Petro, *Aftershocks of the New: Feminism and Film History* (New Brunswick, N.J.: Rutgers Univ. Press, 2002).

6. Friedberg, *Window Shopping,* 202; Projansky, *Watching Rape,* 86.

7. Friedberg, *Window Shopping,* 202; Projansky, *Watching Rape,* 86.

8. bell hooks, "Good Girls Look the Other Way," in *Reel to Real,* 11.

9. Lee did not seem to sustain this multifaceted portrayal of women in *25th Hour.*

10. bell hooks, "Artistic Integrity: Race and Accountability," in *Reel to Real,* 75.

WORKS CITED

Adorno, Theodor, and Max Horkheimer. "The Culture Industry: Enlightenment as Mass Deception." Reprinted in *Cultural Studies Reader* (2nd ed.), edited by Simon During, 32–42. London: Routledge, 1993.

Agee, James. *Agee on Film: Criticism and Comment on the Movies.* New York: Modern Library, 2000.

Alleva, Richard. "City of Angels." *Commonweal* 124, no. 18 (1997): 18–19.

———. "Real Actors v. Real Slobs: *Twilight* and *The Big Lebowski.*" *Commonweal* 125, no. 7 (1998): 22–23.

Amott, Teresa, and Julie Matthaei. *Race, Gender, and Work: A Multicultural Economic History of Women in the United States.* Boston: South End Press, 1991.

Ansen, David. Review of *L.A. Confidential. Newsweek,* Oct. 27, 1997, 68–70.

Arnold, Chuck. "The Numbers Game." *People Weekly,* Feb. 23, 1998, 136.

Arthur, Paul. "Let Us Now Praise Famous Yokels: *Dadetown* and Other Retreats." *Cineaste* 23, no. 1 (1997): 30–33.

Ascher-Walsh, Rebecca, et al. Review of *Twilight. Entertainment Weekly,* Feb. 20, 1998, 52.

Bauer, Erik. "The Mouth and the Method." *Sight and Sound,* March 1998, 7–9.

Beauvoir, Simone de. *America Day by Day.* Translated by Carol Cosman. Berkeley and Los Angeles: Univ. of California Press, 1999.

Benjamin, Walter. "The Work of Art in the Age of Mechanical Reproduction." In *Illuminations: Essays and Reflections,* 217–251. Translated by Harry Zohn. Edited by Hannah Arendt. New York: Schocken Books, 1968.

Bergan, Ronald. *The Coen Brothers.* New York: Thunder's Mouth, 2000.

Bogle, Donald. *Toms, Coons, Mulattoes, Mammies, and Bucks: An Interpretive History of Blacks in American Films.* 4th ed. New York: Continuum, 2001.

Borde, Raymond, and Etienne Chaumeton. *A Panorama of American Film Noir, 1941–1953.* Translated by Paul Hammond. San Francisco: City Lights Books, 2002. Originally published by Éditions de minuit (Paris), 1955.

Burr, Ty. "The Wizard of Odd." *Entertainment Weekly,* Aug. 23, 1996, 132.

Carter, Steven. "Flare to White: *Fargo* and the Postmodern Turn." *Literature and Film Quarterly* 27, no. 7 (1999): 238–244.

Chafe, William H. *The Paradox of Change: American Women in the 20th Century.* Oxford: Oxford Univ. Press, 1991.

Chandler, Raymond. "The Simple Art of Murder." In *The Simple Art of Murder,* 1–18. New York: Random House, 1988.

Christopher, Nicholas. *Somewhere in the Night: Film Noir and the American City.* New York: Free Press, 1997.

Cook, David. *A History of Narrative Film, 1889–1979.* New York: Norton, 1981.

Cook, Kevin, and March Mravic. "Fight Cult." *Sports Illustrated,* Nov. 1, 1999, 31.

Corliss, Richard. Review of *Jackie Brown. Time,* Dec. 22, 1997, 80.

Cripps, Thomas. *Hollywood's High Noon: Moviemaking and Society before Television.* Excerpted in Ross, *Movies and American Society.*

———. *Making Movies Black: The Hollywood Message Movies from World War II to the Civil Rights Era.* New York: Oxford Univ. Press, 1993.

———. *Slow Fade to Black: The Negro in American Film, 1900–1942.* New York: Oxford Univ. Press, 1977.

Crowther, Bosley. Review of *Out of the Past.* In *The New York Times Film Reviews, 1913–1968.* Vol. 4. New York: Times Books and Arno, 1970.

Dargis, Manohla. "Russell Crowe's Special Brand of Masculinity." *New York Times,* Mar. 4, 2001 (late ed., East Coast), 2A.1.

Diawara, Manthia. "Noir by Noirs: Towards a New Realism in Black Cinema." In *Shades of Noir,* edited by Joan Copjec, 261–278. London: Verso, 1993.

Doherty, Thomas. "*Fargo.*" *Cineaste* 22, no. 7 (1996): 47–48.

Dowell, Pat. "Cast Helps Keep *Twilight* from Fading." *Army Times,* Mar. 23, 1998, 42.

Eco, Umberto. "Casablanca: Cult Movies and Intertextual Collage." *SubStance* 47 (1985): 3–12.

Elias, Justine. "Up, Out, and Away." *Village Voice,* May 3–9, 2000, 1.

Everett, Anna. *Returning the Gaze: A Genealogy of Black Film Criticism, 1909–1949.* Durham, N.C.: Duke Univ. Press, 2001.

Faludi, Susan. "It's *Thelma and Louise* for Guys." *Newsweek,* Oct. 25, 1999, 89.

Flinn, Caryl. "Sound, Woman, and the Bomb: Dismembering the 'Great Whatsit'

in *Kiss Me Deadly.*" *Screening the Past,* June 2000. <http://www.latrobe.edu
.au/screeningthepast/reruns/rr0600/cfrr10b.htm> (accessed May 12, 2004).

Flinn, Tom. "Daniel Mainwaring: An Interview." In *The Big Book of Noir,* edited
by Ed Gorman, Lee Server, and Martin Greenberg, 65–68. New York: Carroll
and Graf, 1998.

———. "*Out of the Past.*" In *The Big Book of Noir,* edited by Gorman, Server,
and Greenberg, 69–76. New York: Carroll and Graf, 1998.

Fraiman, Susan. *Cool Men and the Second Sex.* New York: Columbia Univ. Press,
2003.

Friedberg, Anne. *Window Shopping: Cinema and the Postmodern.* Berkeley and
Los Angeles: Univ. of California Press, 1993.

Gabbard, Krin. *Black Magic: White Hollywood and African American Culture.*
New Brunswick, N.J.: Rutgers Univ. Press, 2004.

Gabbard, Krin, and Glen O. Gabbard. "Play It Again, Sigmund: Psychoanalysis
and the Classical Hollywood Text." *Journal of Popular Film and Television*
18, no. 1 (1990): 7–17.

Gerston, Jill. "Pam Grier Finally Escapes the 1970's." *New York Times,* Dec. 21,
1997 (late ed., East Coast), sec. 2.

Giroux, Henry A. "Private Satisfactions and Public Disorders: *Fight Club,* Patriarchy, and the Politics of Masculine Violence." *JAC: A Journal of Composition
Theory* 21, no. 1 (2001): 1–31.

Goldstein, Richard. "Mr. Natural: Is Masculinity a Cultural Construction or a
Biological Fact? Science (and Sci-Fi) Enter the Gender Fray." *Village Voice,*
Oct. 20–26, 1999.

Goodwin-Kelly, Mary Kate. "Pregnant Body and/as Smoking Gun: Reviewing the
'Evidence' of *Fargo.*" Paper presented at the Society for Cinema and Media
Studies Conference, Atlanta, Ga., March 2004.

Green, Philip. *Cracks in the Pedestal: Ideology and Gender in Hollywood.* Amherst:
Univ. of Massachusetts Press, 1998.

Greenberg, Harvey. *The Movies on Your Mind: Film Classics on the Couch from
Fellini to Frankenstein.* New York: Dutton, 1975.

Guerrero, Ed. *Framing Blackness: The African American Image in Film.* Philadelphia: Temple Univ. Press, 1993.

Hannsberry, Karen Burroughs. *Femme Noir: Bad Girls of Film.* Jefferson, N.C.:
McFarland, 1998.

Harris, Oliver. "Film Noir Fascination: Outside History, but Historically So."
Cinema Journal 43, no. 1 (2003): 3–24.

Harvey, John. "Out of the Light: An Analysis of Narrative in *Out of the Past.*"
Journal of American Studies 18, no. 1 (1984): 73–87.

Hassan, Ihab. *The Postmodern Turn: Essays in Postmodern Theory and Culture.* Columbus: Ohio State Univ. Press, 1987.

Hemingway, Ernest. "The Killers." In *The Short Stories of Ernest Hemingway,* 279–289. New York: Scribners, 1938.

Hensley, Dennis. "He's Sew Fine." *Advocate,* Nov. 23, 1999, 62–66.

Heywood, Leslie, and Jennifer Drake. Introduction to *Third Wave Agenda: Being Feminist, Doing Feminism.* Minneapolis: Minnesota Univ. Press, 1997.

Hirsch, Foster. *Detours and Lost Highways: A Map of Neo-Noir.* New York: Limelight Editions, 1999.

hooks, bell. *Black Looks: Race and Representation.* New York: Routledge, 1992.

———. *Outlaw Culture: Resisting Representation.* New York: Routledge, 1994.

———. "Postmodern Blackness." *Postmodern Culture* 1, no. 1 (Sept. 1990), http://www.iath.virginia.edu/pmc/text-only/issue.990/hooks.990.

———. *Reel to Real: Race, Sex, and Class at the Movies.* New York: Routledge, 1996.

James, Darius. *That's Blaxploitation! Roots of the Baadasssss 'Tude (Rated X by an All-Whyte Jury).* New York: St. Martin's Griffin, 1995.

Jameson, Fredric. "Postmodernism and Consumer Society." In *The Anti-Aesthetic: Essays on Postmodern Culture,* 111–125. Edited by Hal Foster. Seattle: Bay Press, 1983.

"Japanese Woman Seeking Fictitious Loot From Movie *Fargo* Mysteriously Dies." *Salt Lake Tribune,* Dec. 9, 2000, A21.

Johnson, Brian. "Bare-Knuckled Knockout." *Maclean's,* Oct. 25, 1999, 86–87.

Jones, Kent. "A Critic's Heart Is an Ocean of Longing." *Film Comment* 34 (March–April 1998): 24–25.

Kaplan, E. Ann, ed. *Women in Film Noir.* New ed. London: British Film Institute, 2000.

Katz, Ephraim. *The Film Encyclopedia.* 2nd ed. New York: HarperCollins, 1994.

Katz, Jackson. "Advertising and the Construction of White Male Masculinity." In *Rereading America: Cultural Contexts for Critical Thinking and Writing* (4th ed.), edited by Gary Colombo, Robert Cullen, and Bonnie Lisle, 458–466. Boston: Bedford, 1998.

Kauffmann, Stanley. "Primal Stuff." *New Republic* 221, no. 19 (Nov. 8, 1999), 64.

———. "Some Crime, Some Comedy." *New Republic* 214, no. 22 (May 27, 1996), 28–29.

Kilday, Gregg. "Why I Hated *Fight Club.*" *Advocate,* Nov. 23, 1999, 62.

King, Barry. "Articulating Stardom." *Screen* 26, no. 5 (1985): 27–50.

Klawans, Stuart. Review of *L.A. Confidential. Nation,* Oct. 13, 1997, 34–35.

Kracauer, Siegfried. "Die kleinen Ladenmädchen gehens in Kino." In *Das Ornament der Masse,* 279–294. Frankfurt am Main: Suhrkamp, 1977.

Lang, Robert. *Masculine Interests: Homoerotics in Hollywood Film.* New York: Columbia Univ. Press, 2002.

Lawson, Terry. "*L.A. Confidential* Star Retains Her Sultry Image after a Two-Year Break." Knight-Ridder/Tribune News Service, Sept. 15, 1997, 915.

Lehman, Peter. "Crying over the Melodramatic Penis: Melodrama and Male Nudity in Films of the '90s." In *Masculinity: Bodies, Movies, Culture,* edited by Peter Lehman, 25–41. New York, Routledge: 2001.

Levine, Josh. *The Coen Brothers: The Story of Two American Filmmakers.* Toronto: ECW Press, 2000.

Lott, Eric. "Racial Cross-Dressing and the Construction of American Whiteness." In *The Cultural Studies Reader,* edited by Simon During, 2nd ed., 242–254. London: Routledge, 1999.

———. "Whiteness: A Glossary." *Village Voice,* May 18, 1993.

———. "The Whiteness of Film Noir." *American Literary History* 9, no. 3 (Autumn 1997): 542–566.

Lotz, Amanda. "Communicating Third-Wave Feminism and New Social Movements: Challenges for the Next Century of Feminist Endeavor." *Women and Language* 26, no. 2 (2003): 2–9.

Lucas, Blake. "*Out of the Past.*" In Silver and Ward, *Film Noir,* 218–219.

Macek, Carl. "*Raw Deal.*" In Silver and Ward, *Film Noir,* 238–239.

Malkin, Marc S. "Why I Loved *Fight Club.*" *Advocate,* Nov. 23, 1999, 66–67.

Martin, Richard. *Mean Streets and Raging Bulls: The Legacy of Film Noir in Contemporary American Cinema.* Lanham, Md.: Scarecrow Press, 1999.

Maslin, Janet. "*Fargo.*" *New York Times on the Web,* March 8, 1996.

———. "*Twilight:* A Round of Championship Bantering, Senior Division." *New York Times on the Web,* March 6, 1998.

Mayne, Judith. *Cinema and Spectatorship.* London: Routledge, 1993.

McCarthy, Todd. "*Twilight.*" *Variety,* March 2, 1998, 83.

Micheaux, Oscar. "The Negro and the Photo Play." In Ross, *Movies and American Society.*

Mulvey, Laura. "The Myth of Pandora: A Psychoanalytical Approach." In *Feminisms in the Cinema,* edited by Laura Pietropaolo and Ada Testaferri, 3–19. Bloomington: Indiana Univ. Press, 1995.

———. "Visual Pleasure and Narrative Cinema." In *Visual and Other Pleasures,* 14–26. Bloomington: Indiana Univ. Press, 1989.

Murphy, Kathleen. "Totems and Taboos: Civilization and Its Discontents According to Lee Tamahori." *Film Comment* 33 (1997): 26–31.

Naremore, James. *More than Night: Film Noir in Its Contexts.* Berkeley and Los Angeles: Univ. of California Press, 1998.

Neale, Steven. *Genre and Hollywood.* London: Routledge, 2000.

Newman, Kim. "*Fargo.*" *Sight and Sound* 6, no. 6 (1996), 40–41.

O'Neill, Brenda. "What Do Women Think?" *Herizons: Women's News and Feminist Views* 16, no. 2 (2002): 20–23.

Osteen, Mark. " 'The *Big* Secret': Film Noir and Nuclear Fear." *Journal of Popular Film and Television* 22, no. 2 (1994): 79–90.

Palmer, R. Barton. *Hollywood's Dark Cinema: The American Film Noir.* New York: Twayne, 1994.

Peachment, Chris. "Past Imperfect." Review of *Out of the Past. New Statesman,* Aug. 21, 1998, 40–41.

Petro, Patrice. *Aftershocks of the New: Feminism and Film History.* New Brunswick, N.J.: Rutgers Univ. Press, 2002.

———. *Joyless Streets: Women and Melodramatic Representation in Weimar Germany.* Princeton, N.J.: Princeton Univ. Press, 1989.

Place, Janey. "Women in Film Noir," In Kaplan, *Women in Film Noir,* 47–68.

Plagens, Peter. "*Twilight.*" *Newsweek,* Mar. 16, 1998, 72.

Polan, Dana. Address, Point Blank Conference, University of Arizona, Tucson, May 2000.

Poland, David. "Flash of Genius or Mistake? (The Final 82 Seconds of the Original Robert Aldrich Motion Picture *Kiss Me Deadly* Are Discovered by Glenn Erickson)." *Entertainment Weekly,* June 27, 1997, 129.

Porfirio, Robert. "*The Killers:* Expressiveness of Sound and Image in *Film Noir.*" In *Film Noir Reader,* edited by Alain Silver and James Ursini, 176–187. New York: Limelight Editions, 1996.

Prince, Stephen. *Classical Film Violence: Designing and Regulating Violence in Hollywood Cinema, 1930–1968.* New Brunswick, N.J.: Rutgers Univ. Press, 2003.

Projansky, Sarah. *Watching Rape: Film and Television in Postfeminist Culture.* New York: New York Univ. Press, 2001.

Rabinowitz, Paula. *Black and White and Noir: America's Pulp Modernism.* New York: Columbia Univ. Press, 2002.

Rainer, Peter. "Nothing under Its Hats: *Mulholland Falls* Is Numbskull Noir Only a Dirty Harry Could Love." *Los Angeles Magazine,* May 1996, 141.

Ray, Robert B. *A Certain Tendency in the Hollywood Cinema, 1930–1980.* Princeton, N.J.: Princeton Univ. Press, 1985.

Roediger, David R. *The Wages of Whiteness: Race and the Making of the American Working Class.* Rev. ed. London: Verso, 1999.

Romney, Jonathan. "LA Lore." *New Statesman,* Dec. 4, 1998, 38.

Rooney, David. "*Fight Club:* An Adrenaline Rush of a Movie." *Variety,* Sept. 13, 1999, 47.

Ross, Steven J., ed. *Movies and American Society*. Blackwell Readers in American Social and Cultural History. Oxford: Blackwell, 2002.

Said, Edward. "Opponents, Audiences, Constituencies, and Community." In *The Politics of Interpretation*, edited by W. J. T. Mitchell, 7–32. Chicago: Univ. of Chicago Press, 1983.

Schickel, Richard. "The Conditional Knockout." *Time*, Nov. 11, 1999, 83.

Sedgwick, Eve Kosofsky. *Between Men: English Literature and Male Homosocial Desire*. New York: Columbia Univ. Press, 1985.

Shargel, Raphael. "The Social Outrage Season." *New Leader*, Nov. 1, 1999, 18–19.

———. "*Twilight*." *New Leader*, Mar. 9, 1998, 21.

Shugart, Helene A., Catherine Egley Waggoner, and D. Lynn O'Brien Holstein. "Mediating Third-Wave Feminism: Appropriation as Postmodern Media Practice." *Critical Studies in Media Communication* 11, no. 2 (2001): 194–210.

Siegel, Deborah L. "The Legacy of the Personal: Generating Theory in Feminism's Third Wave." *Hypatia: A Journal of Feminist Philosophy* 12, no. 3 (Summer 1997): 46–75.

Silver, Alain, and Elizabeth Ward, eds. *Film Noir: An Encyclopedic Reference to the American Style*. 3rd ed. Woodstock, N.Y.: Overlook Press, 1992.

Silverman, Kaja. *Male Subjectivity at the Margins*. New York: Routledge, 1992.

Simon, John. Review of *L.A. Confidential*. *National Review*, Oct. 27, 1997, 56.

———. Review of *Twilight*. *National Review*, Apr. 6, 1998, 58.

Smith, Paul. "Eastwood Bound." In *Constructing Masculinity*, edited by Maurice Berger, Brian Wallis, and Simon Watson, 77–97. New York: Routledge, 1995.

Sobchack, Vivian. "Lounge Time: Postwar Crises and the Chronotype of Film Noir." In *Refiguring American Film Genres: Theory and History*, edited by Nick Brown, 129–170. Berkeley and Los Angeles: Univ. of California Press, 1998.

Stables, Kate. "The Postmodern Always Rings Twice: Constructing the *Femme Fatale* in '90s Cinema." In Kaplan, *Women in Film Noir*, 164–182.

Stein, Joel. "The Emasculation Proclamation." *Time*, Oct. 25, 1999, 46.

Sterritt, David. "Hollywood's Violence Club." *Christian Science Monitor*, Oct. 22, 1999, 15.

Straayer, Chris. "*Femme Fatale* or Lesbian Femme: *Bound* in Sexual *Différance*." In Kaplan, *Women in Film Noir*, 151–163.

Tasker, Yvonne. *Working Girls: Gender and Sexuality in Popular Cinema*. London: Routledge, 1998.

Taubin, Amy. "L.A. Lurid." *Sight and Sound*, Nov. 1997, 11.

———. "The Old 'Hood.'" *Village Voice*, March 17, 1998, 64.

———. "21st Century Boys." *Village Voice*, Nov. 19, 1999, 43.

Thomas, David. Review of *L.A. Confidential. Esquire,* Oct. 1997, 50–51.

Thomas, Deborah. "How Hollywood Deals with the Deviant Male." In *The Movie Book of Film Noir,* edited by Ian Cameron, 59–70. London: Studio Vista, 1992.

Thomson, David. "Dead Lily." *Film Comment* 33, no. 6 (1997): 16–19.

Tonkin, Boyd. "*Mulholland Falls.*" *New Statesman,* Sept. 6, 1996, 43.

Tucker, Ken. "You Can Leave Your Hat On: The Detectives Are Defective in Nolte's *Mulholland Falls.*" *Entertainment Weekly,* May 3, 1996, 62.

Wager, Jans B. *Dangerous Dames: Women and Representation in the Weimar Street Film and Film Noir.* Athens: Ohio Univ. Press, 1999.

Willis, Sharon. "Hardware and Hardbodies: What Do Women Want?" In *Film Theory Goes to the Movies,* edited by Jim Collins, Hilary Radner, and Ava Preacher Collins, 120–128. New York: Routledge, 1993.

Wood, Robin. "Creativity and Evaluation: Two Film Noirs of the Fifties." In *Film Noir Reader 2,* edited by Alain Silver and James Ursini, 98–105. New York: Limelight Editions, 1999.

Wosk, Julie. *Women and the Machine: Representations from the Spinning Wheel to the Electronic Age.* Baltimore: Johns Hopkins Univ. Press, 2001.

Wrathall, John. Review of *L.A. Confidential. Sight and Sound,* Nov. 1997, 45.

———. Review of *Mulholland Falls. Sight and Sound,* Sept. 1996, 48.

Zizek, Slavoj. *The Art of the Ridiculous Sublime: On David Lynch's "Lost Highway."* Walter Chapin Simpson Center for the Humanities Short Studies. Seattle: Univ. of Washington Press, 2000.

INDEX

Dargis, Mahohla, 81
De Niro, Robert, 144, 150
Dead Reckoning, 48
Decker, Albert, 41
Deep Cover, 34
Del Rio, Delores, 124
Dennis, Nick, 65
detectives. *See* investigators/detectives in
    film noir
Detours and Lost Highways, 97
Devil in a Blue Dress, 83, 164n29
DeVito, Danny, 79
Diawara, Manthia, 31
D.O.A., 64
Doane, Mary Ann, 156
Doherty, Thomas, 129, 135, 137
domesticity/domestic space in film noir:
    in *Fargo,* 140; in *Fight Club,* 102; in
    Jackie Brown, 148; in *The Killers,* 43–
    44, 46, 47, 48, 50, 63; in *Mulholland
    Falls,* 92, 96–97, 99; in *Out of the Past,*
    58, 61, 63; in *Twilight,* 125
Douglas, Kirk, 8, 53, 54
Douglas, Michael, 8
Drake, Jennifer, 27
DuBois, W. E. B., 30

Eastwood, Clint, 49
Ebert, Roger, 7
Eco, Umberto, 75, 86–87
editing, film, 91
Elias, Justine, 50–51
Ellington, Duke, 34
Ellroy, James, 79
erotic triangles in film noir, 55, 102, 117,
    118, 121
Esposito, Giancarlo, 125
ethnicity. *See* race
Everett, Anna, 30, 33

Faludi, Susan, 103, 112
Far from Heaven, 158
Fargo, 9, 10, 32, 127, 129–141, 158, 171nn24,
    33; music in, 130–131, 134, 170n4
Fatal Attraction, 9

FBI, 96
female agency in film noir, 4, 22, 27, 31, 88,
    103, 126, 157; in *Casablanca,* 77, 78; in
    L.A. Confidential, 84–85; in *Mulholland
    Falls,* 92, 94
femininity: black, 58, 146–147; as enigma,
    68; in neo-noir, 10, 26, 114; in retro-
    noir, 9, 26, 76, 81, 92, 99; white, 125,
    140
feminism, 8, 27–28, 68, 75–76, 87, 105–
    106, 145, 155, 156–157, 158–159. *See also*
    postfeminism; second-wave feminism;
    third-wave feminism
Feminisms in the Cinema, 68
femme attrapée, 20, 148, 165n15, 171n46;
    definition of, 4; in *Casablanca,* 78; in
    Gun Crazy, 46; in *The Killers,* 8, 40, 43,
    44–46, 48, 49, 52; in *Kiss Me Deadly,*
    69; in *Mulholland Falls,* 95–96; in
    Out of the Past, 54, 59, 60, 61, 62, 131,
    165n17
femme fatale, 19, 22, 86, 132, 161–162n16,
    162n24, 165nn8,15, 171n46; in classic
    film noir, 2, 3, 28, 42, 51–52, 126; con-
    tainment of, 87–88, 112–113; fate of,
    4, 19–20; in *Fight Club,* 102, 103, 104;
    in *Jackie Brown,* 143, 148, 150; in *The
    Killers,* 8, 40, 44–45, 49, 52; in *Kiss Me
    Deadly,* 8, 69–70; in neo-noir, 17, 23,
    26–27, 126; in *Mulholland Falls,* 94; in
    Out of the Past, 8, 53, 56, 57, 58, 60, 61;
    pastiche, 6, 18, 27, 76, 83, 88, 94, 97,
    157; in retro-noir, 32, 81; resistance of,
    to socially acceptable gender roles, 29,
    76, 123; and sexual performance, 5–6,
    9; in *Twilight,* 118, 120
Femme Fatale, 9, 162n24
Femme Noir, 1, 54
Fight Club, 6, 9, 32, 81, 88, 99, 101–114, 118,
    138, 157, 158
Film Encyclopedia, 1, 55
film noir, 3, 10, 79–80, 88, 102, 117; con-
    nection of, with the Weimar Street
    film, 23; definitions of, 3, 13–18, 161n9;
    Richard Martin's taxonomy of, 21–26;

rural settings in, 61, 131–132. *See also* classic film noir; neo-noir; retro-noir; postclassic film noir

Film Noir, 20, 40, 59, 162n1, 163n2

Fincher, David, 105, 110

Fiorentino, Linda, 5, 9

flashbacks, use of in film noir, 41, 43, 51, 54

Flinn, Caryl, 69, 167n23

Flinn, Tom, 54, 166n6

Fonda, Bridget, 150

Ford, Glenn, 48, 165n8

Forster, Robert, 144

Fraiman, Susan, 35, 146, 172n13

Franklin, Carl, 34, 164n29

Friedberg, Anne, 13, 17, 25, 26, 151–152

Gabbard, Glen O., 82

Gabbard, Krin, 82, 135, 137, 138, 171n33

Gardner, Ava, 8, 40, 41, 64

Garner, James, 117, 119, 120, 122

Garrison, Ednie Kaeh, 19

gender in film noir, 2, 20–21, 103, 156, 157, 159; in *Fargo,* 127; in *Jackie Brown,* 154; in *Kiss Me Deadly,* 64, 70; in *L.A. Confidential,* 83; and misogyny, 107–108, 114; in neo-noir, 10, 16; in postclassic noir, 3, 6, 8, 18; in retro-noir, 9, 16, 27–28; in *Thelma and Louise,* 119; in *Twilight,* 117

Genre and Hollywood, 14–15, 23, 162n1

German street films. *See* Weimar cinema

Gerston, Jill, 143, 144

Gibbons, Cedric, 124

Girl 6, 158

Giroux, Henry, 104, 105, 111, 112

Gladiator, 81

Goldstein, Richard, 101

Goodwin Kelly, Mary Kate, 171n24

The Graduate, 103

Grahame, Gloria, 165n8

Green, Philip, 1, 3, 8, 10, 21, 79–80, 145

Greer, Jane, 8, 53, 54, 64

Grier, Pam, 5, 10, 143, 144–145, 147

Griffith, Melanie, 95

Grist, Leighton, 22–23

The Guilt of Janet Ames, 76

Gun Crazy, 4, 20, 46, 131, 165nn8,18

Hackman, Gene, 117, 118, 122

Hamilton, Lisa Gay, 149

Hannsberry, Karen Burroughs, 54

Hanson, Curtis, 82

Harlow, Jean, 96

Harper, 9

Harris, Oliver, 41, 43, 49, 52, 164n7, 165n24

Harris, Theresa, 57

Harvey, John, 60, 62

Hassan, Ihab, 15

Heavy, 132

Heidegger, Martin, 24

Hemingway, Ernest, 39, 40, 52, 164n3

Henreid, Paul, 78

Heston, Charlton, 172n18

heterocentrism, 3, 108, 110, 157, 158, 159

Heywood, Leslie, 27

High Sierra, 124

Hirsch, Foster, 97, 98

Hispanics in film noir, 31, 32–33, 35, 58, 79, 82, 83, 95. *See also* nonwhites in film noir; "otherness" in film noir; race in film noir

Hitchcock, Alfred, 64

Hollywood, 3, 4, 10, 31, 34, 54; endings, 112, 123

Holstein, D. Lynn O'Brien, 17

homme attrapé, 28; choices of, and consequences, 20, 148; definition of, 4; in *Fargo,* 138; in *Fight Club,* 113; in *Jackie Brown,* 144, 153; in *The Killers,* 40, 46, 48, 49, 50, 59, 62; in *Out of the Past,* 59, 62; in *Twilight,* 126–127

homme fatal, 28, 76, 78, 86; absence of, in retro-noir, 18; in *Body Heat,* 23; definition of, 4; disdain of, for working-class or middle-class existence, 29, 123; fate of, in noir, 20–21, 27; in *Fargo,* 138; in *Fight Club,* 113; in *Jackie Brown,* 154; in *The Killers,* 49, 50–52; in *Kiss Me*

Deadly, 64; in *L.A. Confidential,* 86; in *Mulholland Falls,* 93, 97; in *Out of the Past,* 8, 54, 55–56, 62, 64, 80; in *Twilight,* 124

homoeroticism in film noir. *See* homosexuals in film noir; queer readings of film noir

homophobia, 77, 93, 146, 157

homosexual characters in film noir, 21, 32, 76, 77–78, 86–87, 92, 93. *See also* "otherness" in film noir; queer readings of film noir

homosocial relationships in film noir, 66, 77, 79, 83, 85, 86, 92, 93, 97, 99, 108, 113, 122–123, 124

hooks, bell, 3, 10, 146, 153–154, 155, 156, 158–159

Horkheimer, Max, 155, 156

The House on 92nd Street, 64

Hurt, William, 23

Huston, Virginia, 165n17

In a Lonely Place, 167n12

independent films, 21

interracial relationships, 154

investigators/detectives in film noir, 40, 41, 46, 48–49, 54, 64, 65, 78, 82, 123, 125; in *Fargo,* 127, 129–130, 133, 134, 141, 158, 171n24

Jackass: The Movie, 168–169n2

Jackie Brown, 5, 9, 10, 16, 26, 35, 141, 143–154, 158, 159, 172nn13,18; music in, 146, 147, 148, 154

Jackson, Samuel L., 143, 144

James, Darius, 143

Jameson, Fredric, 17, 22

Japanese cinema, 32

jazz clubs/nightclubs in film noir, 8, 34, 45, 53, 57, 58–59, 66–67, 83, 95

Johnson, Brian, 105, 111

Jones, Angela, 5

Jones, Kent, 147, 148, 153

Joyless Streets, 24, 25

Juice, 34

Kaes, Anton, 24

Kane, Irene, 124

Katz, Ephraim, 56

Katz, Jackson, 81

Kauffmann, Stanley, 96, 105

Keaton, Michael, 151

Kilday, Gregg, 108, 110

Kill Bill: Vol. 2, 171n1

The Killers, 4, 8, 39–52, 63, 64, 76, 96, 118, 120, 121, 123, 131, 144, 148, 153, 165nn8, 32

Killer's Kiss, 124

The Killing, 4

Kim, Joon B., 110

King, Barry, 119

Kiss Me Deadly, 8, 63–71, 91, 97, 99, 119, 166n7, 167nn24, 26

Klawans, Stuart, 83

Klute, 9

Kracauer, Siegfried, 168n1

L.A. Confidential, 6, 9, 16, 26, 33, 35, 71, 75–89, 93, 94, 103, 110, 118, 121, 157, 158

Lake, Veronica, 79, 83

Lancaster, Burt, 8, 40, 50–51, 55, 64

Lantana, 158

The Last Seduction, 5, 9–10, 162n25

Lautner, John, 124

Lawson, Terry, 83

Leachman, Cloris, 64

Lee, Spike, 158–159

Lehman, Peter, 109

Leonard, Elmore, 146

Levine, Josh, 131, 132, 136, 138

lighting effects in film noir, 3, 8, 14, 59, 68–69, 117, 118, 121, 122, 161n8, 162n2

location shooting, 60, 117

Loggins, Art, 67

Lone Star, 132

The Long Goodbye, 16, 162n17

Lorre, Peter, 77, 86, 167n6

Lott, Eric, 5, 29, 31, 147

Lotz, Amanda, 27, 28, 163n31

Lucas, Blake, 59

Lupino, Ida, 124
Lynch, John Carroll, 133

Macy, Willliam H., 130, 138
Madsen, Michael, 92, 93
Mailer, Norman, 110
Mainwaring, Daniel, 53, 55
makeup (film), 68–69
Malcolm X, 34
Malkin, Marc, 108
Malkovich, John, 97
The Man Who Wasn't There, 16, 132, 158, 171n46
El Mariachi, 32–33
Martin, Richard, 14, 15, 21–26
Martindale, Margo, 124
Masculine Interests, 66
masculinity in film noir, 4, 22, 23, 125, 164n14; black, 147; in *Fargo,* 140; in *Fight Club,* 102, 107–110; of the homme fatal, 20–21, 64; and homosexuality, 66; in *The Killers,* 48, 49; in *Mulholland Falls,* 9, 92; in neo-noir, 114, 123; parallel versions of, in *Casablanca* and *L.A. Confidential,* 80–81, 85–86; and race, 138; in retro-noir, 26, 32, 76, 83, 86; studies, 156–157; sympathetic, 59, 80; white, enhanced by contact with black culture, 31, 58, 66–67
Maslin, Janet, 7, 120, 138
Matthaei, Julie, 6, 58, 67
Mayne, Judith, 30, 109
McCarthy, Todd, 117, 121, 125
McDormand, Frances, 5, 129, 132, 171n46
Means Streets and Raging Bulls, 14, 21
Meatloaf, 103
Meeker, Ralph, 64
Memento, 82, 158
Mexico (as a setting in film noir), 53, 58, 118, 147
Miami noir, 33
Micheaux, Oscar, 30
middle class. *See* class in film noir: middle
Mildred Pierce, 77

minorities in film noir. *See* Asians in film noir; blacks in film noir; Hispanics in film noir; "otherness" in film noir; race in film noir
misanthropy in film noir, 8, 67, 70
mise-en-scène, 45, 48, 96, 138, 143
misogyny in film noir, 8, 67, 101, 107–108, 113, 114, 154, 156, 157
Mitchum, Robert, 8, 48, 53, 54, 55, 64, 80
modernism, 24, 25. *See also* neo-modernism; postmodernism
Moore, Dickie, 59
More Than Night, 13, 15, 23, 32, 64, 92, 162n22
Morissette, Alanis, 27
Moss, Kate, 27
Mulholland Drive, 9, 158
Mulholland Falls, 6, 9, 16, 26, 64–65, 71, 88, 91–99, 102, 110, 118, 157, 168n1
Mulvey, Laura, 6, 7, 8, 68, 70, 156
Murphy, Kathleen, 94, 96

NAACP, 31, 67
Naremore, James, 13, 15, 23, 31, 32, 34, 57, 59, 65, 66, 91, 92, 125, 162n22
A Narrative History of Film, 149
narrative structure in film noir, 3, 8, 14
National Association for the Advancement of Colored People. *See* NAACP
Nazis, 79, 167n6
Neale, Steven, 14–15, 23, 162n1, 164n5
neo-modernism, 23–24
neo-noirs, 14, 71, 123, 124, 129, 131, 134, 141, 158; *Body Heat* as representative of, 23–24; choices in, and consequences, 148–149, 154; class in, 10, 158; definition of, 16; the femme fatale in, 6, 27, 126, 150; gender in, 10, 28, 157–158; queer readings of, 21; race in, 10, 35, 150, 154, 158; reactionary/nostalgic elements in, 17, 26, 117–118, 125–126; retro-noir masquerading as, 9, 102; revisionary yet also reactionary (*Twilight*), 117–118, 125–126. *See also* postclassic noir

Newman, Kim, 138
Newman, Paul, 117, 118, 120, 122
nightclubs. *See* jazz clubs/nightclubs in film noir
night-for-night photography, 14, 161n8
Nobody's Fool, 117, 132
Nolte, Nick, 92
nonwhites in film noir, 5, 9, 31–32, 35, 157–158, 165n32; in *Casablanca,* 77, 79, 88; in *Fargo,* 10, 135–138, 141; in *Fight Club,* 110, 113; in *Jackie Brown,* 10; in *The Killers,* 41, 47, 52; in *L.A. Confidential,* 82, 88; in *Mulholland Falls,* 99; in *Out of the Past,* 58; in retro-noir, 75–76, 157–158; in *Twilight,* 10, 118, 125
Norton, Ed, 103
nostalgia in film noir, 5, 17, 26, 35, 75, 79, 89, 99
Notorious, 64
nuclear noir, 63, 64–65, 71, 91, 97

objectification of women, 6, 16, 84, 88, 99, 154, 158; in *Casablanca,* 76, 77, 79; in *Fight Club,* 105, 106, 108
O'Brien, Edmond, 41, 48
Old School, 168–169n2
Once Were Warriors, 99
O'Neill, Brenda, 27
Osteen, Mark, 65
"otherness" in film noir, 29, 32, 79, 125, 137–138. *See also* nonwhites in film noir; queer readings of film noir; race in film noir
Outlaw Culture, 153
Out of the Past, 4, 8, 48, 52, 53–62, 63, 64, 76, 118, 120, 121, 131, 148, 165n17, 166n29, 170n6

Palahniuk, Chuck, 103, 112
Palminteri, Chazz, 92, 97
Pandora's box, 64, 68, 70
A Panorama of American Film Noir, 7–8, 39, 40, 53, 63
Park, Steve, 135
Parks, Gordon, 34

Parks, Rosa, 67
pastiche femme fatale. *See* femme fatale: pastiche
patriarchy, 3, 44, 56, 146; defiance of, by femmes fatales and hommes fatals, 19–21; lack of resistance to, by femmes attrapées and hommes attrapées, 4, 20, 62; as promoted in *Fight Club,* 9, 88, 102, 113, 138; as supported by retro-noirs, 10, 16, 18, 27–28, 76, 88, 89, 157; as undermined by neo-noirs, 6, 10, 16, 154, 158
Peachment, Chris, 59
Pearce, Guy, 82, 168n20
Penn, Chris, 92, 93
Peterson, Caleb, 57
Petro, Patrice, 7, 24, 25, 156–157
Pitt, Brad, 101, 102
Place, Janey, 19, 60
Plagens, Peter, 124
Point Break, 9
Porfirio, Robert, 45
postclassic noir, 8–9, 35, 49, 91, 155, 158, 159; as discussed in *Dangerous Dames,* 3–4; gender roles in, 6, 16, 26–27, 114; and nostalgia, 17; race in, 28, 30–35; Richard Martin's discussion of, 14, 21–26. *See also* neo-noir; retro-noir
postfeminism, 7, 27–28, 103, 105–106, 155, 157, 163n31, 169n8. *See also* feminism; second-wave feminism; third-wave feminisim
The Postman Always Rings Twice, 4
postmodernism, 7, 8, 13, 16, 17, 18, 19, 27, 154, 155, 157, 158; as compared to neo-modernism, 22–26; *Mulholland Falls* as exemplar of, 98–99
The Postmodern Turn, 15
Presnell, Harve, 130
Pretty Woman, 108
Prince, Stephan, 64, 161n10
private eyes. *See* investigators/detectives in film noir
Production Code, 4–5, 6, 149, 161n10, 167n24

Projansky, Sarah, 105, 106
Pulp Fiction, 5, 35, 146, 147

queer readings of film noir, 156–157; in
    Casablanca and *L.A Confidential*, 77–
    78, 86–87, 93; in *Fight Club*, 108–110;
    in *Kiss Me Deadly*, 66, 70–71, 166n7,
    167nn19,24; in *Mulholland Falls*, 93,
    97–98

Rabinowitz, Paula, 1, 3, 5, 15, 31, 58
race in film noir, 5, 7, 29–35, 156–157, 159;
    as conflated with class, 5, 76, 79; in
    Fargo, 135–138; in *Fight Club*, 110–112,
    114, 157; ignored, in Martin's taxonomy
    of noir, 21, 22, 26; and integration, 34,
    58; in *Jackie Brown*, 146–147, 153–154;
    in *The Killers*, 52; in *L.A. Confidential*,
    79, 82–83; in *Mulholland Falls*, 92; in
    Out of the Past, 57–58; in postclassic
    noir, 3, 8, 18; reactionary treatment
    of, in retro-noir, 9, 88–89; revision-
    ary treatment of, in neo-noir, 10; and
    segregation, 57; and stereotypes, 10,
    32, 83, 118, 136–137; in *Twilight*, 125. *See
    also* Asians in film noir; black culture;
    blacks in film noir; Hispanics in film
    noir; nonwhites in film noir; "other-
    ness" in film noir; racism; whiteness in
    film noir
Race, Gender, and Work, 6
racism, 30, 35, 58, 113, 114, 138, 146, 153, 156,
    158, 159, 164n3. *See also* nonwhites in
    film noir; "otherness" in film noir; race
    in film noir
Rage in Harlem, 34
Rainer, Peter, 91
Rains, Claude, 78
Raw Deal, 20
Ray, Robert, 77
reactionary tendencies in film noir, 3,
    7, 17, 75, 87, 99, 112, 114, 126, 141, 156,
    157, 158; and the femme fatale, 6; and
    Fight Club, 9; in gender images, 16,
    26; and *L.A. Confidential*, 86; and

nostalgia, 35, 89; in postfeminism,
    27–28, 103; and *Twilight*, 125. *See also*
    retro-noirs
Reel to Real, 156, 159
Reservoir Dogs, 92
retro-noirs, 71, 85, 93, 94, 102, 123; defi-
    nition of, 3, 16; the femme attrapée
    in, 95–96; the femme fatale in, 6, 76,
    88, 95; homosocial relationships in,
    109, 122–123; race in, 32–33, 35, 110–112;
    reactionary/nostalgic impulses of, 8,
    10, 17, 22, 27–28, 75–77, 79, 87–88, 92,
    99, 126, 157, 158, 159; violence against
    women in, 80–81. *See also* postclassic
    noir
Returning the Gaze, 30
revisionary tendencies in film noir, 7, 9,
    16, 17, 71, 125, 158; and appropriation,
    26, 35. *See also* neo-noirs
Robinson, Jackie, 30
The Rockford Files, 120
Rodgers, Gaby, 68
Rodriguez, Robert, 32
Roediger, David, 29–30
Roeper, Richard, 7
Romeo Is Bleeding, 22
Romney, Jonathan, 121, 125
Rooney, David, 108
Ruedrud, Kristin, 130
Rum Punch, 146
Russell, Rosalind, 76

Said, Edward, 156
Sarandon, Susan, 5, 10, 117, 118, 132
Scarlet Street, 20
Schreiber, Liev, 124
Scorcese, Martin, 22, 25, 34
Scott, A. O., 7
Scott, Hazel, 34
Scott, Lizabeth, 69
Sea of Love, 22
second-wave feminism, 19, 27–28, 80
Sedgwick, Eve Kosofsky, 77
sexism, 25, 110, 146, 156, 158, 159
sexuality in film noir, 20, 22, 32, 59, 153,

159, 163n2, 167nn19,24; and black masculinity and femininity, 147; in *Fight Club*, 102–110; in *The Killers*, 43, 50; in *Kiss Me Deadly*, 66, 69–71; in *L.A. Confidential*, 84, 85; in *Mulholland Falls*, 96, 97; and the 1990s femme fatale, 5–6, 9, 17, 161–162n16, 162n24; in *Out of the Past*, 55, 59, 60, 62; in *Twilight*, 118, 120, 121. *See also* homosexual characters in film noir; queer readings of film noir
Shaft, 34
Shargel, Raphael, 105, 118
Shaw, Anabel, 46
Shugart, Helene A., 17, 27
Siegel, Deborah L., 19
Silver, Alain, 65
Silverman, Kaja, 7
Simon, John, 83, 121
Siodmak, Robert, 40, 52
Sling Blade, 132
Smith, Jamie, 124
Smith, Paul, 49
Sobchack, Vivian, 43–44, 48
Society for Cinema Studies, 156
Somewhere in the Night, 57
sound (film), 69
Spacey, Kevin, 82
Spillane, Mickey, 64, 167n24
Stables, Kate, 5–6, 161n16
Stein, Joel, 103
stereotypes, racial and ethnic. *See* race in film noir: and stereotypes
Sterritt, David, 113
Stiffed, 103
Stone, Sharon, 5
Stormare, Peter, 130, 135
The Story of G.I. Joe, 55
Straayer, Chris, 20, 21, 29
The Strange Love of Martha Ivers, 54
Strathairn, David, 84
subjectivity, female, 21, 22, 23, 25, 26, 28, 43, 84, 159
subjectivity, male, 4, 21, 23, 25, 26, 28, 76

Tamahori, Lee, 99
Tarantino, Quentin, 34, 35, 143, 145–146, 171n1, 172n13
Tasker, Yvonne, 17, 19, 20, 23
Taubin, Amy, 82, 108, 110, 121
Taxi Driver, 22, 23
That's Blaxploitation!, 143
Thelma and Louise, 103, 119, 169n5
They Won't Believe Me, 54
Third Wave Agenda, 27
third-wave feminism, 7, 19, 27–28, 155, 158, 163n31, 169nn1, 8
Thomas, David, 83
Thomas, Deborah, 46
Thomson, David, 70
Toms, Coons, Mulattoes, Mammies, and Bucks, 34
Tonkin, Boyd, 92, 98
Touch of Evil, 8, 172n18
Tourneur, Jacques, 53
Tucker, Chris, 150
Tudor, Andrew, 15
Turner, Kathleen, 23
25th Hour, 172n9
Twilight, 5, 9, 10, 16, 33, 117–127, 135, 141, 158, 169n1

Van Peebles, Melvin, 34
voice-over narration, 3, 23, 54, 102, 117, 118
violence in film noir, 20, 22, 26, 96, 158; in *Fargo*, 130, 135, 139–140; and the femme fatale, 76; in *Fight Club*, 88, 101–103, 104, 108–110, 112–113; in *Jackie Brown*, 144; in *The Killers*, 39–41, 45; in *Kiss Me Deadly*, 64; in *L.A. Confidential*, 80–81, 83; in *Mulholland Falls*, 9, 88, 92, 93, 99; in *Out of the Past*, 59, 62; in Quentin Tarantino films, 34, 146; in *Twilight*, 121–122, 124

The Wages of Whiteness, 29
Waggoner, Catherine Egley, 17
Walker, Bill, 41
Wang, Wayne, 32

Ward, Elizabeth, 65
Washington, Denzel, 82
Watching Rape, 105
Weimar cinema, 3–4, 7, 23–25, 168n1
Welles, Orson, 8
whiteness in film noir, 5, 22, 24, 29–30, 125; in *Fargo,* 135; in *The Killers,* 52
white supremacist capitalist patriarchy. *See* patriarchy
Willis, Sharon, 119
Wilson, Dooley, 78
Window Shopping, 13, 16, 25, 151
Winston, Hattie, 149
Witherspoon, Reese, 118
Womack, Bobby, 146, 154

"woman as redeemer," 45, 60, 63. *See also* femme attrapée
Women and the Machine, 47
women's movement. *See* feminism
Woo, John, 32
Wood, Robin, 66
working class. *See* class in film noir: working
World War II, 2, 30, 47–48, 58, 77
Wosk, Julie, 47
Wrathall, John, 92
Wright, Frank Lloyd, 124, 125

Zizek, Slavoj, 6
"zoot suit" riots, 31